ISBN 88-8398-030-1

Florence, Italy
www.e-p-a-p.com
www.europeanpress.it

Giotto's Harmony: Music and Art in Padua at the Crossroads of the Renaissance

Eleonora M. Beck

European Press Academic Publishing

For Liz, Sophie and Alexander

Acknowledgements

I wish to thank Pomona College for the Arnold and Lois S. Graves Award for Excellence in Teaching in the Humanities, which funded my research in Padua. I owe a great deal of gratitude to Fiorenza Gilioli, who helped with the Latin transliterations and translations, and to Maristella Lorch and Darma Tercinod, who worked on the Italian translations. Thank you to the staff at the Biblioteca Civica in Padua, the Biblioteca Marciana in Venice, and the Newberry Library in Chicago. I am grateful to Elena Furin and Gianni Bonatto, who introduced me to the beauty of Padua. I wish to express my deepest appreciation to Zdravko Blazekovic for his eloquent presentation and to David Anderson for his support of this project.

Thank you to Barbara Skipworth and Elise Gautier, who meticulously and thoughtfully edited the manuscript, and to Rebecca James and Emilia Allen, who compiled the bibliography and the illustrations. Thank you to my father for his steadfast support of my research. Finally, I am grateful to Curtis Johnson for securing a subvention from Lewis & Clark College to help cover publication costs.

Contents

Foreword

Crossovers in Paduan Narratives: Music and Visual Art Between Antiquity and the Renaissance

Old cities are like people: they have their histories and heroes, their periods of prosperity and decay; their lives can be strict and abstinent or exuberant and decadent. Still, we rarely associate them with and remember them by more than a few vestiges of their pasts: sometimes this is a great piece of architecture, at other times a significant event that occurred there. If not for treaties signed at Rapallo, Dayton, or the Trianon châteaux in the park of Versailles, these places would remain points of no significance in our collective geographical mind, and hardly anybody would remember Magenta, Solferino, or Waterloo if not for major military victories (or defeats) that occurred there.

Padua is most frequently associated in the mind of people today with Saint Anthony the Hermit, the celebrated Portuguese Franciscan missionary, who happened to die in its vicinity at the age of thirty-six and because of his saintly acts was canonized in 1232, only a year after his death. His grave in the Basilica Il Santo has been for centuries a major gathering point for pilgrims from all of Europe. Those versed in art history will probably associate Padua first with the chapel built by Enrico Scrovegni, and exorbitantly frescoed by Giotto di Bondone. In the collective memory of present-day music lovers, the town usually remains silent until the arrival there of Giuseppe Tartini in the early 1720s, who served as the *primo violino e capo di concerto* at Il Santo. It was none other than Tartini who made Padua famous among many of his violinist contemporaries as a place where they could receive the best violin instruction in all of Europe. Although Padua's cultural history in the Trecento and Quattrocento is tremendously interesting, its musical aspect somehow has not occupied the interest of more than a few music historians. Preserved sources of music by Paduan masters from that time are scarce, and archival information about musical life, no more abundant, making it hard to determine the place of music in the cultural life of the city. Searching for historical facts in notary records we have, however, failed to recognize how musical science and musical art blended at the time with an array of other disciplines – ranging from visual art, literature, and mathematics to astrology and philosophy – into an exquisitely refined union.

An attempt to reconstruct an accurate and detailed view of music in Trecento and Quattrocento Padua is a complex one involving investigations into multiple and dissimilar kinds of evidence. It is necessary to read the narrative inherent in the lyrics of popular musical genres of the time, look at the context of music in large narrative visual cycles, recognize the subtext of treatises on music theory, figure out the influences to which their authors were exposed, and detect repercussions of these treatises in changes of musical thinking. The six studies included in this collection examine such a cultural context of music in Padua at the advent of the early modern period. The book should be read against the background of two characteristics that dominate the cultural history of Padua during this time: the re-examination and revival of the city's antique history, and the creation of powerful visual narratives along the axis of Giotto – Palazzo della Ragione – and Donatello. Both of these aspects provide valuable clues not only to the understanding of music at the time, but also about the reception of music theory among the visual artists. This work proposes several new views on the influences that might have guided artists in designing their narratives involving music, in the center of which was the critical thinking of the composer and music theorist Marchetto da Padova and the physician and astronomer Pietro d'Abano.

Since little of the town's ancient architecture has been preserved, the fact that Padua's history goes back to antiquity might be today easily overlooked. The situation was, however, much different during the Trecento, and the town was then extremely proud of its ancient heritage, fostering the revival of classical artistic forms. The claim that Patavium had been founded by Trojans fleeing after the sack of their city – which goes back to Virgil and the Roman historian Livy – was possible to support with archaeological evidence. In 1283 a skeleton identified as the Trojan hero Antenor was unearthed, and in his honor a Gothic cenotaph was erected in the city. Later on, Livy's tomb was supposedly discovered in the vicinity of the town, and his remains were carried in a triumphal procession through the city in 1443. Against such a backdrop, Padua searched for its identity in a revival of ancient aesthetics and sciences. A university was established in 1222 and venerated throughout the Western world, creating a focal point for intellectuals well informed about classical antique texts. Paduan humanists and patricians collected antique medals, coins, and gems, and assembled sylloges of inscriptions transcribed from ancient buildings and tombs. It comes, therefore, as no surprise that the antique medal was in the Renaissance period first revived by Francesco Carrara II in 1390 to commemorate his recapture of the city. In a similar way, antiquarianism provided the decisive influence on manuscript decorations, rich with the flavor of antique lettering, festoons, and decorative putti. Commissioned in the same spirit, from Donatello, was the monument to the Venetian condottiere Erasmo da Narni, called Gattamelata, who died in Padua in 1443. The work, modeled after the late second-century Roman sculpture of Marcus Aurelius (at that time still identified as the emperor Constantine), was erected in 1453 on the piazza facing Il Santo, and represents the first such equestrian statue in Renaissance Italy.

The period of republican government in Padua ended in 1318 with the appointment of Giovanni da Carrara as the *capitaneus et dominus generalis*. After a brief period of rule by the della Scala family of Verona (1328-1337), the Carrara family firmly established its government until Venice conquered the town in 1405. This was the epoch when the city was flourishing and prosperous to an extraordinary degree because the Carrara family provided patronage to some of the most notable figures of European humanism, including Petrarch. Padua was then one of the most important centers of painting in northern Italy, able to attract a significant number of painters from other Italian towns and some from France and Germany. It is not an accident that the two artists who probably made the most lasting artistic impact on the city, Giotto and Donatello, came here from Florence. The workshop of Francesco Squarcione attracted students from all of northern Italy and both Adriatic coasts. By one account, among his 137 students were Andrea Mantegna, Marco Zoppo, and the two *Schiavoni*, Giorgio Schiavone (Juraj Čulinovic) from Šibenik and Bernardo Parenzano from Poreč in

Istria. Squarcione's home and studio were supposedly filled with pieces of ancient sculptures and architectural fragments, which he either brought from his extensive travels in Italy and Greece or of which he made casts. Naturally, he passed on his fascination for antiquity to his students, who were particularly well trained in the representation of architectural elements in their correct perspective and in the sculptural treatment of human figures. Paintings produced in his school are replete with decorative elements, such as reliefs, medallions, garlands of fruits and flowers, and incrustations.

The period of Paduan proto-Renaissance was a juncture between old and new, antiquity and modernity, stylization and realism. On one hand, the town was extremely proud of its ancient history and used every opportunity to make references to its Greek and Roman roots, never missing a chance to celebrate ancient heroes in street festivals. On the other hand, its university atmosphere was fertile ground for the broadening of intellectual vistas and creating an environment that laid the groundwork for the Renaissance. It therefore comes as no surprise that the treatises which are today the key sources for the understanding of the theoretical background of Paduan music look backward to antiquity and forward to Renaissance traits. Both Marchetto da Padova and Pietro d'Abano were connoisseurs of the Aristotelian philosophy of nature, placing it in the foundation of their treatises. Pietro's *Conciliator* (1303) and *Expositio problematum Aristotelis* (1310) and Marchetto's *Lucidarium in arte musicae planae* (1317/18) and *Pomerium in arte musicae mensuratae* (before 1319) opened new paths in music theory, assigning to Marchetto the position of the most prominent music theorist between Guido and Tinctoris. As a chapter in this volume demonstrates, Marchetto's and Pietro's fingerprints are detectable in Paduan visual narratives for almost a century and half. Instruments that Giotto, Giusto de' Menabuoi, and Donatello included in their visual narratives might appear to us arbitrarily chosen, but seen against Marchetto's tripartite division of musical sound – harmonic music produced by human voice, organic music produced by air set in vibration by the breath, and rhythmic music not produced by the voice or breath – a pattern emerges indicating that the artists might have been organizing them according to rules of music theory.

Today, Padua is packed with visual narratives that, in different ways, document its prosperous past. Chronologically, the earliest is the gargantuan fresco cycle by Giotto at the Cappella degli Scrovegni (1303-1305). This is not only Giotto's most important work but also signifies the dawn of the new aesthetics in visual arts that exploded at the beginning of the Trecento. The composite of 39 fresco panels, representing another junction where the old and new diverge, tells stories assisted by figures that appear to the viewer alive and interactive; one can recognize their emotions, identify the varieties of trees or birds surrounding them, and be part of the atmosphere. Aristotle's philosophy of nature was crucial here, influencing Giotto's attempt to replicate nature in art as closely as possible. In this effort, his aesthetics go hand-in-hand with Marchetto's, which guided the theorist in explaining his proposals for writing music notation, meant to better capture in compositions the natural inflections of voices. Although seemingly simple in their message, Giotto's compositions are imbedded with their own codebook, which his contemporaries were able to read with no more effort than we read narratives in our comic books. However, at a distance of seven centuries from the creation of these works, we are rarely fully aware of what they might have meant to their original viewers. We easily recognize the biblical story they represent, but also easily forget (if we ever knew) what they can tell us about life at the time they were painted. We might not even think that the saintly lives they represent replicate vistas and situations which Giotto knew from the streets and porticos of the *città porticata* or ceremonies in which he himself might have participated celebrating church feasts. Knowing the possibility that Giotto – the leading painter of his time, praised by Dante and Boccaccio – might have encountered Marchetto – the leading Paduan composer of the time – helps us better understand subtleties in the works by the two artists.

Padua's visual narratives did not stop with Giotto. Just as he was finishing the Cappella degli Scrovegni, in the center of the town – between the *Piazza delle erbe*, *Piazza della frutta*, and the *Mercato del vino* – Giovanni degli Eremitani was remaking (1306-1308) the interior of the Palazzo della Ragione, built in 1218. Three rooms on the upper floor were combined into one huge space seventy-eight meters long, twenty-seven meters wide, and twenty-seven meters high, becoming the largest pensile hall in Europe. According to literary sources, the frescos decorating its inner walls were commissioned from Giotto, who produced them during his second stay in the city. The cycle, apparently modeled by Pietro d'Abano, was destroyed during a fire at the hall in 1420, leaving only a few panels undamaged. The new narrative, which still decorates the walls, was immediately painted by Nicolò Miretto and Stefano da Ferrara.

Johan Huizinga pointed out in his epochal 1921 *Herfsttij der Middeleeuwen* that "the life of medieval Christendom is permeated in all aspects by religious images. There is nothing and no action that is not put in its relationship to Christ and faith."[1] And, indeed, nothing can document this statement better than the extensive amalgamation of saints and astrological influences presented in 333 panels on the walls of the Palazzo della Ragione

[1]Citation in Huizinga 1996, 174.

(Salone). Just as it was important to know which saint would be in charge of the protection during a particular day or month, no less crucial was the position of the planets and constellations. It should therefore not be surprising that planetary iconography was frequently appearing in comprehensive compositions such as the one depicted on the walls of the Salone, which is the rarest example of an entirely preserved large-scale medieval astrological cycle. Each of the twelve sections, referring to the twelve months, opens with the image of the apostle of the month, followed by the allegorical representation of the month, its zodiacal sign, the planet and constellation, and finally, images showing labors and influences associated with that period of the calendar.

The understanding of celestial movements was particularly important because not only were they considered significant in a fatalistic context, determining the future, talents, skills, and occupations of a newborn child, but they were also providers of optimal circumstances for the pursuit of taking certain actions in daily life. Whereas today's pedagogues would be concerned about the most appropriate age for a child to begin studying music or the most suitable method of teaching solfège, medieval teachers, in order to ensure good results in teaching music, used to adjust their curriculum according to the favorable position of the planets. For example, the Arabic astrologer 'Alī ibn Aḥmad al-'Imrānī (Haly) offered in his treatise *De electionibus horarum laudabilium*, translated into Latin in 1134, a whole chapter "on teaching songs and those things which pertain to pleasure."

> Someone has said that it is necessary when playing the lyre that the Moon should be in Capricorn; but in striking the drum (atambur) and other [instruments] similar to this it should be in the last part of Leo; and in blowing trumpets it should be in signs lacking voice. For the signs having voices are good for modulating songs and speeches, and this is especially true for Gemini and Virgo.[2]

Anticipating planetary effects throughout the year was therefore important, and even Paduans who might not know how to read – and even if they did, calendars were not available in print – had here a handy guide through their lives, ranging from saints that protected them to planets that influenced them. And what would be a more appropriate place to have such a reminder of beneficial and pernicious days than the palace where judges delivered justice and deadbeats had to sit humiliated on the stone of shame and, dressed only in shirt and pants, repeat "cedo bonis" in front of at least

[2] The treatise was translated into Latin by Albraham bar Ḥiyya, in Barcelona in 1134. The chapter is in its original Latin text, and the English translation published in Burnett 1993, 7-8.

one hundred people, before being banished from the city into an uncertain future. For us today, some of the personifications of these influences look vague and abstract, and we can identify them only by inquiry into contemporaneous literature, but to their contemporaries they were an easily understandable codebook.

Trecento music theory, visual compositions, philosophy, and sciences were rooted in antiquity, and astrology was no exception. One of the most widely circulated astrological works was *Kitāb al-madkhal al-kabīr ʻalā ʻilm aḥkām al-nujūm*, written in Baghdad in A.H. 234 (AD 848) by Abu Maʻshar (known also by the Latin name of Albumasar), who was born in Balkh in Khorasan (now in Iran) in A.H. 173 (AD 787) and died almost a centenarian, in al-Wāsit (central Mesopotamia) in A.H. 272 (AD 886). The treatise, which summarized the entire ancient knowledge of the stars, was the principal source for later Western astrology, making Abu Maʻshar the supreme authority on astronomy and astrology, first among the Arabs, and then in the West. During a period of only ten years, the treatise was translated into Latin twice, first in 1133 by John of Seville (Johannes Hispalensis) as *Liber maior introductorius ad scienciam indiciorum astrorum*, and then in 1140-1143 by Hermann of Dalmatia as *Introductiorium maius in astronomiam.* The work interprets the influences of heavenly bodies on the sublunar world along the lines of Aristotelian physics and cosmology, and therefore it was a particularly important agent in the dissemination of Aristotle's doctrine. At the time the treatise was translated in Spain, Aristotle was not known in the West, and therefore none other than Abu Maʻshar became the channel through which Aristotelian natural philosophy entered the West, some twenty years before any specific work of Aristotle's was actually translated into Latin.[3]

Although Hermann's translation was more widely disseminated through the West, both translations were used as sources for later ones. Ibn Ezra (also known by the Latin name Avenarius, c.1093-1167) translated the treatise into Hebrew. In 1272 Hagin von Mecheln translated Ibn Ezra's version into French, and, his text was, in turn, a source for the 1293 Latin translation by Pietro d'Abano. Although it is impossible today to determine how much of the chart showing celestial influences depicted on the walls of the Salone in its current state is the reconstruction of the destroyed original designed by Pietro and painted by Giotto, it is fairly certain that at one time Paduans had in the hall where they conducted their business one of the best reference guides on what may or may not happen in their lives. And this reference guide bridged the millennium and a half between antique sciences and their mirrored reflection at the dawn of the Renaissance.

[3]Lemay 1962, 40.

Although astrology was for the Paduans an important tool in planning their activities, the power of saintly protection remained just as highly appreciated. Upon the canonization of Saint Anthony in 1232, Paduans began to build a sanctuary dedicated to him, and the basilica with eight-tiered domes was finished around 1300. Nevertheless, it took another century and a half for the completion of the high altar, designed between 1446 and 1450. Donatello, who had the ultimate gift for dramatic narrative, pushed the composition of the Santo altar further than any earlier artist. Six life-size standing bronze figures of saints had possibly been placed on either side of the central group of the seated Virgin and Child, all enclosed in an open tabernacle by eight columns of classical form. He obviously intended to have the figures seen as occupying a unified space and connected through gestures and emotion. Such a composition was only a step away from the representations of saintly gatherings, known as *sacra conversazione*, which emerged in northern Italy in the middle of the fifteenth century. Realism was an important quality at the time, and saints on altar retables were supposed to appear as if they had just come down to meet the pious folk in their devotion.

Somewhere in the original Santo altar, four rectangular bronze reliefs showing Donatello's vision of miracles that Saint Anthony produced during his lifetime were inserted. Again, Donatello could not have avoided antiquity in the composition, and in the background inserted elements of complex classical architecture, superimposing them in the foreground with crowded scenes witnessing Saint Anthony's holy acts. These reliefs were interspersed with twelve panels of music-making angels, four symbols of the evangelists, and a panel showing the image of the dead Christ mourned by two angels. Because of its innovative format and a variety of compositional and figurative ideas, the high altar of one of the most visited churches of northern Italy undoubtedly had a great influence, spreading beyond Paduan artists. However, its dismantling in 1579 made its original appearance a mystery and left us unsure of the novelties it introduced. Since art historians have not yet arrived at a solution regarding the original appearance of the altar, evidence that provides Marchetto's references about the classification of musical instruments might offer clues for a reconstruction of the arrangement of Donatello's music-making angels.

The influence of Donatello's Paduan work radiated in several directions, and the first to fall under his spell were his assistant Niccolò Pizzolo, working on the terra-cotta altarpiece of the enthroned Virgin and Child with saints in the funerary chapel of Antonio degli Ovetari at the Chiesa degli Eremitani (1449-1453), and Andrea Mantegna who, among his first major works, painted the fresco on the chapel's wall communicating scenes from the life of Saint James. The composition, destroyed in a 1944 bombing, closely follows Donatello's manner of narrating the story and, just like the scenes of miracles of Saint Anthony on the Santo altar, an effort was made here to execute with great detail vast vistas of Roman architecture and Roman costumes. Marco Zoppo (1433-1478), another Squarcione pupil, also could not have escaped Donatello's shadow, particularly apparent in his *Virgin and Child* of 1478 (Wimborne Madonna; Musée du Louvre).

A somewhat oversized and monumental likeness of the Blessed Virgin is placed against the background of a classical niche decorated with festoons, surrounded by four music-making angels on the parapet. In our context, it is particularly important that the appearance of the angels closely resembles, down to some details of costume, their counterparts on Donatello's Santo altar discussed in this volume. A similar influence is detectable in the composition of *Virgin with Child* from c. 1461 by Giorgio Schiavone (1433/36-1504), today at the Walters Art Gallery in Baltimore. Although Schiavone liberated himself in this composition from references to antiquity, such as architectural arches or even SPQR initials which appear in his other Madonna compositions, on the parapet on each side of the Virgin is included a Donatellesque angel, one playing a short-neck fiddle and the other a lute. Such compositions of Virgin with Child surrounded by angels are, in a way, governed by similar premises as *sacra conversazione.* Instead of saints, the divine space that surrounds the Virgin is connected here to the mundane space of the worshiper through the angels playing music or, in other compositions, offering fruits. But unlike the putti on festoons and imposts, who appear ageless, the ages of angels playing music or offering Christ fruit are easily recognizable and, in these cases, could be same as the age of Christ, with whom they interact. Although they do have wings, they are firmly sitting or standing on the ground, as any wingless human would do. Soon after, painters began including angel musicians in *sacra conversazione* who were usually realistically shown youths, losing all celestial attributes as, for example, on paintings of the Virgin by Giovanni Bellini and, later, Vittore Carpaccio and Giovani Battista Cima da Conegliano. Although the size of these angels is often reduced compared with the saints, when perceived independently in their own right all, of their proportions are correct, and the ratio between them and the instruments they are holding is normally realistic.

As they are now, at the beginning of the third millennium – when important historical situations remain engraved in our collective memory museum with images rather than literary texts, and certain written genres which historians once used in their research are vanishing from their current diet – visual narratives were, in early modern Padua, an important medium through which to perceive biblical history and its morals, determine favorable and unfavorable celestial sways, and record historical chronology or the deeds of illustrious Padua citizens and their guests. Visual narratives were a convenient tool for communicating messages at a time when written books were expensive and rare, and literacy might not have been at its best among common people. The tapestry of visual narratives in Paduan public and private spaces is extraordinary. They appear in different renditions, shapes, and sizes, providing us (if we know how to read them) with evidence of just about everything happening in the town. In some places, it feels almost as if Paduans had a need to counterbalance their old stories with the new ones, constantly creating new accounts around them. For pilgrims coming today to Il Santo, Donatello's dramatic visions of miracles that Saint Anthony produced during his life might remain overshadowed by the more flashy narrative of the *ex voti* hanging around the saint's grave in the Santissimo Chapel, documenting Saint Anthony's many posthumous miracles. Few will know today how to read without an explanation the extensive astrological iconography at the Salone and what would be the meaning of this synthesis between saints and celestial symbols. Still, the impact of this composition is so strong that it could easily overshadow another narrative told on the outside of these same walls, where shields carved in stone pay tribute to past captains and governors of the city. Similarly, the history of the university is documented with the names of rectors and graduates posted on the building facade. These narratives sometimes documented history in progress, and other times created visions of historical events seen in retrospect, such as in the monumental presentation of illustrious personalities from Padua's history surrounding Prato della Valle. Traces of the Roman Zairo Theater at the southern edge of the city where in the late seventeenth century replaced by a large public park which was somewhat later encircled with life-size sculptures of eminent Paduans and their guests.

Each of these narratives tells its own story and, in so doing, applies different means to achieve the most convincing result in advancing its agenda. Different media in the process invariably cross over, making it often difficult for us to understand subtleties of the conveyed message and to learn why something appears the way it does. Even the literary language set in madrigals might be only somewhat comprehensible to today's listener, who easily misses references to individuals from the Paduan Trecento society or allusions and allegories obvious to their original listeners. To read the coded language and messages, one needs to apply different methodologies and skills, which can be particularly difficult when the text is distanced from us in time and loaded with symbolism and forgotten references. After reading the present volume, Tartini will still retain in our collective memory his iconic place, but explained and interpreted narratives will bring the Paduan proto-Renaissance closer to us, making it just as important an item in our museum of music history.

Zdravko Blažeković
The Graduate Center, City University of New York

Introduction

For more than sixty years, between the demise of Ezzelino da Romano in 1260 and the beginning of the reign of the Carrara family in 1328, the city of Padua enjoyed freedom from tyrannical leaders and warring factions. The city flourished in an unprecedented manner during this "golden age": major construction took place within its walls, including the building of the Scrovegni Chapel and the expansion of the already gargantuan Palazzo della Ragione. Paduans renovated ancient Roman bridges and roads and reconstructed city doors. The trade of wool, once a vital part of the ancient Roman markets, was reinvigorated, and Padua's exports in textiles and agricultural products were restored to their classical grandeur. In the intellectual arena, Trecento Padua boasted one of Europe's most venerated universities. The city could count Marchetto da Padova, Dante Alighieri, Giotto di Bondone, playwright Albertino Mussato, and medical doctor and astronomer Pietro d'Abano among its luminaries.[1]

Music flourished in Padua during this period. A *schola cantorum* existed in the late thirteenth century under the direction of a *magister scholarum* (responsible for the instruction of grammar and music) and a *cantor*, who directed the performances of plainchant (Petrobelli 1977, 441-442). Two extant manuscripts preserve a substantial repertory of sacred music documenting theatrical productions of New Testament stories – the so-called *uffici drammatici* (dramatic offices) – musical settings of feasts, including those of the Annunciation, Resurrection, and Ascension. Although most of the extant music is monophonic, a unique note-against-note polyphonic style, dubbed *cantus planus binatim* by F. Alberto Gallo, can also be found in this repertory. The Rossi Codex, the earliest compilation of secular Italian music, is also believed to have originated from the Padua and greater Veneto regions. Marchetto da Padova, the greatest Italian theorist of the Trecento (and, as will be newly documented in this work, a friend of Robert

[1]Dante resided in Padua between March and September of 1306 – at the same time that Giotto was completing the frescoes in the Scrovegni Chapel (Gloria 1865, 21).

of Anjou), composed several motets during this period, including the three-part *Ave regina celorum.* Marchetto contributed significantly to the new notational practices of the Ars Nova in his influential treatises the *Pomerium artis musicae mensuratae* and *Lucidarium in arte musicae planae*, in which, among other important lessons, he insisted that musical notation capture to the greatest extent possible the intent of the composer. Marchetto wrote in the *Pomerium*: "Art imitates nature as far as it can (as Aristotle said in book II of the *Physica*). I shall prove this with an example: he who paints a lily or a horse strives as far as he can to paint it so as to resemble a horse or a lily in nature."[2]

Like Marchetto's new theories of notation, Giotto's renderings of music-making in Padua capture musical instruments, players, singers, and musical settings more realistically, unlike earlier representations, which were generally stylized, merely decorative, and infrequent. Artists primarily represented music in relation to the Book of Revelation and the Coronation of Mary. It will be argued that Giotto introduced several important musical prototypes for generations of subsequent painters. These scenes include the *Wedding Procession*, the *Feast of Herod*, and the many angel choirs that grace Italian frescoed ceilings. Giotto also painted the instruments as if he had carefully observed them in his studio, and rendered them in such detail that they can be studied by musicologists as reproductions of actual artifacts of the period.

This book, *Giotto's Harmony*, explores the philosophical and cultural intersection between artists and intellectuals of Padua during its golden age, and the resulting formulation of an Italian pre-humanist musical aesthetic. The book focuses on the work of Giotto, Marchetto da Padova, and Pietro d'Abano. Padua's unique intellectual fervor and proximity to Venice drew these titan celebrities together; the richness of their cross-disciplinary work places Padua at the forefront of musical pre-humanism. While pre-humanist endeavors in Padua have long been established,[3] musical pre-humanism is a term I introduce in this book to describe the burgeoning musical culture of early Trecento Padua. Paduan pre-humanist contributions will be viewed as the vanguard of musical development in Italy, rather than as a footnote

---

[2]Translated in Gallo 1985, 115-116. "Et tunc assumimus secundum principium: ars imitatur naturam in quantum potest (per Phylosophum, secundo Physicorum). Probatio per exemplum: nam qui depingit lilium vel equum, nititur ipsa depingere in quantum potest ad similitudinem equi seu lilii naturalis" (Da Padova 1961, 50). For more about Marchetto and Giotto, see Beck (February) 1999, 7-24. The titles of treatises are found in English, Latin, and Italian in this book. It has proven impractical to place them all in the same language. Instead, I refer to titles found in the bibliography.

[3]Kristeller (1985, 1-18) discusses Paduan humanism and scholastism. Palisca (1985, 51-67) calls Pietro one of the precursors of musical humanism.

to the musical culture of Florence. Indeed, I maintain that the musical Renaissance, which is often believed to have its origins in the much later work of Dunstable and Dufay, has its roots in Padua's pre-humanist tradition.

The first two chapters of this book present the philosophical and intellectual underpinnings of Paduan musical culture. Chapter 1 establishes the landscape of Padua's Greek and Roman musical ancestry as resurrected in the Trecento by the medieval chroniclers Rolandino, Da Nono, and Cortusi, and by Renaissance writers Ongarello and Scardeone. Examples include the excavation and veneration of Roman architectural foundations, such as the Scrovegni and Prato della Valle, and the furtherance of the lore of Padua's founding by Antenor, the brother of Achilles. Antenor's bones were exhumed in the late thirteenth century, and his sarcophagus, inscribed with dedicatory words by poet and pre-humanist Lovato Lovati, was placed in the center of Padua.

This archaeological spirit certainly influenced the type of music performed in Trecento Padua. Paduan chronicles document its citizens engaging in public celebrations in imitation of the city's Roman tradition. Large celebrations with musical accompaniments filled the streets. The many trumpet processions that took place in Trecento Padua are further vestiges of Roman practice. Archival evidence suggests that Paduan confraternities paid trumpeters to play at their reunions. During the popular Feast of the Annunciation, the music of which survives in manuscripts of the *uffici drammatici*, the clerics were accompanied in their procession to the Scrovegni Chapel by musicians playing brass instruments who were expected to perform their services without pay. The plays of Albertino Mussato, based on the classical themes of Seneca, also contained choruses and processions accompanied by instruments.

Chapter 2 explores a second primary influence in the development of musical pre-humanism in early Trecento Padua: the scholastic study of the natural sciences, or the so-called Aristotelian philosophy of nature. The University of Padua was renowned for its faculty of the natural sciences, hailing among its famous students Albert the Great and Witelo. It will be demonstrated that Marchetto da Padova, who was at the forefront of the Italian Ars Nova, and, as will be established, the first Italian musical pre-humanist, appropriated Aristotelian philosophy in his *Lucidarium* (1317 or 1318) and *Pomerium* (before 1319). While earlier French theorists had been influenced by Aristotelian dialectic and modes of argument, Marchetto uniquely emphasized the "scientific" language and methodology of Aristotle's philosophy. Pietro d'Abano was the most renowned Paduan to embrace the study of Aristotle's *Physica* and *Metaphysica* and was dubbed the "second Aristotle" by Savonarola. Also a capable music theorist, Pietro d'Abano incorporated Aristotle's and Boethius's views of nature and music into his formulation of scientific theories in his *Conciliator* (1303) and *Expositio problematum Aristotelis* (1310).

The next three chapters explore the manner in which Aristotelian philosophy and the cultural influences described above are manifested in the primary musical and figurative artifacts of the period. Chapter 3 examines the extant musical repertory – specifically, the written tradition of the madrigal and caccia. In this chapter, I argue that the early madrigal found its original inspiration in what I call the shepherd motif. From its inception, the madrigal exhibited a strong connection to the classical pastoral tradition. The anonymous writer of the *Capitulum applicatis verbis*, who was active in the Veneto region around 1315, describes the madrigal as follows: "The texts of madrigals should be about shepherdesses, flowers, orchards, garlands, fields and the like, but in good subject-matter, language and expression."[4] Antonio da Tempo, a Paduan lawyer and man of letters, described the etymology of "madrigal" as originating from *mandriale* or *mandria* (herd).[5] This chapter will trace the evolution of the madrigal in Padua, with particular attention given to a "cycle" of poems originating from the Veneto region that share the name Anna and the tree *perlaro*. The music of Maestro Piero, Giovanni da Cascia, Jacopo da Bologna, and later Bartolino da Padova and Johannes de Ciconia, will be a primary subject of inquiry in tracing the proto-Renaissance spirit of rebirth and science in Padua.

In addition to its literary connections, the shepherd image – and by extension the woman spinning wool – was central to the spirit of Padua, whose citizens prided themselves in the city's rich agricultural surroundings in the delta of the Po River (from which Padua derives its name). The wool motif is found in numerous pieces of art from the period. Giotto incorporates a prominent figure of a woman spinning wool in his *Annunciation to Anna*, and sheep and shepherds abound in his *Joachim Retires to the Sheepfold* and *Sacrifice to Joachim*, all three in the Scrovegni Chapel. One also finds a *mandriano* (shepherd) as part of the representation of the month of August in the astrological ceiling of the Salone della Ragione. Could the word *madrigal* have its origin in the town of Mandria (just five kilometers southwest of Padua), just as *tarantella* derives from the town of Taranto?

Chapters 4 and 5 examine Giotto's depictions of music-making in his fresco painting, taking as a starting point the representation of music be-

[4]Translated in Gallo 1985, 121. "...cuius verba volunt esse de villanellis, de floribus, arbustis, sertis, utere et similibus, dummodo sit bona sentencia, loquela et sermo" (Debenedetti 1906-1907, 80.)

[5]Da Tempo 1977, 70.

neath the figure of *Justice* in the Scrovegni Chapel. *Justice* sits in a niche surrounded by classical and Gothic decorations. In a marble-like space beneath her, three females sing and dance to the playing of a tambourine. On the opposite wall sits *Injustice*, an old corrupt judge on a crumbling seat, bordered by cracking medieval ramparts. Beneath him the once placid world has been disrupted, the women beaten, and the music stopped. It will be shown that the origin of this enigmatic program lies within a reading of Cicero's *De Republica* as transmitted in the *City of God* by Augustine. Classicism pervades Giotto's *Justice*, which emphasizes balance of the musical scene in contrast to the chaos of a corrupt medieval life. The connection between music and justice established in the frescoes is paramount to the understanding of many subsequent representations of music in the Trecento, including Ambrogio Lorenzetti's dancing women in the *Effects of Good Government in the City* in the Sala della Pace in Siena and Boccaccio's ballatas for the end of each day in the *Decameron*.

Chapter 5 begins with an exploration of the musical figures in the primary narrative pictures of Giotto's Scrovegni Chapel frescoes and their relationship to the work of Marchetto da Padova. It will be demonstrated that Giotto repainted musical instruments in these works, shortening trumpets in *Wedding Procession* to tone down the visual "sound" in his pictures. It is noteworthy that the faint outlines of longer trumpets have been replaced by reedlike instruments. The depiction of music as emblematic of temperate behavior in Giotto's fresco reflects pre-humanist beliefs as expounded by Pietro d'Abano and Marchetto da Padova. Giotto may have been inspired by Marchetto to make this change. Indeed, F. Alberto Gallo (1974) has suggested a connection between Giotto and Marchetto, noting that Marchetto's motet the *Ave regina celorum/ Mater innocencie* was written for the opening ceremonies of the Scrovegni Chapel. In addition, the unique relationship between the composition of the motet and the structure of Giotto's frescoes will be brought to light: among other similarities, the tenor of the motet contains the same number of longs (39) as the number of narrative frescoes in Giotto's series.

The second half of chapter 5 examines other representations of music-making in the work of Giotto, such as the cycle of paintings in the Upper Church of Saint Francis of Assisi, the Peruzzi Chapel, the Stefaneschi Polyptych, and the Baroncelli Polyptych, and Marchetto's and Pietro's influence on these works. It will be argued that an understanding of the meaning of the musical elaborations in Giotto's work is central to the artist's conception of time and space, and this interdisciplinary complexity in his frescoes is echoed in Bruce Cole's description of Giotto as an "auditory painter" whose "narratives are often filled with implied sound" (1996, 345).

Chapter 6 contemplates representations of music in Padua after Giotto. Three primary works will be examined: the astrological frescoes in the Salone della Ragione, Giusto de' Menabuoi's frescoes and polyptych in the Baptistery of Padua, and Donatello's bronze altar in the Church of Saint Anthony of Padua. These works have been chosen because (1) they contain extensive and varied depictions of music, (2) they were influenced by the prevailing theories of Pietro d'Abano and Marchetto da Padova, and (3) they illustrate the transition from late medieval to Renaissance style in Padua. The chapter begins with the Salone della Ragione frescoes, whose program was believed to have been inspired by Pietro d'Abano. While scholars have scrutinized the structure and significance of the frescoes as a whole, little has been written about the significance of the musical scenes. Not only do they capture evidence of where and when music was performed, they provide information concerning the relationship between the performance of music and what was believed to be the influence of the planets on earthly actions. In unraveling the musical signification of these frescoes, I propose that they capture the prevailing pre-humanistic theory, expounded by Pietro d'Abano, Cecco d'Ascoli, and Dante, that music and astrology be viewed as legitimate sciences rather than as frivolous or degenerate activities.[6]

Giusto de' Menabuoi's frescoes and polyptych in the Paduan Baptistery will serve as example of the influence of Giotto's new musical realism in the work of this Paduan artist. Giusto's frescoes have been dubbed a "crowning" achievement in late medieval art, and it will be newly shown that their composition was also based on the prevailing musical theories of Marchetto, who was still influencing artists and music theorists fifty years after his death.

Finally, the chapter will examine the work of Donatello in the Church of Saint Anthony of Padua and demonstrate the influence of Giotto's musical realism in the mature Renaissance, again with a nod to Pietro and Marchetto. Donatello's bronze altar is replete with musical angels, and it will be suggested that the prevailing musical tradition in Padua informs the work, leading to a new hypothesis regarding the original placement of the angels on the altar. Like Giotto, the Tuscan Donatello came to Padua in the midst of a brilliant career and contributed significantly to Paduan culture.

In conclusion, *Giotto's Harmony* will summarize the contributions of the Paduan pre-humanists that led to a flourishing of realistic renderings of music-making. Giotto's work in Padua will be situated at the forefront of

[6]Cecco d'Ascoli, a professor of astrology at Bologna, was familiar with Pietro's writings since the two universities had many ties in the Middle Ages (Siraisi 1973, 16). Dante's *Convivio*, written between 1304 and 1308 (during his time in Padua), contains an important passage (2.13.20-25) concerning the musical properties of Mars and its relation to the trivium and quadrivium.

a new realistic movement in painting – echoed in musical notation – that flourished in Padua and had as its philosophical underpinning the scholastic writing of Aristotle as transmitted by Pietro and Marchetto, placing Padua at an important crossroad of the Renaissance, where music infused the narrative with drama.

Chapter 1

Reclaiming the Musical Artifacts of Padua's Greek and Roman Past

In his influential *Renaissance and Renascences in Western Art*, Erwin Panofsky (1960, 151) noted the impact of classical artifacts on painting:

> Looking out of his "window" the painter learned to perceive the products of Roman art – buildings and statues, gems and coins, but above all reliefs – as part and parcel of his visible and reproducible environment, as "objects" in the literal sense of the word (objectum, 'that which is set against me').

A similar impulse may be discerned in the musical repertory and theory of Trecento and Quattrocento Padua, where the imitation of Greek and Roman vistas and the renaissance of classical theoretical ideals thoroughly inform Paduan musical culture. Madrigal and caccia texts preserved in the Rossi Codex, a compilation of secular music composed in the first decades of the fourteenth century, contain numerous allusions to mythic creatures and luscious vistas that evoke a glorious pastoral past. Motets written by Johannes Ciconia in the early fifteenth century exalted the splendor of early modern Padua. Paduan music theorists Marchetto da Padova, Pietro d'Abano, and Prosdocimo Beldomandis infused their observations with nods to Aristotle, Cicero, and Boethius, to name a few. Paduans reenacted memories of Roman musical customs with large gatherings in their piazzas and streets, at the same time that theorists laid the groundwork for the Italian Ars Nova, a movement associated with new rhythmic and notational practices in the early Trecento.

Chroniclers captured evidence of festivals, weddings, and contests that featured elaborate musical accompaniments based on Roman traditions. In his history of Padua, Giuseppe Gennari noted that like their Roman ancestors, Paduans took particular joy in *spettacoli.* Writing about an otherwise uneventful winter of 1300, Gennari observes:

> Also in Padua, even though there existed no occasion or victory or marriage, great and pleasurable festivities were organized in February. Our chroniclers do not provide any other reason except that they were done to publicly celebrate Padua's maximum liberty.[1]

Beautiful women took to the streets:

> The ladies with tightly shaped and highly ceremonial costumes were escorted from the newly made balconies of the palace, and with their presence they increased the gaiety and the splendor of the festivity, which ended with a rich banquet that included 400 guests, among them aristocrats and common people.[2]

Gennari claims that these Paduan celebrations, like their Roman precursors, were designed to keep Padua's citizens engaged in public duty:

> The citizenry loved spectacle, and Augustus, an excellent political man, could not have found a better way to remind the Romans of the loss of liberty than to maintain the abundance of Rome, and maintain the citizens' devotion with frequent games and joyful festivities.[3]

What was Padua's perceived Greek and Roman inheritance and how did it influence composers and music theorists in the Trecento and early Renaissance? This chapter will examine and piece together visual, historical, and

[1]Author's translation unless otherwise specified. "Anche in Padova, benchè con ci fosse occasione alcuna o di vittorie ottenute, o di nozze, nel febbraio di quest'anno furono fatte grandi allegrezze e piacevoli intertenimeni. I nostri Cronisti altra raggione non ne rendeono se non che si fecero *in publicam laetitiam propter Paduae maximam libertatem"* (Gennari 1804, 88).

[2]"Le gentildonne attillate ed in tutta gala vi assistettero da' ballatoi del palazzo nuovamente fatti, e colla loro presenza accrebbero gaiezza e splendore alla festa, la quale terminò con un lauto banchetto di quattrocento persone tra nobili e popolari" (Gennari 1804, 88).

[3]"Il popolo ama perdutamente gli spettacoli: e Augusto eccellente politico non trovò mezzo più acconcio per fare che i Romani della perduta libertà si dimenticassero, che mantenere l'abbondanza in Roma, ed intrattenere i cittadini con frequenti giuochi ed allegre feste" (Gennari 1804, 88).

musical artifacts associated with Roman and Greek tradition that were revived and elaborated upon in the Trecento and Quattrocento by Paduan chroniclers and historians, including the history of the founding of Padua, as told by Renaissance chroniclers Scardeone, Ongarello, and Livy, Padua's famous son. The reconstruction of Paduan classical heritage will lay the foundation from which an interdisciplinary picture of Paduan music and theory will emerge in later chapters.

The *Historiae de urbis Patavii*, written in 1560 by Bernardino Scardeone (1478-1574), provides a captivating description of Paduan music history from the Roman period to the Renaissance. His chapter "De claris musicis Patavinis" begins with a brief introductory section in which he brings to the fore the most important names associated with Paduan music:

> Up to this point enough has been said concerning poets and writers of our ancient Latin and Etruscan languages. Now follow the musicians of our city, who because of the nature of the location and the talent of the city (like the doctors) were and are still numerous and abundant and cannot be separated from the divinity of the place.[4]

Certainly the number and quality of musical practitioners attest to Padua's eminence in music.

> This is abundantly confirmed in our time, which has brought to light many ancient musicians, singers, horn, trumpet, and cither players and the same type of concert players of great talent.[5]

Scardeone argues that Paduan musicians were the first to revive ancient texts and customs in the Trecento:

> Later, and I do not know for what reason this took place, something that must seem very extraordinary, how it came to be that all the famous arts and disciplines, once made completely extinct in Italy by the Gothic furor, became resuscitated for the first time in Padua from their tomb. It happened! So we see that Pietro d'Abano was the first among the others to bring to Italy many medications from his sojourn in Greece; Albertino Mussato among others was almost

[4]"Hactenus de Poetis, atque de Latinae et Hetruscae linguae scriptoribus dictum est satis. Succedant his modo Musici, quibus civitas nostra pro natura loci, et urbis genio (quod et de medicis superius dictum est) mirifice semper abundavit, abundatque in praesenti:ut nunquam a se ipsa, atque a suo ipsius loci genio discedere omnino possit"(Scardeone 1979, 295-296).

[5]"Hoc autem abunde nobis aetas haec nostra probat, quae plurimos Musicos, cantores, cornicines, tibicines, cytharoedos, et id genus concentuum peritissimos in lucem protulit" (Scardeone 1979, 295-296).

> the first to bring the ornaments of poetry and the charm of Latin reason.[6]

This passage is revelatory for several reasons. Scardeone places Padua at the forefront of the Renaissance revival, noting that the "famous arts and disciplines" were resuscitated in Italy for the first time in Padua. He calls the period prior to the Trecento "the result of Gothic furor," seemingly differentiating Italy's accomplishments from those of France. Interestingly, Scardeone mentions Pietro and Mussato in this section dedicated to music, indicating that he acknowledges their contributions to music, even though they were best known for their successes in other disciplines. Pietro, a philosopher and doctor, described the properties of music in his writing; Mussato, a playwright and statesman, brought a musicality found in ancient drama into his poetry. By incorporating these figures into his discussion of music, Scardeone attests to the interdisciplinary nature of the musical culture of his native city.

In addition to Pietro and Mussato, Scardeone praises several figures connected to early literature in the vulgate, including Brandino Padovano and Antonio da Tempo. He notes that Brandino Padovano "was the first among Italians to embellish the vulgate."[7] Dante describes Brandino in chapter 14 of *Volgare eloquenza* as if he had known him personally. He writes: "of whom we see one, who has forced himself to let go of his maternal language to reduce himself to speaking the vulgate: and this is Brandino Padovano."[8] Scardeone next invokes the name of Antonio da Tempo, a lawyer and writer, whose volume *Delle rime volgari* (1332) examines the types of music and texts that flourished in the Trecento. Scardeone explains that da Tempo "demonstrated a multifarious variety of modes in the harmony of the vulgate."[9]

Indeed, according to Scardeone, da Tempo was the first to determine the Italian doctrine of the variation of rhyme. His contributions to music will be further examined in chapter 3.

[6] "Porro nescio quo fato contigerit quod mirum admodum videri debet, ut omnes praeclarae artes ac disciplinae, quae olim Gothico furore penitus in Italia extrinctae fuerant, Patavii primum attollere potissimum oculos, et reviviscere, atque e sepulchro quodammodo exsurgere visae sint. Sicut enum diximus Petrum Aponum primum ante alios per multa secula profugam medcinam e Graecia in Italiam traduxisse: et Albertinum Musatum prae caeteris fere primum ad poetis ornatum, historiaeque ac orationis Latinae condimentum recens quodpiam attulisse" (Scardeone 1979, 295-296).

[7] "Et Brandinum Paduanum exornare elocutionem vulgarem apud Italos primum tentasse" (Scardeone 1979, 295-296).

[8] "... tra i quali abbiamo veduto uno, che si è sforzato partire dal suo materno parlare, e ridursi al volgare cortigiano: e questo fu Brandino Padovano" (Dante 1868, 35).

[9] "Et Antonium Tempum in rhythmicis eiusdem linguae concentibus, multiplicem modorum varietatem monstrasse" (Scardeone 1979, 295-296).

With respect to music theory, Scardeone lauds the contributions of Marchetto da Padova:

> So also we may affirm that in this same generation Marchetto da Padova brought forth the first foundations of music, which like the other sciences of which I have spoken about to this point, was kept in exile by the tyrannical Gothic monstrosity.[10]

Scardeone maintains that Marchetto was significant in the history of Paduan music because he dedicated himself to the scientific study of music and championed serious musical study by fleshing out its principles in his *Lucidarium* and *Pomerium*. Scardeone explains that Marchetto was known first as a philosopher and second as a great practitioner of music: "Marchetto da Padova, the first and most learned philosopher and man of music, honored his patria and Italy greatly with his celebrated art."[11]

Scardeone also applauds the talents of Prosdocimo Beldomandis:

> Worthy of no less praise in the material of music, but gifted with even greater abilities in all the other liberal arts, is the brilliant Prosdocimo Beldomandis, of a noble Paduan family: an excellent musician, distinguished philosopher, and famous astrologer. He published an excellent treatise on the spheres.[12]

Before concluding his brief biographies of Trecento and Renaissance Paduan composers and musicians, among them Marchetto, Prosdocimo Beldomandis, Antonio Lydio, Antonio Martorello, Antonio Rota, Francesco Portenario, and Annibale Patavino, Scardeone furnishes the reader with several classical stories in praise of music:

> Therefore, in my task of having to laud musicians, it is not easy to speak about the faculty of dancing and singing: music in Greek times was held in great consideration, and they believed that the greatest erudition and nobility consisted in the strings and the voices.[13]

---

[10]"Ita quoque affirmare possumus Marchetum Paduanum olim in eo rudi seculo prima Musices fundamenta jecisse: quae et ipsa sane sicut et aliae scientiae, di quibus hactenus dixi, ex tyrannica illa Gothorum immanitate penitus exulabant" (Scardeone 1979, 295-296).

[11]"Ornavit ergo hac tam celebri arte patriam, atque Italiam fere primus Marchetus, cognomento Paduanus, doctissimus philosophus, simil et Musicus" (Scardeone 1979, 297).

[12]"Non minori laude in ea re, in caeteris vero artibus liberalibus majori etiam peritia per ea ipsa tempora claruisse fertur Prosdocimus Beldomandus, e nobili familia Patavina ortus: egregius Musicus, et eximius philosophus, et clarus astrologus. Edidit tractatum sphaerae pulcherrimum" (Scardeone 1979, 297).

[13]"Verumenimvero ut aliquid de Musices laudibus (quum sim de Musicis dicturus) attingam, non est parvi facienda pulsandi atque canendi facultas: quae olim apud Graecos tanti fuerat, ut ipsi summam eruditionem et nobilitatem, in nervorum vocumque concentibus esse putarent" (Scardeone 1979, 295-96).

He provides an example:

> At one time the inhabitants of Mitilene, when they became the rulers of the sea, made a pact that if their citizens became traitors, the punishment was that it was prohibited to traitors' sons to study literature and to play the cither in public.[14]

He cites a story, as retold by Cicero, to demonstrate music's lasting impression:

> How, as Cicero writes, Epanimondas, the most glorious prince of Thebes, was greatly praised because he played the lira very harmoniously. And Themistocles, first among the Athenians, was judged to be ignorant because he hid the lira during banquets, while Socrates, who began to study the lira when he was already an old man, showed himself to be clumsy in the art of music, as if he had never tried it.[15]

Waxing Platonic, Scardeone observes:

> Nothing corresponds to our minds as much as rhythm and sounds, because of which we get excited, we become enraged, we calm down, and we languish.[16]

Scardeone's unearthing of Padua's classical and medieval histories and his emphasis on the city's auspicious location near the Po River delta were vital in reestablishing Padua's cultural preeminence. A potent municipality was reconstructed, rich with tradition and worthy of respect. One of the primary stories ubiquitously told by Paduan chroniclers, including Scardeone, Sertorio Orsato, Guglielmo Ongarello, and Angelo Portenari, was Livy's account of the founding of Padua. Padua was a flourishing Roman municipality according to Livy, who lived in the decades surrounding the birth of Christ.[17]

---

[14]"Unde olim Mitylenaei, qui quum maris imperio potirentur, commilitonibus suis ac sociis civitatibus, si in sanciendo foedere defecissent, hanc poenam esse voluerunt, ut liberi desertorum, et literas discere, et cytharam pulsare publice prohiberentur" (Scardeone 1979, 295-296).

[15]"Quid?(ut scribit Cicero) Epaminondas gloriosissimus ille Thebanorum princeps vehementer laudatur, quod fidibus concinne admodum caneret. Et Themistocles primus ille inter Athenienses, cum inter epulas recusasset lyram, habitus est indoctior, Socratem vero constat iam aetate provectum, fidibus operam dare coepisse, satius esse indicantem, eius artis usum fero, quam nunquam percepisse" (Scardeone 1979, 295-96).

[16]"Nihil tam cognatum nostris mentibus, quam numeros et voces: quibus et excitamur, et incendimur, lenimur et languescimus" (Scardeone 1979, 295-96).

[17]Livy was born in 59 BC, the year of Caesar's first consulship, and died in Padua in 17 AD (1919, IX). The following information about Padua's ancient history is extracted from Sommer's evocative and supremely useful book, a compilation of archival and published facts from Paduan chroniclers and archives. In the text, citations are from the Loeb Classical Library editions.

In the first volume of *From the Founding the City*, Livy provides an early account of the origins of his hometown:

> Antenor [of Troy], with a company of Eneti who had been expelled from Paphlagonia in a revolution and were looking for a home and a leader – for they had lost their king, Pylaemenes, at Troy – came to the inmost bay of the Adriatic. There, driving out the Euganei, who dwelt between the sea and the Alps, the Eneti and the Trojans took possession of those lands (1.1.2-3).[18]

Antenor founded Padua, according to Livy, after the destruction of Troy. Paduan Guglielmo Ongarello, in his fifteenth-century *Cronaca*, amplifies the story with a quotation from Albertino Mussato: "Antenor was a King from the family of the Great Priam" ("Rex fuit Antenor Priami de sanguine Magni"). Ongarello explains that Antenor was a descendant of the family of Priam and "this argument is made because of the emblem that Antenor carried, the golden lilies in a blue background, the emblem of Troy."[19] According to Ongarello, Antenor "made Padua a beautiful city from the remains of the Euganean people."

The story of Padua's founding by Antenor, one of the city's most well-known tales, was revived in the late Duecento by Lovato Lovati (1237-1309). In 1274, a decree of the Republic of Padua ordered the construction of a new hospital for orphans. While excavating the ground to begin the project, a coffin was found containing the body of a warrior in armor, together with more than 3,000 Venetian lire in silver (Sommer 1935, 7-8). A judge and poet, Lovato Lovati was instrumental in determining that the remains were those of Antenor, and he presided over the selection of the body's new location and its magnificent tomb. Ongarello informs us of a curious story regarding Lovato's discovery. A Paduan proverb circulating at the time read: "When the goat speaks, the wolf will respond, and Antenor will rise again."[20] The citizenry believed that Antenor would never be found because the goat doesn't speak to the wolf, and the wolf in turn would not understand. But as Ongarello explains, the chief goat notified *lovo* – that is, Lovato – of the tomb's whereabouts. A celebration was organized, in which the coffin was paraded through the streets, accompanied by all the men and women of the town, to the house of Lovato, whose words, inscribed on the tomb, are still legible:

[18] Virgil, in his *Aeneid*, also describes the founding of Padua by Antenor, at 1.242-249.

[19] "Et questo argomento fano per l'arma, che portava Antenor zoè tre zigi d'oro in lo campo azurro, la qual era arma della Casa de Troglia" (Ongarello, 5). Fabris (1937, 167 and following) purports that "Ongarello's" treatise was written in the second half of the sixteenthth century, and was probably authored by Francesco Refatto da Padova.

[20] "Quando el capra parlerà el Lovo responderà, Antenor se leverà" (Ongarello, 101).

> The famous Antenor, for the good of the people/ Transferred here Venetian and Roman fugitives,/ Expelled the Euganeans,/ founded the city of Padua/ And here is kept in a little marble home.[21]

The announcement of the discovery of Antenor's tomb was of such importance that Brunetto Latini wrote about it in his *Il Tesoretto* (1.39): "Then Antenor and Priam left with a great company of men, and they went to the Marsh of Treviso, and there they built another city which is called Padua, where the body of Antenor lies, and where his sepulcher is still today."[22] The consecration of this tomb by the Paduans as that of Antenor fueled an already prosperous city government intent on transforming the once gloomy city governed by a tyrannical Ezzelino into a new free republic. Later, the sword found in Antenor's tomb was donated to Alberto della Scala, head of the Scaligeri dynasty, as an example of Paduan pride in its past (Pignoria 1625, 92).

Scholars credit Lovato and Albertino Mussato with initiating the prehumanist movement in the last decades of the thirteenth century in Padua. Robert Weiss, in *The Dawn of Humanism in Italy* (1947, 5), argues that these luminaries were the first practitioners of a new humanist movement in all of Italy. Weiss notes that it is no coincidence that these men, all interested in reviving ancient thought, were connected with the law. He explains, "Their application of the Digest and Code to contemporary problems led them to see Roman civilization as a living thing" (5). John Kenneth Hyde, in his seminal *Padua in the Age of Dante* (1966, 283-303), also views Lovato and Mussato, contemporaries of Pietro and Marchetto, as the precursors of full-fledged Renaissance Humanism, calling them pre-humanists because of their knowledge, their work as translators, and their commitment to the revival of ancient texts. In Antenor's retrieval and ceremonial burial we see the first sparks of the new humanist interest in reconstituting Padua from the ashes of tradition.[23]

Livy and later Paduan chroniclers explain that before the arrival of Antenor and prior to the Roman conquest, a people called the Euganei (Greek for "of noble origin"), descendants of the Etruscans, inhabited the Italian peninsula. Among these chronicles is Sertorio Orsato's *Historia di Padova*,

---

[21]"In ditus Antenor patrie vox visa quietam/ Transtulit huc Henetum/ Dardamdumque fugas/ Expulit Euganeos, Patavium condidit Urbem/ Quem tenet hic humili marmore casa domus" (Ongarello, 101).

[22]Latini 1993, 27.

[23]Also fueling the passion for the rebirth of their classical past in the beginning of the fourteenth century was the unearthing of Livy's tombstone. It was housed in the atrium of the basilica of Saint Giustina, where the brother of Albertino Mussato, the playwright, was the abbot (Billanovich 1976, 23).

which consists of a compilation of citations excerpted from classical histories and begins with a consideration of the Euganei:

> That part of the world, in which the city of Padua was established, from that point was distinguished by the names first Euganea, then Gallia Transpadana, then Venezia, and now Lombardia.[24]

The Euganei lived in the hills bordering Padua to the southwest. They were prosperous, as Orsato's quotation from Pliny's *Natural History* evidences: "The Euganei were so numerous and powerful in this area that they owned thirty-four castles."[25] Their name has been retained in the unusual hills that overlook the city, and their name is still found in the small town of Brusegana, once called Burgus Euganeus, which in remote years was an important agricultural center. The Euganei lived a pastoral life, naming their towns "Taurilia" (now Torreglia), "Bovaria" (now Boara), "Villa Tauria" (now Villatora), and most notably for the history of music, "Mandria," which lies to the west of the city and to which we will return (Sommer 1935, 91). The Euganei are significant in the history of music because their name is commonly found in the Trecento madrigal texts examined in chapter 3.

Named for the Po River (in Latin called Padus), Padua flourished in the rich delta region between the Alps and the Apennines.[26] The Po is Italy's most majestic river, flowing from the Western Alps to the Adriatic Sea. Polybius's *Histories* describes it in some detail:

> It has a larger volume of water than any other river in Italy, since all the streams that descend into the plain from the Alps and Apennines flow into it from either side, and is highest and finest at the time of the Dog-star, as it is then swollen by the melting of the snow on those mountains (1922, 2.16.8-10).

In book 3 of his *Natural History*, Pliny notes the origin of the word *Padus*. He writes: "One is ashamed to borrow an account of Italy from

[24]"Quella parte del Mondo, in cui edificata Padova si trova; da quando cominciò ad essere distinta con nomi, prima Euganea, indi Gallia Transpadana, poi Venezia chiamossi, ed ora Lombardia vien detta" (Orsato 1678, 1).

[25]"E furono gli Euganei in queste parti così numerosi e possenti, che vi hebbero trentaquattro castelli se dice il vero Plinio Hist.Nat.lib.3 Cap. 20" (Orsato 1678, 2).

[26]Ongarello provides several colorful origins for Padua. "Lately, it is believed to be called Padua because when it was founded there were many white swans, which augured that the city should be founded; and it is Patavium, that is place founded by the birds. Others say that it is a German word, which means warm baths." "Ultimamente perchè quando fu edificata si dimostrò in quello luogo molti cisani bianchi, per li quali loro tolsero augurio che lì si dovesse edificare, fo dopo chiamata Patavia, id est Patavium, zoè luogo dimostrato per oselli: alcuni altri, che sia parola Todesca et voglia dire luogo de bagni caldi" (6).

the Greeks; nevertheless, Metrodorus of Scepsis, says that the river has received the name Padus because in the neighborhood of its source there is a quantity of pinetrees of the kind called in Gallic dialect *padi*" (Pliny 1942, 3.16.122). The poetical association concerns the story of Phaëthon, who fell into the Po; the weeping-poplar trees and the black clothing of the inhabitants near the river, it is said, still dress thus in mourning of the young man (Polybius 1922, 3.16.13-14).[27] Pliny also observed in his chapter "Wonders of Fountains and Rivers" that "green grass grows in the hot springs of Padua, frogs in those of Pisa, fishes at Vetulonia in Tuscany near the sea" (Pliny 1938, 106.227-228).

Sertorio Orsato records that numerous ancient literary testimonies spoke of the extraordinary richness of the region: "The fertility of the land and the rural mastery of the Patavians, the ample forests, vines, grains, olive trees, pastures, orchards, alongside the products of fishing in the rivers and lagoons provided affluence and wellbeing to the population."[28]

For instance, Polybius in his *Histories* 2.15 writes in the second century BC of the triangle of land formed by the Alps, the Apennines, and the two seas, the Adriatic and the Mediterranean: "Its fertility is not easy to describe." And later, "The cheapness and abundance of all articles of food will be most clearly understood from the following fact. Travelers in this country, who are put up in inns, do not bargain for each separate article they require, but ask what is the charge per diem for one person" (1922, 2.15.3-5). In Martial's *Epigrams* (1920, 10.93), we find the region mentioned once again, this time in verse translated as: "If before me, Clemens, you shall behold Helicaon's Euganean shores, and the fields decked with vine-clad trellises, carry to Sabina of Atesta poems unpublished as yet, and that too newly arrayed in purple wrapper."[29]

Strabo, in his *Geography*, selects Padua as the "best of all cities" in the Veneto region (1923, 5.1.7). He cites a recent census (probably of 14 AD) telling that Patavium had five hundred knights, and in addition, in ancient times, used to send forth an army of one hundred and twenty thousand. With regard to the richness of the land, Strabo acknowledges that Paduans sent to Roman markets clothing of all sorts and many other things that "show what a goodly store of men it has and how skilled they are in the arts"

---

[27]The Greeks called the river Eridanus. "It is navigable for about two thousand stades from the mouth called Olana; for the stream which has been a single one from its source, divides at a place called Trigaboli, one of the mounts being called Padua, and the other Olana" (Polybius 1922, 2.16.10-11).

[28]"... fertilità dell'agro e della perizia rurale dei patavini, ampie foreste, viti, cereali, ulivi, pascoli, frutteti davan coi prodotti della pesca fluviale e lagunare, agiatezza e benessere alla populazione" (Orsato 1678, 48).

[29]Helicaon is Antenor's son.

(1923, 5.1.7). Like other writers, Strabo notes the fine quality of the wool exported from the city, observing that Paduans cultivated the "medium" type of wool, from which were made "expensive carpets and covers and everything of this kind that is wooly either on both sides or only on one" (1923, 5.1.12). Wool was the foremost export of the town, and Martial, in *Epigrams* 14.143, speaks of the splendid thickness of Paduan tunics. Paduan merchants were, in fact, sent to Rome to clothe the citizens of that city. Though the Paduan wool trade seemed to wane during the early Middle Ages, Angelo Portenari records, in his *Della felicità di Padova*, that its export once again became profitable in the middle of the thirteenth century, after Ezzelino's death:

> It is read in the first volume of statutes of the community of Padua that in the year 1265, a little after the death of Ezzelino, under whose tyranny the manufacturing and the arts were left desolate, the manufacture of wool was reinvigorated.[30]

He observes that the wool trade resembled the grandeur of that of ancient times: "There has, then, always been a very proficient wool factory in this city" ("Essendo dunque stato in ogni tempo il lanificio molto essercitato in questa città"). So it was that Ubertino da Carrara put into place incentives for shepherds to cultivate wool:

> Ubertino of Carrara, the third ruler of Padua, wanting to reestablish Padua's ancient reputation in the year 1343, granted many privileges to exceptional wool merchants and in particular decreed that this company of artisans have the ability to elect a magistrate, who will adjudicate on the issues concerning this company, and that this magistrate will be the judge in any civil cases regarding the company.[31]

Padua's prominence in the wool trade survived through the Dark Ages to reach its pinnacle with the Carraresi, who gave prizes to shepherds raising the most sheep (Portenari 1623, 142). Padua's rich history in the wool trade sheds light on Giotto's inclusion of a spinner of wool in his fresco the *Annunciation to Saint Anne* in the Scrovegni Chapel, as well as on the

---

[30] "Parimenti legge nel primo volume delli statuti della Communità di Padova che nell anno 1265, cioè poco dopo la morte di Ezzelino, sotto la cui tirannide gli artifici, e le arti tutte restarono desolate, l'arte della lana era ritornata in piedi" (Portenari 1623, 215).

[31] "Ubertino da Carrara terzo Signor di Padova volendo rimetterlo nell'antica reputazione concesse, nell'anno 1343 molti privilegi, a eccezionali mercatanti di lana, e in particolare decretò, che essa arte havesse facoltà di eleggere un magistrato che tutte le cause ad essa arte spettanti dovesse giudicare il qual magistrato fosse anco giudice in ogni forte di cause civile nel foro all'ufficio del Orso" (Portenari 1623, 216).

many references to shepherds in Paduan musical texts of the Trecento.[32] Padua was a great center of trade, and under Augustus was perhaps, next to Rome, the richest town in Italy.

In addition to its reputation as a trading city, Livy describes with great relish the strength of his native people in fending off the advances of the Spartan Cleonymus (302 BC):

> ...for three maritime villages of the Patavini were situated there along the riverbank. Disembarking there they [Spartans] left a small body of men to defend the boats, burnt the houses, made spoil of men and cattle, and, lured on by the sweets of pillage, advanced to a greater and greater distance from their ships (Livy 1926, 10.2.9).

The Spartans were soundly defeated by the Patavians:

> Cleonymus sailed off with barely a fifth part of his ships intact. In no quarter of the Adriatic had his attempts succeeded. There are many now living in Patavium who have seen the beaks of the ships and the spoils of the Laconians which were fastened up in the old temple of Juno. In commemoration of the navel battle a contest of ships is held regularly, on the anniversary of the engagement, in the river that flows through the town (Livy 1926, 10.2.14-15).

Patavians were also famous for their love of theater in the Roman period. According to Cesira Gasparotto (1951, 48), Paduans were known for their performance of *ludi*, also called *caetasti*, which were celebrated every thirty years. These are described by Tacitus in his *Annals*, and were said to have been instituted by Antenor (1937 16.22). They are essentially dramatic representations of the character of Certamen. Tertullian's scathing attack on the overuse of spectacle in Rome contains vivid accounts of the nature and origin of the *ludi*. He writes in *De Spectaculis*, "From Etruria, the Romans fetch the performers, and with them they borrow also the time and the name – the *ludii* are so called from the Lydians" (Tertullian 1931, 5). Indeed, Etruscan culture exercised great musical influence on Roman musical culture. Ancient casters of bronze, the Etruscans are credited with introducing the *tuba* (trumpet), *cornu* (a g-shaped horn), and *buccina* (trumpet or horn, precise appearance is unknown) to the Romans, who adopted these instruments in military and secular ensembles. Early trumpets with a straight tube and wide bells are depicted on the walls of ancient Etruscan tombs.[33]

[32]Sheep are also prominent in Giotto's *Joachim among the Shepherds, Joachim's Sacrifice*, and *Dream of Joachim*.

[33]Meucci (1985, 387) writes that Roman trumpets were generally a meter and a half long and played during military maneuvers such as the attack and retreat, during combat, and during changing of the guard.

Tertullian explains that *ludi* derives from playing: "Even if Varro derives the *ludii* from *ludus* (that is, from playing) – just as they used to call the Luperci *ludii* because in play they run hither and thither – he nevertheless reckons this playing of the youths as belonging to festal days, temples and matters of religion" (1931, 5). Tertullian describes festivals in honor of Father Liber (Bacchus) as the Liberalia, and games originally held in honor of Neptune as Consualia. Romulus derived the Ecurria from horses and named general festivals for Neptune, Jupiter, Latiaris, and Flora. Royal birthdays, victories of state, and municipal festivals also contained games (Tertullian 1931, 6-7).

Few artifacts are extant regarding actual Roman musical performance. We have several fragments of song texts and rather vague indications about how they should be performed (Comotti 1965, 48).[34] These include sacral poems, convivial songs (accompanied by the *tibia*), songs in honor of victorious generals, and funerary lamentations. Although the actual Roman instruments may not have survived, vestiges of venues in which Roman music was performed remain standing in Padua. The two primary edifices are the Arena and the Prato della Valle (and surrounding buildings), which chroniclers cite as the location for Roman festivities and theatrics. In the shadows of the crumbling walls and archways, ancient viaducts and passageways, each venue inspired images of spectacles, theater, and triumphant civic reunions among Paduans in the Trecento and early Renaissance.

The most prominent Roman venue is the Arena, an ancient amphitheater now serving as a public garden, and made famous by Giotto's frescos in the Scrovegni Chapel. The Arena has an internal space 76 meters long and 39 meters wide, with external walls 134 meters long by 97 meters wide (Sommer 1935, 129). Between the walls corridors and ladders once existed, and above the stands platforms were erected on which the spectators, whose numbers may have reached several thousand, sat. Evidence indicates that gladiators took part in combats here: writing on a carved stone, found while constructing the still glamorous Caffè Pedrocchi, tells that a woman named Purricina made a sepulchre for her gladiator husband, who died in combat at the *Arena patavina.*

This site remained intact until 601, when it was destroyed by the Longobardi. Subsequently the ruined space was used for public functions until it was donated to Milone, Vescovo of Padua, in 1090, who in turn sold it to the Dalesmanini family.

This family built a large palazzo alongside the Scrovegni Chapel, in which the Foscari counts of Venice lived after 1400. The Arena and the Chapel became public property in 1880. Centuries of invaders destroyed

[34]For more on Roman music, see Smoldon 1965, 29-31.

most of the other Roman edifices, although four Roman bridges and numerous streets remain intact.

Ongarello observes that the Arena was constructed "avanti Christo" and that this location was covered from one side to another ("da torno a torno", 8). Above the cover, which was completely paved ("la quale era tutta selegiata"), a huge number of people could stand – according to Ongarello, almost the entire population. Under the covering were merchants' shops, with special guards standing watch. "In the middle of this building was a huge piazza, where games were played, and the feasts of the pagans, and in the middle was an enormous hole where water flowed."[35]

Angelo Portenari's *Della felicità di Padova* echoes and elaborates on Ongarello's account, describing the construction of the Arena and the kind of performances held in the space in ancient and modern times. He writes:

> The spacious and round edifice called the Arena is an extremely old theater commonly thought to have been built before the birth of Christ. In it public spectacles were celebrated. It had around it porticos of stone made in vaults upon which the public watched. It had two large doors, one in the middle and one on the side, as one can still see at certain places in the walls of square stone.[36]

Indeed, Portenari describes music in his recipe for reviving Padua's classical successes: "For recreation, the arts of dancing, playing instruments, singing, in comedies, spectacles, and public games."[37] Livy's *From the Founding of the City* 7.2, a fascinating account of the origin of theatrical performances in the Roman kingdoms, illuminates the type of performances that took place in the Paduan Arena. According to Livy, theatrical performances were first introduced into the culture as a superstitious gesture to appease the wrath of the gods, who had persecuted Rome with pestilence. Actors were brought in from Etruria, who "danced to strains of the flautist

[35]"Sopra la coperta la quale era tutta selegiata poteva stare grandissima quantità de persone et quasi tutto il popolo, et sotto la detta copertura erano le botteghe de mercadanti, le quali anchuo si chiamano fonteghi, dove tutta la notte stasea special guardie per custodia delle dette mercantie: et tutto detto luogo se serrava con due porte, nel mezzo di detto edificio era una grandissima Piazza, dove se faceva li zoghi e le feste dei Pagani, in mezzo della quale era una fossa grandissima con un buso ... dove scorreva tutta l'acqua de detto edificio" (Ongarello, 8).

[36]"L'edificio spatioso e ampio di figura rotonda da noi chiamato Arena è un teatro antichissimo edificato per commune opinione avanti la natività di Cristo, nel quale si celebravano li spettacoli publici. Havea intorno portici di pietra fatti in volto sopra li quali stava il popolo a vedere. Havea due gran porte, l'una per mezzo l'altra, e era cinto, come ancora in qualche parte si puo vedere, da muraglie di pietra quadrata" (Portenari 1623, 96).

[37]"Per la ricreatione, l'arti di ballare, sonare, cantare, le commedie, li spettacoli, e li giuochi publici" (Portenari 1623, 121).

and performed not ungraceful evolutions in the Tuscan fashion" (Livy 1924, 7.2.4).

Young citizens soon began to imitate the actors. These performers were called *histriones*, from the Tuscan word *hister* (player). Their compositions were called *saturae* (medleys), which Livy describes as "full of musical measures, to melodies which were not written out to go with the flute, and with appropriate gesticulation" (1924, 7.2.7). According to Livy (1924, 7.2.8-10) the performances evolved into a kind of pantomime with music, and he recounts that a certain "Livius," having broken his voice by being obliged to repeat the sounds too often, put a boy in front of the musicians to sing a monody, while he performed with gestures.

For Livy, this practice was the beginning of the tradition of chanting in consort with the actors' movements. With the increased influence of Greek theater in the middle of the third century BC (after the occupation of southern Italy as a result of the victory in the First Punic War), Romans became more systematic in their inclusion of music in theatrical productions. In tragedy, spoken dialogues were alternated with sections of sung parts as solos and duets. The chorus did not retain as central a role in Roman theater as in Greek, and music was limited to a soloist playing a *tibia* (flute). Comedic solo parts predominated, practically eliminating the need for the chorus. Instead, instrumental pieces were inserted between acts. *Tibiae*, the double *auloi*, generally accompanied the songs. Terence includes stage directions in his comedies that note the use of the *tibiae pares*, of equal length: the *tibiae impares*, tuned on different pitches and the *tibiae sarranae*, or Pheonician.[38] Mime, pantomimes and new types of performances that engaged a primary soloist, originated as an art form in the first century BC. Actors interpreted events of daily life or parodied mythical stories. These scenarios were accompanied by a chorus and orchestra of *tibiae, citharae*, pipes, and percussion instruments. Similar orchestras also gave outdoor concerts with added military instruments, including the *tuba, lituus, buccina*, and *cornu*. In his *Epistles*, Seneca describes a musical scene, "To be sure, I am referring to the chorus which the old-time philosophers knew; in our present-day exhibitions we have a larger number of singers than there used to be spectators in the theaters of old. All the aisles are filled with rows of singers; brass instruments surround the auditorium; the stage resounds with flutes and instruments of every description; and yet from the discordant sounds a harmony is produced" (1920, 84.10).

Portenari and Ongarello discuss theatrical events with musical accompaniments in their descriptions of the types of spectacles performed near the Arena. Portenari writes:

[38]Terence quoted in Comotti 1965, 51.

> Next to this theater [Arena] was a place called the Satiro because in this type of space representative of scenes in forests and Satiric poems were recited.[39]

Portenari notes that this Roman tradition continued into the seventeenth century: "in the same way that at the present time pastoral scenes are reenacted."[40]

A similar, amplified description is found in Ongarello's commentary:

> In the Arena a few families were paid and asked to watch over the said space. It was there, where the Church of the Eremitani stands, that a space where those who sang in Latin, or in the vulgate, stood, which they called the satyr. In said Satyr were those who listened to the singing and those who sang, as it usually happens with such things for the privilege given by the Bishops of Padua for the Emperor Henry IV.[41]

As described by Ongarello, the people of Padua traditionally found pleasure in listening to narrators or singers of stories and romances. For instance, there exists from the early fourteenth century a fragment from an anonymous Paduan of the first part of *La Prise de pampelune*, based on the Charlemagne legend (Hyde 1966, 292). One can imagine from both Livy and Ongarello that the reciting of this legend was accompanied by music in the evocative environment of the Arena.

A lively theatrical community existed in early Trecento Padua, spearheaded by the aforementioned Lovato and Mussato. Lovato immersed himself in the plays of Seneca and is credited with their first revival in the fourteenth century (Weiss 1947, 7). Petrarch rated him one of the leading poets of his generation (Hyde 1966, 291). Lovato's most famous pupil was Albertino Mussato, whose name was derived from the nine Muses. Born into a poor Paduan family in 1262, Mussato earned a living by copying books for university students. Soon people in power discovered his genius and he was urged to dedicate himself to law. He eventually worked for the Republic of Padova, and was sent to Rome as an ambassador to Pope Boniface VIII.

---

[39]"Contiguo a questo teatro era un luogo chiamato il Satiro, perche in questa sorte di luoghi era la scena rappresentante paese boscareccio per recitarvi poemi Satirici" (Portenari 1623, 96).

[40]"...come al presente si fanno le scene delle favole pastorali" (Portenari 1623, 96).

[41]"In questa Rena erano comprate, e collocate dal Pubblico alcune famiglie, che guardavano il detto luogo. Item era la', dove al presente è la Chiesa [de' PP. Eremitani], un luogo, dove quelli, che cantavano o per lettera, or per vulgare, stavano e chiamavano il satiro, in lo quale Satiro staseva quelli che udiva a cantare, e colui che cantava, come appare queste cose per lo privileggio concesso alli Vescovi di Padova per Henrico Imperatore IV" (Ongarello, 8).

He is most famous for his tragedy *Ezzelino* and wrote twelve other books of history, including *Le imprese di Enrico VII of Luxembourg*, inspired by the tragedies of Seneca and Livy's histories. Hyde (1966, 299) writes that Mussato "was aware of the classical writers Livy, Salust and Seneca, not as equals but as models to be imitated." Mussato defended classical mythology, and according to Hyde, argued it as "embodying the same immortal truths as Christianity, claiming that the poets of antiquity had performed the same functions as the theologians."

Tertullian's *De Spectaculis* provides other insights into Roman theatrical practice. He observes that one's walk on the path to the theater – filled with a miserable mess of incense and blood – was accompanied by the "tune of flutes and trumpets" (1931, 10). In addition, he notes that there was a difference between the performance of theater and the performance of music. He explains their different components in terms of pagan ritual: Venus and Bacchus are the patrons of the arts of the stage: "those features of the stage peculiarly and especially its own, that effeminacy of gesture and posture, they dedicated to Venus and Liber" while the musical component of the performance, "done with voice and song, instrument and book, is the affair of the Apollos and the Muses, the Minervas and the Mercuries" (Tertullian 1931, 10).

Minerva is closely aligned with the playing of the *tibia*. In his *Fasti*, Ovid has Minerva telling the story that she was the first to produce music of the *tibia longo* by piercing boxwood with holes wide apart (1976, 6.695 ff.). When she saw her reflection in the water, her virgin cheeks puffed up, and she threw the flute away; it fell beside the riverbank. Marsyas found it and began to play, bragging among the nymphs and challenging Apollo. Vanquished by Apollo, Marsyas was hanged and skinned.

Both Livy and Ovid recount the story of Minerva, who founded the order of fluteplayers, and the festival held in their honor. The story relates that the flute-players were quite popular in ancient times, performing in temples, games, and mournful funerals. Soon their popularity began to wane, and a decree was issued stating that no more than ten could play at funerals. Angered, the players left Rome and stayed at Tibur. Ovid recounts, "The hollow flute was missed in the theater, missed at the altars; no dirge accompanied the bier on the last march" (1976, 6.699). To ensure their return to Rome, a plan was hatched to get the players intoxicated. They were then taken back to Rome and dressed in masks and long gowns to conceal their true identities. Upon their return the Senate approved their music-making, and a festival in masks and gowns continued in their honor.

Tertullian formulates a tantalizing argument on the subject of gods and music. He suggests, as in the case recounted by Ovid, that demons stole the credit for inventing instruments and became gods because they received the credit. "Demons from the very beginning thought for themselves, and among the other pollutions of idolatry devised those of the spectacles for the purpose of turning man from his Lord and binding him to their own glorification, and so inspired ingenious arts" (1931, 10). The demons then lent the arts their names:

> For no others but they would have devised what should turn to profit; nor would they have given the arts to the world at that time through the agency of any other men than those by whose names and images and legends they determined they would negotiate the trick of their own consecration (Tertullian 1931, 10).

In speaking about the games (Olympian games in honor of Jupiter – these were called Capitoline games in Rome), Tertullian also notes the uses of trumpets. The games were held in a stadium under the auspices of the nine Muses, Minerva, Apollo, and Mars, and with a "trumpet they imitate[d] the circus" (1931, 11).

Tertullian's remarks concerning Roman musical practice are echoed in a famous and spectacular celebration that occurred in Padua in 1466, mentioned by all the chroniclers (Sommer 1935, 17-18). Noble Paduans took part in the festivities, which featured representations of popular mythological scenes. They began with a parade from the Piazza dei Signori to the Prato della Valle, and featured a gigantic figure and an equally enormous wooden horse pulled by fifty pair of oxen. Behind them was a train of pagan divinities, monsters, and heroes, among them the Cyclops, the Chimera, the Nine Muses, and Cibele. The last in line was a figure of Antenor, the founder of Padua, surrounded by noblemen and horses. The only souvenir of this celebration is the wooden horse, now found in the Salone della Ragione, said to be the work of Donatello and remembered by Giorgio Vasari. Donatello spent a decade in Padua between 1443 and 1453, where he worked on the bronze altar for the Church of Saint Anthony of Padua, on the aforesaid wooden statue of a horse, and on the equestrian statue of Condottiere Gattamelata. The *Gattamelata* is surely inspired by classical models, primarily Marcus Aurelius in Rome, and is the earliest free-standing post-classical bronze equestrian monument.

The gargantuan Prato della Valle, the final destination of these festivities of 1466, is another prominent vestige of Padua's Roman ceremonial heritage. Hailed as the largest Italian piazza within city walls, the space borders the southernmost part of Padua near the ancient Santa Giustina church. An expansive area of greenery within the bustling city, it consists of an oval ringed by water and a series of statues. The marble statues commemorate famous Paduans and distinguished visitors to Padua, among them Pietro, Livy, Andrea Mantegna, Giuseppe Tartini, Francesco Petrarca, and Galileo Galilei.[42]

Medieval and Renaissance chroniclers speak of several ancient structures in conjunction with the still accessible Prato della Valle, among them a coliseum called the Zairo; a temple to Concord, mentioned by Albertino Mussato; a second coliseum, associated with the Church of the Santo; and the remains of a circus.[43]

In 1441 Ongarello describes the existence of an ancient theater under the Prato della Valle:

> Those walls that appear above the Prato della Valle are of a coliseum that was in the said location, where people could stand to watch the festivities that took place there, as it was similarly done in the city of Rome; this coliseum was called Zairo, as found in public records, which now are found in the Church of Saint Giustina.[44]

Ongarello also explains that music was part of the festivities in the theater:

> The citizens of Padua came together to watch festivities, first in the Arena to see the battles made by beasts, that is, lions, pigs, bulls, and similar animals. Also in this Arena there was a place where histories were sung, and gentle things, which were called the Satyrs, because the Satyrs and the poets sang the things they had composed, and Henry the Emperor gave the Arena with the Satyr to Milone, Bishop of Padua, in 1090.[45]

---

[42]For the history of the statues, see Puppi 1986, 160-174.

[43]Ongarello (9) observes that there was a coliseum connected to the Church of the Santo, in which feasts and dances took place, "Coliseo del Santo se fasea comunemente le altre feste e danze." Indeed, priests and citizens took stones from the coliseum to build the church. "Un' altro Coliseo e quale comenzava alla detta porta et fenia quasio appresso segrado del Santo del quale Coliseo, cavando molte volte li Cittadini et lidetti fratti del Santo Antonio trovavano maravigliosi fondamenti et molti tiene per opinione che li fondamenti della Gesia del Santo fossero fatti delli muri del detto Coliseo."

[44]"...quelli muri che apparono sopra il Prato della Valle, sono de un Coliseo, che era in lo detto luogo dove le persone podevano à torno à torno stare à vedere le feste che se faceano in quello, come per simile se ne vede nella cittade di Roma: et quel Coliseo se chiamava Zairo, come appar per publici Instromenti, li quali de presente sono in la Gesia de Santa Giustina" (Ongarello quoted in Bosio 1986, 39).

[45]"...se adunavano i cittadini di Padova per vedere le feste, e primo in la Rena per vedere le battaglie, che facevano le bestie, cioè lioni, porci, tori e simili animali. Item era in quella Arena un luogo, dove se cantava le historie, e le cose gentili, che si chiamava el Satiro, perchè li Sàtiri, e li Poeti si cantavano le cose avevano fatte, e quell'Arena con il Satiro, Enrico Imperatore nel 1090 donò a Milone Vescovo di Padova" (Ongarello, 9 quoted in Stratico 1795, 7).

Giacomo Cavacci maintains that the term Zairo is a corruption of the term Satyro, found in a document of 26 February 1090, which refers to an antique theater. The edifice stood until the sixteenth century, when to pay off old debts, the city of Padua transported the stones from the ancient theater to Venice as material for the construction of the foundation of the Rialto bridge (Bosio 1986, 39). The exact date of the theater's construction is not ascertainable, but scholars believe that it was built at the end of the first century AD, during the Augustinian epoch (Bosio 1986, 41). Spectacles and *ludi scaenici* were performed in this space, with both comic and tragic representations.

The grassy expanse comprising the Prato della Valle proper served as a space for festivities in Padua in the late Middle Ages (Stratico 1795, 21). The chronicler Rolandino notes that a great spectacle was made in 1208 for the days of the Pentecost. A game of the "uomo Selvatico" was also played as citizens decked out in new vestments held great feasts with "balli e danze."[46] Another famous spectacle performed in the Prato during the thirteenth century involved a decree establishing that each year on the 19th of June (the anniversary of the capture of Padua's suburbs), the *Podestà* and his *curia* and *fraglie* go to vespers in the Church of the Santo. The spectacle was followed on the same day by a procession of the Bishop of Padua accompanied by his clerics, who then conducted Mass in the same church. The community of Padua was obliged to donate on June 19 in the public street in the Prato della Valle twelve yards of scarlet cloth, one hawk, and one pair of gloves. To win these prizes the participants had to run to Mass, and the first to arrive at the church was given the scarlet cloth, the second, the hawk, and the third, the gloves.

Gennari mentions the Prato della Valle in the description of Paduan festivities of 1300:

> The dances, jousts, military maneuvers, and games, entertainments of all kinds, performed not only on the Prato della Valle, but in the public piazza, rendering that day deserving of remembrances.[47]

Interestingly, Ongarello also notes the presence of another coliseum, called del Santo, in which "dances and other celebrations were commonly conducted" ("se faceva comunemente tutte le altre feste, e danze"), a description not corroborated by other chroniclers.[48] There are, however, in-

[46]As related in Stratico 1795, 21.

[47]"Balli, giostre, armeggiamenti, e giuochi sollazzevoli d'ogni maniera eseguiti non già sul Prato della Valle, ma nella pubblica piazza, rendettero quel giorno degno d'essere ricordato" (Gennari 1804, 88).

[48]Ongarello, quoted in Stratico 1795, 7.

dications of a Roman circus that existed near the Prato della Valle, where Paduans delighted in racing horses.

If the area of the Prato was covered with Roman ruins, the neighborhood that encompassed the Palazzo della Ragione exhibited the "new" flourishing medieval town. One of the most conspicuous symbols and centers of civic life in all of the Veneto, the Palazzo della Ragione was begun in 1218-1219, and it has continued to undergo modifications and additions through the centuries. The Palazzo satisfied many exigencies of the city. First, it stood as a representation of central government and the administration of justice. Second, it allowed shops to be systematized in and around the outside of its first floor. In the Palazzo we see a representational meeting of powerful civic forces: the rule of justice and the powerful merchant class distributing its wares. Portenari provides an elegant description of the edifice:

> The Palazzo della Ragione of Padua has no equal in beauty, grandeur, and artfulness in the entire world. It has a huge room, in a long island, 256 feet long, and 86 feet wide. It is held up by ninety pilasters of baked rock, disposed in four rows, and connected by agreeable arches and vaults, under which there are two paths on each side and one traversing it in the middle, and forty shops, where wool, furs, and other commodities are sold. On the outside part, there are about fifty shops delegated to warehouses of flour, cloth, and other silk goods. These shops have beautiful porticos before them, fabricated with vaults, sustained by columns of bright stones, and covered with tiles. The Palazzo has four staircases, two on the east and two on the west, of circa fifty stairs each, by which one climbs to the two stunning long galleries. Since the Palazzo is built upon vaults, it is supported by fifty-six columns of white and red marble covered in lead and adorned by 580 little columns and cornices of the same stone.[49]

The walls of the Palazzo's primary room, called the Salone, contain a cycle of astrological images. First painted by Giotto around 1317 during

[49]"Il palazzo della Ragione di Padova non ha pari in bellezza, grandezza e artificio in tutto il modo. Questo è un gradissimo salone in isola lungo ducento cinquantasei piedi, e largo ottantasei. E sostentato da novanta grandi pilastri di pietra cotto disposti in quattro fila, e congiunti con arche e volte molo bene intese, sotto le quali sono due strade per lungo, e una per traverso, e quaranta botteghe, ove si vendono panni di lana, pellicie, e altri merci. Dalla parte di fuori ha cinquanta botteghe in circa deputate per la maggior parte alli fondachi de farine, e di panni, e d'altre merci di seta, le quali hanno avanti bellissimi portici fabricati a volta, sostentati da colonne di pietra viva, e coperti di tegole. Ha quattro scale, due all'Oriente, e due all'Accidente, per le quali di cinquanta scaglioni ognuna in circa si ascende a due bellissime gallerie lunghe, quanto è il palazzo, fatte a volta, sostentate da cinquantasei colonne di marmo bianco e rosso, coperte di piombo, e adornate intorno da 580 piccole colonne, e cornici dell'istessa pietra" (Portenari 1623, 97).

his second stay in the city, the frescoes were destroyed in a fire in 1420 and repainted during the fifteenth century. Giovanni da Nono, who provided accurate accounts at the beginning of the fourteenth century, observes that the Palazzo went through several structural changes between 1306 and 1309 (Alvarez 1990, 5). These changes were undertaken with a new "astrological" consideration in mind, following the prominent school led by Pietro d'Abano, who is believed to have created the program for the Giotto frescoes that decorated the principal second-floor room, as Portenari and others confirm.

> The paintings that one finds inside the building were invented by Pietro d'Abano, of which there are 400, of many images of diverse things, arts and actions, placed under the twelve signs of the Zodiac, the seven planets and the twelve months of the year, which display the natures of those born.[50]

In many ways the Salone images mirror the ideal city as devised by Lorenzetti in Siena around 1335 in the *Effects of Good Government in the City*, in which justice and the ruling classes of the Nove, Siena's governing body, hover around the everyday events of merchants selling their wares and people chatting in the streets. In the Salone, a calm and quiet aggregate of citizens is pictured acting in the best interests of the city, according to the laws and influences of the celestial bodies. The newly painted space was intended as a kind of *macchina giudiziaria*, integrating the philosophies of the new academic humanists and the exoteric science of astrology.

The Palazzo della Ragione was also the site of important government events. In Gatari's *Cronaca carrarese* we read:

> And so in the Palazzo del Comune of Padua, after accepting the election, it was promised that justice and reason would be maintained for the powerful as well as the weak. And this election took place in the days of our Lord Jesus Christ 1318 in the month of July: of which the election was of such peace and concord in all the community of Padua that it could not be fully written about.[51]

[50] "Le pitture di lui dalla parte di dentro furono inventate da Pietro d'Abano, le quali sono 400, e più imagini di diverse cose, arti e operationi poste sotto li dodeci segni del Zodiaco, 7 pianeti e dodeci mesi dell'anno le quali dimostrano le nature dei nascenti" (Portenari 1623, 98). Michele Savonarola, in the *Libellus de magnificis ornamentis regie civitatis Padue Michaelis Savonarole*, in circa 1446 noted that the artist who repainted the frescoes followed Pietro's original program.

[51] "E così nel palacio dil comune di Padoa, acietata la 'lecione, zurò e promese di mantenere iusitcia e rasione sì al grande come al picolo. E fu questa elicione negli anni del nostro signore Ihesu Cristo mille tresento XVIII, di xxiiii del mese di luio; la quale elecione e acientasone fu di tanta pace e concordia di tuto il comune di Pada, che a pieno

As exemplified in that passage, peace and concord were primary themes for the newly flourishing community of Padua under the rule of the Carrara family. The revival of ancient feasts and celebrations, replete with music, informs the spirit of the new era of freedom and civic pride. Giotto's portrayal of *Justice* and *Injustice* in the Scrovegni Chapel, with its musical predella, provides an early Trecento representation of the connection between music and Ciceronian conceptions of justice. The importance of balance and tranquility, as exemplified in the pastoral quality of the fruitful Paduan countryside, will be seen as a primary influence on the first flourishing of secular music in Padua. An appreciation of Padua's prized history and mythical landscape is fundamental to understanding the musical style of the Tre- and Quattrocento, during which time composers imitate pastoral poetry and absorb classical themes in their texts and musical style. In the next chapter of *Giotto's Harmony*, another primary influence on the formation of a Paduan musical culture will be examined: the adoption of the Aristotelian philosophy of the science of nature, found primarily in Aristotle's *Physica* and *Metaphysica*, as interpreted in the music theory of Marchetto and Pietro, both Giotto's contemporaries.

non si potrebbe iscrivere." Andrea adds that "The Council of Giacomo da Carrara gave the banner of the people, with a red cross in the middle and made him swear on a book of statutes and in the memory of this election, each year they instituted a race with a banner of grain on the street of the Ponte Corbo, and the banner remained on the piazza of the 'biava del zopellaire' " (Gatari 1931, 11).

Chapter 2

Aristotle and the Science of Music in Padua: Marchetto da Padova and Pietro d'Abano

The study of the natural sciences, the so-called *physica et scientia naturalis*, flourished in Padua in the thirteenth century. Founded primarily on readings of Aristotle's *Physica* and *Metaphysica*, the natural sciences were considered the confluence of the Aristotelian philosophy of nature and the new science of observing natural properties (Siraisi 1973, 95-96).[1] The University of Padua was renowned for its faculty of natural sciences, and the chronicler Rolandino notes that several regent masters whose specialty was the natural sciences ("profundi et periti doctores in physica et sciencia naturale") taught at the university in 1262.[2] The physician William of Brescia probably lectured on the natural sciences between 1276 and 1281 in the university. In addition, numerous celebrated writers with both ecclesiastical and scientific interests, including Albert the Great, Witelo, and Engelbert of Admont, came to Padua as students of science before continuing their illustrious careers elsewhere (Siraisi 1973, 112). In the fifteenth century, the

[1]Already in the twelfth century, Latin translations existed in the Veneto region of Aristotle's *Physica, Metaphysica*, and *De Anima* by James of Venice (fl.1136-1148). For more, see Minio-Paluello 1952. For the reception of Aristotle in schools of Western Europe, see van Steenberghen 1955.

[2]Quoted in Siraisi 1973, 22.

university faculty could also boast of the Aristotelians Jacopo da Forlì (d. 1413) and Paolo da Venezia (d. 1429), writer of the remarkably up-to-date *Summa Naturalis.*[3]

Evidence gathered by Nan Carpenter in her *Music in the Medieval and Renaissance Universities* (1972, 39) indicates that music was taught as part of the liberal arts at the University of Padua.[4] The doctorate in arts (*laurea*) was regularly given, and early fifteenth-century professors and humanists advocated the study of music as part of a well-rounded education. Paduan theorists of music, most notably Marchetto da Padova, Pietro d'Abano, and the anonymous author of the *Capitulum applicatis verbis*, borrowed Aristotelian arguments and scientific language from the *Physica, Metaphysica,* and *De Anima* in treatises devoted to the physical properties of music. These authors attempted to understand the complexities of music through the lens of Aristotelian conceptions of nature. In so doing the theorists firmly grounded music in the realms of science and established and promulgated what we now think of as the Italian Ars Nova, the Italian contribution to the advancement of theories regarding rhythmic complexity and notation. Indeed, French music theorists of the thirteenth century such as Johannes Garlandia and Jacob de Lièges included in their theories Aristotelian logical applications and rhetorical gestures found primarily in the *Categorie* and *De interpretatione* (in translations by Boethius).[5]

While chapter 1 explored classical influences on the city of Padua and its musical tradition, this chapter examines the philosophical underpinnings of Trecento music, focusing primarily on Aristotelian influences on the music theory of Marchetto and Pietro. Both theorists were thoroughly steeped in Aristotelian science, and each adopted Aristotle's writings in imaginative ways: Marchetto relied on Aristotle for his arguments describing the newest advances in musical notation in his *Pomerium* and *Lucidarium*; Pietro focused primarily on the effect of music in his *Conciliator* and *Expositio problematum Aristotelis.* Furthermore, both writers were active at approximately the same time; Pietro (1250-1316) was in fact a bit older than Marchetto (b. Padua, 1274?; fl. 1305-26). It is interesting to note, however, that their contributions to Trecento music theory rarely covered the same material. Marchetto was clearly the practitioner of the two, composing music and participating actively in the Paduan musical scene. For his part, Pietro was a besieged medical doctor, philosopher, and astrologer,

---

[3]For Padua's contribution to science in the Renaissance, see Randall 1961.

[4]In 1450 Pope Nicholas V established a chair in music at the university.

[5]For Aristotelian influence on French musical aesthetic, see Page 1993 and Yudkin 1987. The allusion to Aristotle's scientific treatises can be seen in Jacob of Liège, *Speculum musicae.* This is certainly to be understood as a link between the French and Italian intellectual communities.

who described musical properties as part of his encyclopedic understanding of the mechanics of human existence.

In this study, Marchetto's work will be examined first because it is most closely aligned with Aristotle's *Physica*, from which the music theorist derived the distinction between "nature" and "art" used extensively in his explanation of notation in his influential treatise the *Pomerium* (1318-1319). First, however, it is useful to summarize Aristotle's arguments, and more specifically those adapted by Marchetto in the *Pomerium*.

Aristotle's most complete exploration of the natural world appears in the first two chapters of his *Physics*. Aristotle defines "by nature" at the beginning of book 2. He notes, "Of things that exist, some exist by nature, some from other causes. 'By nature' the animals and their parts exist, and the plants and the simple bodies (earth, fire, air, water) – for we say that these and the like exist by nature" (1930, 192b7-11). "By nature" generally applies to things (for Aristotle) whose principles of motion or change are controlled by their own natures (192b14-16). Aristotle then defines nature as relating to change: "nature is a source or cause of being moved and of being at rest" (192b21-22). Aristotle also claims that both an object's matter and its form contribute to its nature in the "shape or form (not separable except in statement) of things which have in themselves a source of motion" (193b2-5).

Aristotle suggests that the physicist, or student of nature, understand the matter and form of things. Like the astronomer, he should know the nature of the Sun and the Moon, and like a mathematician, he should know the limits of a particular object, and, most relevant to this study, he should be familiar with evidence provided by the branches of mathematics, such as optics and harmonics (194a7). Harmonics are a reflection of objects in nature and are, therefore, prime for scrutiny in a scientific manner. Indeed, when discussing the "causes" of change, Aristotle cites the musical example: "the ratio 2:1, and number in general, cause the octave" (195a 30-31).

Objects also exist for Aristotle "by art." "By art," in this context, is anything that is made by man and quite literally an artifact. For Aristotle, what is made is made for some purpose or for some end. "For the word 'nature' is applied to what is according to nature and the natural in the same way as 'art' is applied to what is artistic or a work of art" (192b32). An object may also exist by accident, when it is not in accordance with its nature. For example, in his *Metaphysica* (1928, 1025a14-19) he presents the following musical example:

> Accident means that which attaches to something and can be truly asserted, but neither of necessity nor usually, e.g. if someone digging a hole for a plant has found a treasure.... And a musical man might

> be pale; but since this does not happen of necessity nor usually, we call it an accident.

Aristotle's is not a determined universe. So, for example, if an acorn grows into an oak it is "by nature." If it is carved into a face it is "by art," and if it is eaten by a squirrel it is "by accident," though it may be in the squirrel's nature to eat the acorn. Aristotle expands on this point in the *Metaphysica* (1070a5) as follows:

> For things come into being either by art or by nature or by luck or by spontaneity. Now art is a principle of movement in something other than the thing moved, nature is a principle in the thing itself (for man begets man), and the other causes are privations of these two.

Furthermore, Aristotle does not make a moral judgment about the relative worth of objects by nature or by art. "Things which are formed by nature are in the same case as these produced by art. For the seed is productive in the same way as the things that work by art" (1034a33). The Philosopher sees nature and art working in tandem: "... generally art partly completes what nature cannot bring to a finish, and partly imitates her" (199a17).

In the *Pomerium*, Marchetto thoroughly appropriates Aristotelian discourse on the natural sciences in his innovative discussion of the properties of mensural music, or the duration of notated music. Marchetto borrows three primary Aristotelian arguments found in the *Physica*: the observation of the natural world through the dichotomy between nature and art, the philosophy of the four causes, and the doctrine of opposites. He makes it clear in book 1, chapter 1, that in observing the essence of music he will follow a scientific method ("via scientifica in praesenti opere procedamus" 40).[6] In chapter 3 of the *Pomerium*, in the midst of arguing the nature of the smallest time unit, Marchetto discloses an essential premise of his philosophy of music. He observes that "music was invented by man in a natural way" ("quod contradicat musica, cum sit inventa ab homine per viam naturae, et maxime Philosopho in libro Metaphysicae" 83). For Marchetto music is part of the natural world. He refines this idea by formulating a division between the essence of mensural music, which he calls the notes themselves (39-40), and the accessories to mensural music, which he calls additions to the notes.[7]

---

[6]Page numbers in the text refer to the edition by Vecchi 1961. The translations of the *Pomerium* are by Renner (1980) unless otherwise noted. Renner's thesis serves as a companion to the Vecchi edition, since the thesis contains cross-references to Vecchi's pagination throughout.

[7]"With regard to this first topic, it is known that the notes alone constitute the essence of music (as we will prove, God granting) and all the other [elements] are accessories which

In his dedication letter to Robert of Anjou, King of Naples, Marchetto states that he has engaged the service of Brother Syphantis de Ferraria, of the order of Praedicatorum ("ordinis Praedicatorum, dirigente ducatu"), to help him with philosophical arguments that inform the treatise. Marchetto believes that the novel order and conception of the book will make it more pleasurable for Robert ("[as I] believed that the more properly elegant this book was in [its] format, the more pleasing it would be in your majesty's sight." ("... quantum ad libri ordinem et philosophiae fulcimina rationum, autumnans praesense opusculum tanto fore decentius formalitate venustum quanto maiestatis vestrae conspictibus gratum erit" 36-37.) He contends that his treatise will further clarify how written notation will serve the science of music, and demonstrate to musicians and singers that the rules are not arbitrary but rational.

The first mention of Aristotle's *Physica* within the body of the *Pomerium* appears in book 1, chapter 2, in a discussion of the addition of tails to the notes in mensural music (48). Marchetto extracts the phrase "art imitates nature" from the following explanation in Aristotle to produce one of the most thought-provoking and rich arguments of the entire *Pomerium*. When defining the study of the natural sciences in the *Physica*, Aristotle explains:

> But if on the other hand art imitates nature, and it is the part of the same discipline to know the form and the matter up to a point (e.g. the doctor has a knowledge of health and also of bile and phlegm, in which health is realized, and the builder both of the form of the house and of matter, namely that it is bricks and beams, and so forth): if this is so, it would be the part of physics also to know nature in both its senses (194a22).

Marchetto writes:

> Second principle:art imitates nature as far as it can (as Aristotle said in book II of the *Physica*). I shall prove this with an example: he who paints a lily or a horse strives as far as he can to paint it so as to resemble a horse or a lily in nature.[8]

---

are used in mensural music for reasons to be given below – [accessories] such as tail stems, dots, and the sign which is commonly called musica falsa, or false music." ("Quantum ad primum, est sciendum quod omnia praeter notas, in quibus solum essentialis ratio consistit musicae, ut demonstrabitur Deo dante, sunt accidentia sive accidentalia concurrentia in ipsa musica mensurata, rationibus infra dicendis. Cuius modi sunt caudate, proprietates, pausae, puncta et quoddam signum quod a vulgo falsa musica nuncupatur" [Da Padova 1961, 39-40]).

[8]This passage is translated in Gallo 1985, 115-116. "Et tunc assumimus secundum principium: ars imitatur naturam in quantum potest (per Phylosophum, secundo Physicorum). Probatio per exemplum: nam qui depingit lilium vel equum, nititur ipsa depingere in quantum potest ad similitudinem equi seu lilii naturalis" (Da Padova 1961, 50).

In explaining the Italian notational system, Marchetto compares an artist's imitation of nature in painting with specific notational devices, such as the addition of "tails to the notes." He continues:

> Since, therefore, the written notes pertain to the art of music, although music is in itself an accepted science, it was right that the tails added to the notes, which were written because of the need to hand down the music, should be added to them in accordance with the perfections found in man himself, who instituted this art; for in man is found, in origin, the right and the left... Therefore the tails added to the written notes are rightly added to them on the right and the left, as with respect to man.[9]

Marchetto argues that the written notes capture the intentions of the composer as closely as possible "because of the need to hand down the music" and that for this reason tails should be added to the notes. Furthermore, music should be regarded as a science and adhere to certain rules. In Marchetto's *Pomerium* the notes themselves, the breves and semibreves, exist "by nature" and the accessories (tails and stems added to notes, rests, the *pontellus*, or dot of division, and *musica falsa*, or the addition of the diesis) exist "by art." He then provides several examples to clarify his position. A breve in the first perfect division is equally divided into three semibreves, each having the same value and written alike. But if there are only two semibreves, then naturally the last one, because it indicates the end, contains two parts of the same unit, and the first one, one. Artificially, then, one can double the value of the first semibreve by adding a stem (an accessory).

In borrowing the Aristotelian dialectic of nature and art, Marchetto observes that the value of the neumes (notes) within the *tempus* (measure of time) is "naturally" more perfect toward the end, so a group in imperfect time is equivalent to one in modern notation. Marchetto makes this distinction in his treatise 7, chapters 3 and 4, in which he observes that addition of a tail "artificially displaces the perfection to the beginning. This premise forms the basis of the consideration of all the different divisions of the breve and semibreve in perfect and imperfect time, and he employs this dichotomy when discussing accessories, ligatures, and rhythmic modes:

> Then we say this [time unit] is to be apportioned between the notes either naturally (*via naturae*) or artificially (*via artis*). If naturally,

[9]"Cum igitur ipsae notae scriptae ad artem musicae pertineant, licet ipsa musica de se sit accepta scientia, oportuit ergo quod proprietates additae notis ipsis, scriptis propter necessitatem modi tradendi, adderentur eisdem secundum perfectiones repertas ab ipso homine, qui instituit talem artem. In homine autem primo et principaliter invenitur dextrum et sinistrum" (Da Padova 1961, 51).

> the last note, which is the end, will indicate two parts of the time unit; the reason given above is that the end is always more perfect than the beginning. But if artificially, then it suffices that, when two or more semibreves are grouped together, a complete measure results so that the parts in it equal the whole.[10]

The importance of the end is essential for Marchetto and determines the measurement of the semibreves in imperfect time (102). "And if there are two [semibreves], how are they related to each other?"

> We answer: If they are written in completely the same way, then the last one has two parts of the time unit and the first [has] one. Here is our proof for this. Of those things which fill out the measure of something, as parts fill out the measure of the whole, the one that is last or ultimate in the order of nature always perfects or completes the nature [of] that something. Why?Because [it is] the end, and the end is always what makes a thing ultimately perfect or completed. For everything is in process toward an end [or ultimate state], and when a thing has attained its end, it has attained its perfection or completion. For the end [of a thing] is [its] cause of causes and the most noble of all (Aristotle, book II of the *Physica*).[11]

At the end of this passage, Marchetto notes that his reference to the causes is derived from Aristotle's *Physica*. For Aristotle, cause essentially defines the nature of a particular object. So, for instance, the letters are the causes of the syllables (195a15). In the *Physica*, the Philosopher writes that there are four causes of change (194b23-35):

> In one sense, then (1) that out of which a thing comes to be and which persists is called 'cause', e.g. the bronze of the statue, the silver of the bowl, and the genera of which the bronze and the silver are species. In another sense (2) the form or the archetype, i.e. the statement of the essence, and its genera, are called 'causes' (e.g. of the octave the relation of 2:1 and generally number), and the parts in the definition.

---

[10]"... et tunc dicimus quod hoc applicabitur ipsis notis, aut via naturae, aut via artis. Si via naturae, ultima quae est finis, dicet duas partes ipsius temporis; et ratio supradicata est eo quod finis semper sit perfectior quam prinicipium. Sed si ab arte, tunc sufficit quod in duabus vel pluribus semibrevibus compositis ad invicem, consurgat perfectio mensurandi, qua ipsum totum possit a partibus adaequari" (Da Padova 1961, 104).

[11]"Sed dices: Et si sint duae, quomodo se habent ad invicem? Dicimus quod, si eodem modo per omnia figurentur, tunc ultima semper habet duas partes temporis, et prima unam. Cuius ratio est quia illud quod mensurat aliquid, sicut partes mensurant totum, illud quod est ultimum via naturae semper perficit naturam. Quare? Quia finis, et finis semper est ultima perfectio; nam omnia aguntur propter finem, et quando res habet suum finem, habet suam perfectionem. Finis enim est causa causarum et omnibus causis nobilior (per Philosophum, secundo Physicorum)" (Da Padova 1961, 102).

> Again (3) the primary source of the change or coming to rest; e.g. the man who gave advice is a cause, the father is cause of the child, and generally what makes of what is made and what causes change of what is changed. Again (4) in the sense of end or 'that for the sake of which' a thing is done, e.g. health is the cause of walking about. (Why is he walking about? we say. 'To be healthy', and having said that we think we have assigned the cause.)

Cause explains why an object came to be and is the way it is.[12] (1) The material cause is characterized as "that out of which," or the building blocks of the final product. Therefore, bricks are the material cause of the wall. (2) The formal cause or pattern is that which the matter proximately constitutes, or an archetype of the object. So, for instance, the wall is the cause of the bricks. (3) The third cause concerns a movement or the source of change, the maker of what is made, such as the person who builds the wall. (4) The end or final cause Aristotle suggests is what things are for. This is also the best thing: this is a brick wall that keeps the neighbor's dog out of your yard.

Strikingly, Marchetto's *Pomerium* contains an introductory paragraph found in four different manuscript sources that refers to the four causes:

> There are four causes; they naturally concern material, form, the effect, and their end. The material is the *musica mensurata*; the form is the practice of the subject in this work; the effect is the agent; the final end is the knowledge of mensural music, to sing rationally, and not by passion, as we will see.[13]

This short passage, which is followed by a detailed description of the division and content of each section of the manuscript, is significant because it indicates that the author, or perhaps a scribe, found a distinct connection between the *Pomerium* and Aristotle's natural science. The meaning of the four causes and their relation to the *Pomerium* may be illuminated as follows: (1) the material cause is the constituent parts of mensural music, or neumes, the stems, the dots, etc; (2) the formal cause is its archetype within the *Pomerium,* or the essence of mensural music; (3) the efficient cause is the author of the Pomerium, or Marchetto; and (4) the end is the

[12]On Aristotle's causes, see Wallace 1996, 5-7 and Aristotle 1970, 98-100.

[13]"Quattuor sunt causae, scilicet materialis, formalis, efficiens et finalis: materialis, ipsa musica mensurata; formalis, modus tractandi de ipsa in hoc opere; efficiense, ipse actor; finalis, ut sciatur musica mensurata, etiam et cantari rationabiliter et non pro libito voluntatis, sicut quibusdam videtur" (Da Padova 1961, 31). The sources for the introduction are Bruxelles, Bibl. Royale II 4144; Pisa, Bibli. Univ.606; Roma, Bibl. Vat. Lat. 5322; and Siena, Bibli. Comunale L V 30. On the sources, see Da Padova 1961, 7-19.

purpose of the entire the treatise, "that mensural music be understood and sung by the rules" (31). In summary, the first cause concerns the materials of measured music; the second, the form or essence and the genera or types; the third, the agent or actor creating the change; and the last, the outcome or the end. For Marchetto the end is knowledge, and the change that has occurred in the reader through the process of reading the treatise is the acquisition of this knowledge of music in order to learn to sing rationally and not from passion: essentially to underscore the science of music.

A close comparison of the *Pomerium's* conception and Aristotle's four causes suggests a connection between the two. Could Aristotle's four causes have served as a template for the organization of the *Pomerium*? The *Pomerium* consists of three books, each divided into parts (book 1) or treatises (book 2 and book 3), each part divided into treatises, each treatise further subdivided into chapters. The total number of treatises is thirteen; each contains an introduction, while only some offer a conclusion. The overall layout appears as follows:

Table of contents:

Dedicatory letter

Book 1

Part:	1				2		
Treatise:	1	2	3	4	5	6	7
No. of chapters:	2	3	3	4	3	5	6[14]

Book 2

Treatise:	1	2	3
No. of chapters:	3	1	6

Book 3

Treatise:	1	2	3
No. of chapters:	1	5	4

Epilogue

The manuscript is divided into three books with four parts. The content of book 1 (parts 1 and 2) takes up more than half the treatise, while books 2 and 3 are evenly divided. Book 1, part 1 begins with a description of the "accessories" of music, the tails and stems, rests, *pontellus,* and *musica*

[14]This outline is based on the English translation of the Pomerium (Renner, 1980).

ficta. Though these may seem at first glance like a rather arbitrary list of musical components, they make more sense when viewed as *materialis*, or what Aristotle might define as his first cause, "that out of which a thing is created." From these components, mensural music comes to exist. This is a list of materials, each contributing to the perception of the value of notation. In the introduction to book 1, part 1, treatise 1, we also note that Marchetto suggests that he speaks of the accessory elements of knowledge to arrive at the knowledge of its essence.[15] Once again he echoes Aristotle, this time the *De Anima* (1.50.402b2).

The "Essentials of Mensural Music" ("De essentialibus musicae mensuratae: De tempore") is the title of the second major division of the treatise, book 1, part 2. This section corresponds to Aristotle's second cause ("the form or the archetype, i.e. the statement of the essence, [e.g. of the octave the relation of 2:1, and generally number]"). Marchetto explains the properties of the measured notes. He writes, "Now the essential and intrinsic elements of mensural music are the notes, in which the science of music essentially consists" (61).[16] Again Marchetto contends that it is vital, in the consideration of music as science, to consider what Aristotle would call its "essence." He defines the essence of mensural music as musical time and the different ways in which it can be divided. The components of time consist of the application of a time unit to the notes, the valuation of the altered breve, how the time unit is divided, and examples of divisions of the time unit (62). For Marchetto time is the essential cause of mensural music, and he calls upon Aristotle's *Physica* once again to make his point: "And every measure consists in a certain quantity and [unit of time], for 'time is the measure of motion.' " ["Omnis enim mensura in certa quantitate et tempore est, nam tempus est mensura motus (per Philosophum, quarto Physicorum)" 75-76.]

The following chapters will, therefore, concern themselves with "first, how it is understood [specifically] in music and, [then], how it is applied to the notes so that, as a result, we can see how the notes are understood and measured in mensural music." ("Videndum est igitur de ipso tempore, primo scilicet quomodo in musica accipiatur, et quomodo ipsis notis applicetur, ut per consequens videmus in cantu mensurato quomodo istae notae

[15] "Quoniam, dicente Philosopho in prooemio de Anima, accidentia multum conferunt ad cognoscendum quod quid est, id est, per cognitionem accidentium devenimus in cognitionem essentiae rei. Cum igitur in praesenti opere nostrae intentionis sit cognitionem tradere per rationes essentiae musicae mensuratae, igitur, primo de accidentibus sive de accidentalibus concurrentibus in musica mensurata principaliter est tractandum, deinde de essentialibus musicae praelibatae" (Da Padova 1961, 39).

[16] "Sed substantialia et intrinseca ipsius cantus sive musicae sunt notae, in quibus ipsa scientia musicae essentialiter consistit; de notis igitur est videndum" (Da Padova 1961, 75).

accipiantur et qualiter mensurentur" 76.) In the final chapter of book 2 and throughout book 3, a demonstrable shift in focus takes place in the *Pomerium* from considering the qualities of music to considering the importance of the composer as agent and fashioner of the notes. It could be argued that the shift reflects Marchetto and Syphantis's willingness to portray subtlety and nuance for King Robert by employing Aristotle's four causes as a basis for the organization of the *Pomerium*. The new focus on the composer and the practice of making music may relate to Aristotle's third cause, the actor or agent of change. In these latter books, Marchetto shows the composer to be the agent, who uses the materials and essentials described in the previous section to create a composition, (particularly, the use of these materials in) a piece of discant. As you will recall, the section concerns Aristotle's "primary source of the change or coming to rest," that is, the composer who gives rise to the musical composition (or Aristotle's "father is cause of the child"), or what the *Pomerium's* introduction calls *ipse actor*. It is in chapter 5 of book 2 ("The Difference Between the French and the Italian Practice in Singing According to the Imperfect Time Unit and Whose Practice Is More Reasonable") that Marchetto moves to his famous and enigmatic consideration of the difference between Italian and French practice. "Practice" describes the actions of the agent, the composer, in relation to the materials of mensural music. For Marchetto the primary difference between the two practices concerns the assigning of perfection within the tempus. "For the Italian practice is always to attribute perfection to the end, just as [they do] in proportioning [semibreves] when singing according to the perfect time unit, whereas the French [practice] is to attribute perfection to the beginning."[17]

Marchetto then gives numerous examples of differences between the two practices, saturating his language with references to *via naturae* (without stems) and *per artem* (with stems). For instance, we read:

> If two semibreves are used for the imperfect time unit, then according to both the French and the Italian [practice] they are sung equal. Because these two semibreves are the parts of the first division of the imperfect time unit, they are called naturally major [semibreves], because they are comparable to two of the [three] parts of the first division of the perfect time unit. Artificially, however, a stem can be added to one of [the two semibreves].[18]

---

[17]"Nam Italici semper attribuunt perfectionem a parte finis, sicut fit proportionando eas ad invicem in modo cantandi de tempore perfecto; Gallici vero attribuunt perfectionem a parte principii" (Da Padova 1961, 72).

[18]"Si enim duae semibreves accipiuntur pro tempore imperfecto, tunc, et secundum Gallicos et secundum Italicos, aequaliter proferuntur. Et quia ipsae sunt primae partes

Echoes of Aristotle's fourth cause appear in the conceptions of book 3 of the *Pomerium*, which continues with a discussion of the practice of mensural music with respect to the composition of discant. It is entitled "Mensural Music and Those [Elements] Which We Treat in [Mensural Music] insofar as They Give Rise to a Different Form of [Music]." In this book Marchetto describes how the materials of music are formed to achieve an end: discant, a type of mensural music "sung in a reasonable manner." The end, or final causes, also refers to the end product of Marchetto's efforts: the composition of discant and the scientific knowledge the book imparts to its reader. For Marchetto, the final cause is the knowledge of mensural music, to sing rationally, and not by passion. He explains the use of ligatures and plicas, and other means of tying notes together in a piece of music. Here he lays out rules to be followed by the composer and points out errors made by some. We read, for instance:

> Accordingly, it is clear that it is the essential nature of a ligature to be ascending and/or descending. With this and other statements we intend to refute the error of those who tie together two or more notes in the same space or on the same line.[19]

Book 3 contains many suggestions to composers for writing serious music that follows the scientific principles laid out in the previous books. Indeed, instead of continuing to rely on Aristotle as an authority to buttress his observations, Marchetto frequently evokes the name of Franco, a fellow theorist, to support his claims. The shift to Franco, who also strove to teach his fellow musicians proper practice, signifies a move toward an end, a purpose, that is the proper composition of discant. The epilogue reiterates this end:

> The purposes of this [book were]: to show singers that mensural music is not sung or written arbitrarily, but, considered as a science among, makes use of, and is splendidly ornamented by, its own proper principles, means, and conclusions; to refute errors, propound the truth, and instruct whoever desires to sing the Lord wisely.[20]

---

divisionis temporis imperfecti, ideo dicuntur maiores naturaliter eo quod comparantur duabus primae divisionis temporis perfecti" (Da Padova 1961, 173-174).

[19]"Per quod patet quod essentialis ratio ligaturae est per ascensum et descensum; per quod verbum et per alia intendimus reprobare errorem ligantium in eodem spatio vel in eadem linea plures notas" (Da Padova 1961, 186).

[20]". . . et ipso propter quid est suis rationibus ostendente, in quantum scivi melius compilavi, ut ex eo cantoribus ostendatur quod musica mensurata non pro quocunque libito voluntatis et scribitur et cantatur, sed tamquam scientia inter scientias computata suis propriis principiis, mediis et conclusionibus utitur et clarissime decoratur, errores tollantur, veritas proponantur, et quilibet instruatur cantare Domino cupiens sapienter" (Da Padova 1961, 209-210).

Like Pietro before him, Marchetto chooses scientific terminology over sacred allusions to emphasize the importance of the end of a time unit. Indeed, Marchetto's argument is a fascinating amalgam of traditional Franconian theories of perfection and Aristotelian science. Franco relies on traditional arguments of perfection arising from the allusion of the number three to the trinity. In describing the value of the long in the *Ars cantus mensurabilis*, he writes, "It [the long] is called perfect because it is measured by three 'tempora,' the ternary number being the most perfect number because it takes its name from the Holy Trinity, which is true and pure perfection."[21] Marchetto, however, makes no mention of the Trinity in the *Pomerium*.

Marchetto also borrows Aristotle's contention in the *Physica* that nature and art can work in tandem. The Philosopher notes, "Generally art partly completes what nature cannot bring to a finish, and partly imitates her" (199a17).

After reiterating the dictum "art imitates nature as much as possible," Marchetto argues that composers may combine natural objects and art to produce the desired result:

> Nevertheless, natural things are combined in art in ways in which they are not found in nature; for art combines the goat and the deer to make a goat-deer, and yet they are not the same when [they are] in nature as they are when art uses them as its basis. Therefore, although that thing [i.e., the goat-deer] is not from nature but from art, art took those things [i.e., the goat and the deer] from [among] natural things.[22]

In much the same way, he maintains that composers combine different natural elements of mensural music with art. "We say, therefore, that the musician can change and add to the notes conditions which indicate that they have properties beyond their nature," as, for instance, when a tail is added to a note, altering its nature in an artificial manner.

> So, although he does this artificially, nevertheless he starts with natural things as a basis – i.e., with the parts of the time unit and the notes – and [then artificially] combines [the notes] with different parts

[21]"Perfecta dicitur, eo quod tribus temporibus mensuratur; est enim ternarius numerus intra numeros perfectissimus, pro eo quod a summa trinitate, que vera est pura perfectio, nomen sumspit" (Coussemaker 1963, 119). Translated in Strunk 1965, 142.

[22]"Et tamen naturalia ita componuntur ad invicem in arte, quod non sic reperiuntur in natura; nam hircum et cervum, quae sunt naturalia, ars ad invicem componit, faciendo hircocervum; et tamen talia non sunt simul in rerum natura quae ars habuit simul pro suo fundamento. Unde, licet tale quid non sit a natura, sed ab arte, ars tamen a rebus naturalibus ipsa accepit" (Da Padova 1961, 104).

of time unit; and this [combining] means adding something over and above the nature of those notes and not contrary to their nature."[23]

The idea of combining natural and artificial notation also applies to Marchetto's famous distinction between Italian and French practices of assigning perfection in a unit of imperfect time (Da Padova 1961, 213). In book 2, chapter 5, he argues that "the Italian practice can also be maintained by the argument that they imitate perfection as much as they can (which is reasonable enough) by always comparing the imperfect to the perfect."[24]

Therefore, because proportions according to imperfect and perfect time are similar for completion of the unit, this is a reasonable assertion for Marchetto to make. Again the theorists touch on a very striking point. The difference, essentially, between the Italian and the French style is that the former strives more toward imitating perfection. This Italian style sounds very much like Giotto's style, and effectively captures the difference between the French and Italian manner in the early Trecento. Fourteenth-century French art was characterized by a flowering of the Gothic tradition best known for its stained glass windows, illuminations, and personal, secular miniature painting. This style is noted for extreme linearity, giving the effect of elegance and refinement, and for attention to decorative detail. It is distinctly different from the grand gestures seen in Giotto's frescoes in the Scrovegni Chapel, which show marked influence from classical traditions. Marchetto's statement also parallels Scardeone's claim, explored earlier in this book, that the Paduans saved Italy's arts from the Gothic furor: "Later, and I do not know for what reason this took place, something that must seem very extraordinary, how it came to be that all the famous arts and disciplines, once made completely extinct in Italy by the Gothic furor, became resuscitated for the first time in Padua from their tomb."[25]

Marchetto's discussion of perfect and imperfect time units is also formulated on the Aristotelian doctrine of opposites found in the *Metaphysica*. In chapter 6, "How Semibreves Belong to the Second [of the two second and of two third] Division[s] of the Time Unit," he uses the example of corporeal and incorporeal opposites (and a diagram) to stress that there is no

---

[23]"Dicimus ergo quod musicus potest diversificare et conditiones apponere ipsis notis quae innuant ipsas habere proprietates ultra suam naturam; et hoc facit diversas naturas notarum ad invicem diversimode componendo" (Da Padova 1961, 105).

[24]"Modus etiam cantandi Italicorum potest etiam sustineri, dicendo quod imitantur perfectionem in quantum possunt; quod est rationabile satis, scilicet imperfectum semper reducere ad perfectum" (Da Padova 1961, 173).

[25]"Porro nescio quo fato contigerit, quod mirum admodum videri debet, ut omnes praeclarae artes ac disciplinae, quae olim Gothico furore penitus in Italia extinctae fuerant, Patavii primum attollere potissimum oculos, et reviviscere, atque e sepulchro quodammodo exsurgere vi saesint" (Scardeone 1979, 295-296).

intermediate value between the two time values. Marchetto notes, "that which is included in any one of [two opposites] can never be intermediate between the [two opposites]. For example, corporeal and incorporeal are opposites."[26] Therefore, because every number may be included in two or in three (even and odd), perfect and imperfect time are opposites between which no intermediate quantity may exist. He asserts this point in book 1, chapter 2, when he observes, "in themselves, absolutely, and without reference to any division or multiplication of either, perfect and imperfect time are essentially opposed, as is sufficiently clear from our definition."[27]

Book 2 of the *Pomerium* concerns imperfect time. Once again, the discussion begins with a quotation from Aristotle, this time from the *Topica* [i 10.104a15], "Knowledge of contraries is the same." In this book, Marchetto repeatedly emphasizes the "science of music," noting that the knowledge of music with regard to notes and accessories is "always based primarily and principally on the perfect time unit." He argues that all accidents of music, such as rests, tails, and dots, appear in perfect and imperfect time:

> The reason is this: There is no scientific knowledge, nor even sensory knowledge, of the imperfect except by taking the perfect as norm; for neither by our intellect nor by our senses could we ever know that something is imperfect unless we knew what would be necessary for it to be perfect; it is a fact that scientific knowledge regarding things grasped by the intellect or the senses is always based on the perfect. [The science of] music, therefore, with regard to both notes and accessories, is always based primarily and principally on the perfect unit."[28]

[26]"Corporeum et incorporeum sunt opposita; omne ergo quod includitur in corporeo, necessario opponitur incorporeo, et nunquam potest esse medium inter ipsa duo" (Da Padova 1961, 148).

[27]"Tempus autem perfectum et imperfectum essentialiter opponuntur, per se et absolute et non habito respectu ad aliquam divisionem vel multiplicationem ipsorum, sicut satis patet in diffinitione superius declarata" (Da Padova 1961, 159-160). He explains, "Therefore, it is impossible that any musical time unit can be at once actually and essentially perfect and imperfect, for this implies a manifest contradiction, since it amounts to saying that someone is at once man and a non-man." ("Impossibile est ergo quod realiter et essentialiter aliquod tempus musicum possit esse simul perfectum et imperfectum, ut quidam fingunt, quia hoc esset implicare contradictionem manifeste:esset enim dicere quod aliquis possit esse homo et non homo" 160.)

[28]"Et ratio huius est quia de imperfectis nunquam potest esse scientia mentalis, nec etiam cognitio sensitiva, nisi per comparationem ad perfecta. Nunquam enim nec per intellectum, nec per sensum possemus cognoscere aliquid esse imperfectum, nisi cognosceremus quid esset ei necesse ad hoc ut esset perfectum, ita quod scientia, quantum ad ea quae cadunt sive in intellectu sive in sensu, semper est de perfectis. Musica ergo, et quantum ad notas et quantum ad accidentia, semper est de tempore perfecto primo et principaliter" (Da Padova 1961, 162-163).

Marchetto asserts that because the notation and accessories (rests, stems, and dots) of perfect and imperfect time are the same, the composer should indicate at the beginning of a particular section whether it is perfect or imperfect by using .i. (imperfect) or .p. (perfect), .t. (ternary) or .b. (binary). Interestingly, Marchetto ends the chapter by explaining that mensural music tends to use the perfect, rather than the imperfect, time unit ("a melody will normally use not the imperfect but the perfect time unit"). He stops short of calling imperfect time artificial. This is because imperfect time does not represent a *change* from perfect, but an *object* that is naturally and essentially opposed to it.

The *De Mundo*, a text attributed to Aristotle during the Middle Ages, contains evocative passages describing the harmony produced by opposites:

> Yet some have wondered how it is that the Universe, if it be composed of contrary principles – namely, dry and moist, hot and cold – has not long ago perished and been destroyed. It is just as though one should wonder how a city continues to exist, being, as it is, composed of opposing classes – rich and poor, young and old, weak and strong, good and bad (1931, 396a-b).

In this passage from the *De Mundo* attributed to Aristotle, we find a relationship between the harmony of opposites and the harmony of peace, a conception central to understanding Giotto's depictions of music in the Scrovegni Chapel:

> They fail to notice that this has always been the most striking characteristic of civic concord, that it evolves unity out of plurality, and similarity out of dissimilarity, while it admits every kind and variety. It may perhaps be that nature has a liking of contraries and evolves harmony out of them and not out of similarities (just as she joins the male and female together and not members of the same sex), and has devised the original harmony by means of contraries and not similarities (1931, 396b).

The passage also speaks directly about art and music:

> The arts, too, apparently imitate nature in this respect. The art of painting, by mingling in the picture the elements of white and black, yellow and red, achieves representations which correspond to the original object. Music, too, mingling together notes, high and low, short and prolonged, attains to a single harmony amid different voices; while writing, mingling vowels and consonants, composes them all in its art (1931, 396b).

Marchetto's prologue and epilogue in the *Pomerium* speak of combining disparate voices to produce harmony. In the prologue, he describes heavenly choirs uniting to produce one voice, the hymn of divine glory: "when with harmonious voices and great fervor they sing unceasingly as one voice the hymn of divine glory: 'Holy, holy, holy' " ("dum modulatis vocibus hymnun divinae gloriae 'Sanctus, sanctus, sanctus' ferventius una voce clamare non cessant" 35). The image of antiphonal choirs singing as one also appears in the epilogue. Marchetto quotes Psalm 46.7-8, "I ask all singers: Sing praises to our God, sing praises wisely" ("Rogo omnes cantores: Psallite Deo nostro, psallite, quoniam rex omnis terrae Deus, psallite sapienter" 209). Once again Marchetto urges singers to sing correctly (the fourth cause, according to the introductory notes to the *Pomerium*) when describing the union of voices from the church triumphant and the church militant (209).

In Aristotle's *De Mundo* we find words eerily echoed later by Marchetto:

> The single harmony produced by all the heavenly bodies singing and dancing together springs from one source and ends by achieving one purpose, and has rightly bestowed the name not of 'disordered' but of 'ordered universe' upon the whole. And just as in a chorus, when the leader gives the signal to begin, the whole chorus of men, or it may be of women, joins in the song, mingling a single studied harmony among different voices, some high and some low; so too is it with the God that rules the whole world (1931, 399a).

Pietro d'Abano, the most important Paduan to champion Aristotelian science, also relied on Aristotle's *De Mundo* in his discussion of musical properties. However, as we shall see, Pietro borrowed less methodically from Aristotle's *Physica* than did Marchetto. Rather, Pietro used the *Physica*, together with the *Politics* and *De Mundo*, in fashioning his chapters dedicated to music. Furthermore, Marchetto's and Pietro's theories almost never overlap, which leads to two conclusions: they did not travel in the same intellectual circles; and they were essentially two different types of thinkers, with different backgrounds: Marchetto was a practicing musician, and not affiliated with the university, while Pietro, though a professor, was first a doctor for whom music was one more phenomenon to be understood in the context of a larger world.

As he does for Marchetto, Bernardino Scardeone will serve as Pietro's Renaissance biographer. In his *Historiae de urbis Patavii*, Scardeone describes Pietro's contributions to Paduan history:

> It is said that Pietro was the first person to bring to Italy the study of medicine from Greece after many centuries. He was known as

> a supreme expert in antique magic, natural science, and the art of medicine.[29]

Pietro was the first among the writers in Latin to reconcile medicine and the study of the natural sciences. Scardeone lauds his fellow Paduan:

> It was the case, in fact, that the art of medicine (as Tortellius confirms) was of little value during the time of Avicenna, was not followed at all in Italy for many centuries; [and was] practically unknown and completely obscured in Latin. The first of the Latin writers to regain interest in medicine (as he himself says) was Pietro, a man worthy of admiration in any time; who, reconciling with his doctrine the diverse opinions both in the field of philosophy and medicine, was deemed expert by all his contemporaries, and was given the nickname conciliator.[30]

According to Scardeone's biography, Pietro traveled to Greece as a young man to improve his knowledge of Greek language and literature. He next went to Paris, where he passed exams testing his knowledge of mathematics. Pietro progressed so quickly that when he returned to Italy with a superb reputation in the study of the sciences, he was suspected of practicing magic. Pietro was accused of heresy and necromancy by the doctor Pietro Rigiense, who, according to Scardeone, was jealous of Pietro's fame. While undergoing a second trial in 1315, Pietro died. His body was kept in the Basilica of Saint Anthony of Padua until it was found by his enemies, exhumed, and burned.

Pietro's writings provide the primary evidence for the academic study of music in Padua. Pietro incorporated Aristotle's and Boethius's philosophies into the formulation of his scientific theories in the *Conciliator* (1303) and *Expositio problematum Aristotelis* (1310). The *Conciliator* contains explanations of the functions of the human body and the natural world. Significantly for the study of music, differentia 83 includes a section entitled "Is musical consonance found in the pulse?" Pietro notes that the beat

[29]"Primus omnium qui rem medicam post multa secula in Italiam traduxit e Graecia, Petrus Aponus fuisse perhibetur, qui habitus est et veteris magiae, et naturae rerum, et medicae artis unus omnium consultissimus: quod ex eius sapientissimis scriptis ubique patet" (Scardeone 1979, 227).

[30]"Constat enim artem medicam (ut Tortellius affeverat) ab Avicenae temporibus vilem, et nullius fere pretii in Italia per multa secula fuisse: utpote incognitam ac prorsus obscuram Latinis. Primus ergo inter Latinos, qui nobis conciliavit medicinam (ut ille ait) fuit Petrus Aponus, vir in omni aetate admirandus: qui tum in philosophia tum in his, quae ad medicam disciplinam spectant, diversas conciliando opiniones sua doctrina, habitus est omnium, qui hactenus fuerint, peritissimus, unde sibi a praecipuo opere, et a re ipsa conciliatoris cognomen adeptus est" (Scardeone 1979, 227).

in music and heartbeat share a similar pulse. A summary of Pietro's arguments about pulse can be found in Giuseppe Vecchi's *Medicina e musica, voci e strumenti nel "Conciliator" (1303)* (1967) and Nancy Siraisi's "The Music of Pulse in the Writings of Italian Academic Physicians" (1975).

Of far greater significance to this discussion is Pietro's translation from the Greek, and commentary on, the *Problemata*, a text attributed to Aristotle, which served as the foundation for the study of the natural sciences at the University of Padua.[31] The treatise (and the debate that surrounded it) was almost unknown in Western philosophical thought before Pietro, who helped make it known beyond Italian borders, especially in France. The *Problemata* consists of about eight hundred questions with speculative answers.[32]

In writing the commentary concerning the questions on music, Pietro brought the language of music in line with that of the new Renaissance appreciation of the natural sciences in the universities. The understanding of the complexities of music was now fashioned after the Aristotelian conception of nature. Like Marchetto's *Pomerium*, Pietro's *Expositio problematum Aristotelis* is arranged with a nod to Aristotelian science. In the preface of the book, he notes that the problems are divided into three primary parts. Siraisi (1970, 325) defines the divisions as follows: "1) things against nature, 2) natural things, and 3) things that are not natural – these three divisions apparently corresponding to the various particulae on medical problems, natural science, and such topics as ethics and the liberal arts, respectively." The first 14 particulae are concerned with the human body, disease, and remedies; 15-19 deal with the quadrivium; 20-26 expound on the natural sciences; 27-30 are on ethics; and 31-38 return to the human body.

Pietro reserves his most comprehensive observations about music for particula 19 of the *Expositio*. Problem 1 begins:

> Why is it that people who are sad and those who are happy play the flute?Perhaps so that the sad people feel less pain and the other group more pleasure.[33]

To answer Aristotle's questions, Pietro launches into a thorough investi-

[31] The *Problemata* was translated into Latin by Bartholomeus de Messina between 1258 and 1266. On Pietro's *Commentary*, see Olivieri 1988. On Pietro and music, see Palisca 1985, 51-66.

[32] For recent research on Pietro's *Expositio*, see Cadden (2001). Cadden notes that there are numerous textual variations in the *Expositio*'s sources, and she argues that "they illustrate the range of stances and strategies adopted by those interested in natural philosophy in the fourteenth and fifteenth centuries to deal with material that they or their contemporaries judged unseemly or even shameful" (68).

[33] "Propter quid dolentes et delectantes fistulantur, aut ut hij quidem minus tristentur alij autem magis gaudeant" (D'Abano 1475, 189r).

gation of music, exploring its origins, its history in Greek treatises, and its classifications into three types, *mundana, humana*, and organic (or instrumental), the last of which he further divides into natural (*ut vocalia dicta*) and artificial (*ut organa, pslateriumn atque taliem*). Pietro clearly shows familiarity with the writings of Boethius and Isidore and embellishes their discussion by combining their ideas with Aristotelian philosophy. He continues his problem 1 with the establishment of music as a science, a crucial initial step in aligning his argument with Aristotelian science. Pietro writes:

> After having treated the problems that regard mathematics and rethoric, I will discuss the science of harmony and of music. There is in this same subject a love for oration as in the preceding part, and for the first time greater space is dedicated to musical things. According to Boethius, music is the faculty of perceiving high and low sounds, analyzing them well from the point of view of sensation and rationality. According to Isidore in his etymology, it is the ability to blend [modulare] sounds and singing and it is called also the science of number with respect to sound, which for Isidore derives from muso, the laws from which poetry and music originate.[34]

Pietro then explains the origin of music:

> From here these poets imagined that the daughters of Zeus and Memory were dumb. Indeed if they didn't memorize the sound they could not transcribe it. For others, in truth, it was invented by Moses with water because at one time music was discovered in water and in liquids and was practiced with aquatic instruments. Isidore relates that Moses found it in a tomb before the flood. The Greeks, as we find in Macrobius and Boethius, say that music was invented by Pythagoras when he casually went out and discovered it in the beating of hammers of the ironworkers and the movement of the strings.[35]

[34]"Determinatis problematibus circa mathematica et orationes determinat nunc problemata circa armonicam vel musicam. Eo que in ipsa est quidam amor sermonis ut in priori particula et primitus ad huius maiorem exponem permittuntur quidam coia [sic] sicut quid est musica et que ipsius. Que secudum Boetium musice est armonice facultas drias acutorum et gravium sonorum sensu ac ratione perpendens. Secundum vero Isido [Isidorus] in ethymologijs est peritia modulationis sono cantuque consistens dicitur etiam scientia numeri ad sonos proportionati que secundum ysido dicitur a muso quasi a querendo quia per eam ius carminum que rebatur: unde a poetis" (D'Abano 1475, 189r).

[35]"Unde a poetis Jovis et Memorie filias mutas esse confictum est. Nam si memoria soni non teneant percunt cum non possint scribi: a non nullis vero dicitur a moys quod est aqua: quia olim permitus inventa fuit in illa et in ydrijs sive instrumentis aquaticis similiter exercitata. Refert autem moyses hanc invenisse tubal de stirpe chaym ante diluvium Sed greci ut apparet per Macrobium et Boetium dicunt eam invernisse pythagotici samium sonitu malleorum cum casu in publicum exiret ad fabros et chordarum demum impulsione" (D'Abano 1475, 189r).

Pietro continues with a description of Boethius's famous tripartite division of music:

> Music was then subdivided by the Greeks into mundane, human, and organic or instrumental. In the mundane, one observes the harmonic sounds produced by the heavenly spheres according to the Pythagoreans. The cause the harmonic sound but we cannot perceive it because at birth the sounds were irradiated from our ears to leave room for the noise of the masses, which is perceived a bit as a result of habit, which Aristotle describes in *De Mundo* [2].[36]

His description of *musica humana* alludes to natural science:

> Music is called "humana" when it concerns the concordance of different elements into a unique composition or in the composition of the body, by which (*musica humana*) the nature of form is connected to the body. And the "ronalis" and "irronalis" concordance appears in the Platonic structure. Given a certain soul it will have a constitution in harmony with it. Connected to Platonic philosophy of the soul. In this category music for voice alone pertains, without accompaniment from instruments. The connection between body and soul according to a consonance of natural order happens because it can be said that music may be included in the science of nature.[37]

In this passage, Pietro reiterates music's connection to science and includes a digression to Platonic consideration of the forms. Most interestingly, unlike Boethius, Pietro asserts that this music, especially of the human voice, can be perceived by the human ear.

In his description of *musica instrumentalis,* Pietro makes use of the dichotomy between nature and art expounded upon in Aristotle's *Physica*:

> Instrumental music is the one that is practiced with certain harmonic instruments, and it seems that there exist two types. In fact it is practiced with a natural instrument, which is the human voice, together

[36] "Dividitur autem musica iuxta eosdem in mundanam humanam et organicam vel instrmentalem. Mundana vero attenditur in sono armonico quem causant orbes celestes secundum pitbagoricos cum alijs musicis differenter commoti. Sonum enim armonicum causant sed eum non percipimus dicunt propter quod in auribus nostris a principio nativitatis est complantatus ut in eis apparet malleatoribus strepitum suum vix pricipientibus consuetudine quos Aristo. impugnat celi et mundi # 2" (D'Abano 1475, 189r).

[37] "Musica vero humana dicitur que circa concordantiam elementorum diversorum ad invicem in uno compositio vel compositionem corporis versatur: per ea enim natura spumalis coniungitur corpori: et ronalis concorditer cum irronali coniungitur: quod videtur a platonicis habitum: ponentibus animam quandam armonicam fore consistentiam. Unde dictum est in asso. Colligatio corporis et anime secundum ordinis naturalis consonantiam facta est ut subsistat quare huius musice naturali vident scientie supponi" (D'Abano 1475, 189r).

> with other vocal or artificial instruments. And this last possibility is of many types such as with pressing, as in the viols, or percussion as in the cembali or with the breath as in the trumpets or almost in every way as with flutes, and according to Isidore, harmonic music may be divided into metric and rhythmic, of which the harmonic is distinguished in sound from high and low.[38]

For Pietro, the voice is a natural instrument, while instruments are artificial. This division between "natural" and "artificial" is evidence that Pietro's *Expositio* may be one of the primary influences on Marchetto's groundbreaking *Pomerium*. The distinction between natural and artificial instruments is echoed in Marchetto's understanding of music, and will form the foundation for a new reading of Donatello's musical angels in chapter 6.

Later in problem 1, Pietro discusses the need for educating the citizens in one of four primary areas, namely literature (reciting, oration), music, writing, and painting, returning to the initial question posed at the beginning:

> The student is ordered to learn at least one of the four disciplines that are literature (reciting, oration), music – in fighting and when it is necessary to protract things – writing, and painting. Aristotle asks himself as usual in the form of a problem: for what reason it is useful to feel (experience) the joy and happiness caused by bagpipes and similar instruments in those who are sad and happy.[39]

In answering the question again, Pietro borrows another argument from *Physica*, chapter 2:

> When the body is sad, it suffers less because of the happiness that the playing of instruments produces. While when the soul is already happy, it can experience more happiness thanks to greater harmonic stimulus. We know this is true because the same thing can be the origin of two different consequences, or why do they need a different thing? In the same condition one finds, by chance or by reason, that

[38]"Instrumentalis vero dicitur que quibusdam exercetur armonicis instrumentis: que pritis videtur fore considerationis existens duplex: nam quedam exercetur instromento naturali ut hominis voce cum reliquis organis locutivis aut artificiali. Et illud multipliciter aut tactu ut violis vel pulsu ceu cimbalis: vel flatu ut tubis aut quasi omni modo sicut fistulis que iusta Isidorus dividetur in armonicam metricam et rithimicam quarum armonica grave in sonis et acutum discernit" (D'Abano 1475, 189r).

[39]"... ponitur enim unum quatuor que debet adiscere puer: que sunt lingue luctativa musica et protractativa ceu scribere et pingere. Querit igitur Arist. more consueto problema dicens. Quare dolentes contristantes et delectantes gaudentis que fistulas et simuliter instrumenta delectationem et gaudium inducentia expedit audire" (D'Abano 1475, 189r).

> a sailor remains on the ship and saves it with his presence and reason of saving himself.[40]

In simple language, Pietro notes that a ship depends on the sailor, and if the sailor is on the boat, it can be saved; if he is not there, it sinks.

Problems 3, 5, 6-10, 15, 30, 33, and 38 contain the most relevant passages relating to Trecento musical practice. While it is not in the purview of this present study to cite all the references to Aristotle, following is a summary of the arguments in each of these sections, some of which are the most fascinating, and, if you will, the most Renaissance-minded of Pietro's observations. Briefly, problem 3 essentially introduces the names of the pitches and their relation to the planets, with each note of the scale called by its Greek name. Problem 5 explores the idea of the increased enjoyment of music when the music is familiar. Pietro argues that it is only natural that humans are drawn to the familiar. Problems 15 and 30 concern the performance of music within the theater, which is beyond the scope of this study. Problem 33 explores whether it is easier to sing from the high register to the low or vice versa, with Pietro arguing that it is more natural to sing from the top to the bottom of the scale.

Problems 6 through 10 concern the passions that music can arouse. In many ways, these are the most tantalizing sections of particula 19. In problem 6, Pietro distinguishes between comic and tragic and the kind of music that should accompany each. Pietro writes that it is important to note the two ways to sing harmony (that is, with someone else). One is comedy (*comedia*), the other tragedy (*tragedia*).[41]

Comedy is a type of song that concerns the private matters of humble people, often centered in the countryside or combining, according to the Greeks, the world (*mundo*) and songs (*ode*) to form mundane songs. These

---

[40]"De inde Aut Solvit dicens causam esse ut qui tristantur ac etiam dolent minus contristentur et doleant propter iocunditatem inductam ex sonitu instrumenti in oppositis vero causa est ut magis gaudeam et delectentur si enim aliqui sunt iocundi addita causa iocunditatis ut sistulationis armonice applius delectabuntur. Nosce que illud potest contingere quia idem potest esse causa diversorum aut ratione dispositionis susceptivi: vel quia diversa agat idem vel ratione eius quid per se aut per accidens extat; ut nauta per sui presentiam causa est salutis navis eius vero absentia submersionis 2 Phys" (D'Abano 1475, 189r).

[41]"Quare rationabile existsi que genus cantandi tragicum per ypatem cantetur. Notandum que circa genus armonicum quodumquem duplicem manerium cantandi constare quedam enim est comedia alter tragedia. Est autem comedia canticum agreste que res privatarum et humilium personarum comprehendit et dicitur a cosmos que est villa vel laus secundum aliqous grece tamen mundus et odi cantus quasi mundanus et vulgarus cantus de rebus enim vulgaribus tractat et affinibus et cotidiane locutioni vel dicitur a comestione post cibum enim homines solebant ad eam audiendam convenire" (D'Abano 1475, 190v).

songs concern themselves with vulgar arguments and themes from everyday life. The word *comedy* could derive from *comestion* (eating with), that is, from the banquet; indeed, it was common to hear comedy after dinner. Pietro's description of comedy is reminiscent of the words used to describe the earliest madrigals in the anonymous *Capitulum de vocibus applicatis verbis* and in the work of Antonio da Tempo. Could the madrigal be an outgrowth of comedy and have its origin in the word *mangiare?* As we shall see in chapter 3, the word *madrigal* does have its origin in the Veneto region, and Pietro's explanation is further evidence of its roots in the comic tradition.[42]

In problem 9, Pietro presents an argument that is the precursor to musical philosophies found in Renaissance Florence. He answers Aristotle's question, "Why do we derive more pleasure in hearing monody if it is sung to the accompaniment of the flute or one lyre?"[43]

In Renaissance Florence, Lorenzo de Medici was known for assembling intellectuals at his home to reinvent classical modes of singing. These intellectuals called for the reciting of music to the accompaniment of one primary instrument, usually the lyre. Indeed, the *frottola*, which scholars point to as the precursor of the sixteenth-century madrigal, appears to derive from Lorenzo's practices, and Lorenzo himself, with the help of his teacher Isaac, composed in this genre, as did more famous composers, such as Marchetto Cara. Pietro here implies that this style was known and practiced in Padua in the early Trecento, having its origin in Paduan drama of that time. Pietro responds to Aristotle's question: "if indeed the same song is more pleasing when it is accompanied [by one instrument], it would be even more pleasing to hear it with a great number of instruments."[44]

Aristotle continues with the following question: "Why is it that a singer reaches his goal better when he is accompanied by only one flute or one lyre?"[45]

Pietro answers, "Multiplying the number of instruments does not heighten the pleasure because the singer's voice is covered."[46] Pietro argues that

[42]Tragedy, according to Pietro, is the mode of singing that the poets used for sad occasions and derives its name *tragos*, which is a *capro*, (goat), and *ode*, (song), so that song of the *capro* is derived from this animal, which is sad and funereal.

[43]"Propter quid delectabiliter unitatem cantus audimus: si quis ad fistulam aut lyram cantat et ad chordas ..." (D'Abano 1475, 191r).

[44]"... si enim ad hoc magis idem potius oportebat ad multos fitulatores et adhuc delectabiliter esse" (D'Abano 1475, 191r).

[45]"Aut quia adipiscens manifestius intentionem magis quando ad fistulam aut lyram quando vero ad multos fistulatores aut lyras multas non est delectabile propter id que destruit melodiam" (D'Abano 1475, 191r).

[46]"... et hoc quia in cantu quedam reservantur proportiones ut dicetur commensurate quibus observatis iocunda consurgit armonia que quidem corrumpitur et indelectabilis

when singing alone with the accompaniment of one instrument, the singer maintains a more unified timbre and singing style than when the singer is accompanied by diverse instruments. His comments apply to multiple players and singers as well: "If many sing the same song, they cannot do it in the same manner; it is not enough that the song is identical; the singer also must measure it according to himself and adapt his style to that of the others, so that the song is a result of singers adapting their style to something similar."[47]

In problem 10, Pietro considers the relative merits of vocal and instrumental music. He asks, "Why, if it is true that the human voice is more appealing to listen to than instrumental sounds, is it that it is less pleasing to hear a voice vocalizing without words, than it is to hear instruments?"[48]

Pietro answers that the voice is most pleasing when it is imitative, and here he means when it reflects the meaning of the words. He cites book 7 of Aristotle's *Politics* to defend his position that the voice is more pleasing to hear accompanied by words, by comparing it to Aristotle's comment that without them it is like listening to the birds. ("...birds that sing sounds without significance.")[49]

Problem 38 deals most directly with the issue of nature and music. The original Aristotle reads:

> Why do all men delight in rhythm and melody and concords in general? Is it because we naturally rejoice in natural movements? This is shown by the fact that children rejoice in them as soon as they are born. Now we delight in the various types of melody for their moral character, but we delight in rhythm because it contains a familiar and ordered number and moves in a regular manner; for ordered movement is naturally more akin to us than disordered movement, and is therefore more in accordance with nature. This is shown by the fact that by working and eating and drinking in an ordered manner we preserve and improve our nature and strength, whereas if we do these things irregularly we destroy and derange our nature; for diseases are disturbances of the natural order of the body. Thirdly, we delight in

redditur cum cantas ad multa cantaverit instrumenta" (D'Abano 1475, 191r).

[47]"Que autem inductum est in contrarium prius novum multi possint idem cantare non tamen eodem modo non enim solum requiritur ydentitas ex parte illius que cantatutur; et cuiuslibet cantantis ad se ipsum imo uniuscuiusque et ad alius ad omnes" (D'Abano 1475, 191r).

[48]"Propter quid si delectabilis hominis vox: que sine sermone cantantis non delectabile est: ut vernantium; sed fistula aut lyra?" (D'Abano 1475, 191r).

[49]"Quare si vox humana est delectabilis auditu, unde museus politicorum 8; Delectabilissimus est hominibus cantare; cum quis cantat etiam non preferendo sermonem omnino; aut insignificatium cur enim non est delectabilis vox alicuius vernantium cum sit hominis" (D'Abano 1475, 191v).

> concord because it is the mingling of contraries that stand in proportion to one another. Proportion, then, is order, which, as we have said, is naturally pleasant. Now that which is mingled is always more pleasant than that which is unmingled, especially if, being perceived by the senses, it contains equally the force of both extremes; and in concord the proportion has this characteristic (1927, 920b28-921a6).

Pietro's response to the above passage focuses primarily on the notion of "natural" movement, which he notes is more regular: the more natural the movements, the healthier the person. Furthermore, when someone corrupts this movement and goes about it in a messy fashion, he distances himself more and more from the natural state. Pietro concludes that there is no doubt that illnesses are changes to the natural order of the body. With respect to Aristotle's assertion about "mingling," Pietro concludes that we appreciate consonance because it is the mingling and the harmonization of contraries that create a rapport between people. The result is order, which he declares more pleasing by nature.

To summarize the musical portions of the *Expositio*, Pietro takes as his starting point Aristotle, Boethius, Isidore, and the classical myths, and forges an erudite explanation of music. He focuses primarily on the traditional Greek modal system and nomenclature and coming to an understanding of music's effect as it relates to words and instruments. These considerations may be viewed as the precursors to late Renaissance intellectualizing by Girolamo Mei and Vincenzo Galileo, who established perimeters for opera, and proposed the idea that words accompanied by music are the most effective means of communicating emotion. Galileo's *Dialogo della musica antica, et della moderna* (1581) has much in common with Pietro's *Expositio*, as exemplified by Galileo's description of Greek method and effect (Moyer 1992, 245-262). Pietro's approach to music, however, is from his perspective as a theorist, and professor of medicine and philosophy, rather than that of practitioner, and it is left to Marchetto, the great Paduan theorist, to adopt Aristotelian science in the practice of composing and notating music.

The *Capitulum de vocibus applicatis verbis*, an anonymous treatise fragment that describes the different genres of music popular in the first decade of the Trecento, will serve as transition toward a discussion of the Trecento repertory to be found in chapter 3. As we have seen, Paduans sought to revive ancient Greek and Roman traditions in their musical festivities and in their burgeoning musical theories. The imitation of Roman festivities and the interest in the city's classical history are examples of an archeological spirit rampant at the outset of the Trecento. Furthermore, the appropriation of the doctrines of Aristotle in the music theories of Marchetto and

Pietro propelled music into the forefront of academic study. Both influences may be seen in the anonymous *Capitulum*, which dates from 1315-1320 and originates in the Veneto region. It reads: "as the Philosopher says at the opening of his *Physica*, 'Our knowledge begins from things that are better known.' "[50]

The end of that chapter of the fragment also invokes Aristotle: "as the Philosopher says in the Dialectics, 'Science deals with the universals and the finites.' "[51]

This is followed by descriptions of the most popular genres of vocal music in the early Trecento, the ballata, rotundello, motet, caccia, madrigal, and sonnet. The madrigal is the only genre for which the writer suggests the appropriate song texts. Strikingly, the words are reminiscent of Pietro's description of music for comedy: "The texts of madrigals should be about shepherdesses, flowers, orchards, garlands, fields and the like, but in good subject-matter, language and expression."[52]

It will be seen that these genres are rooted in the imagined landscapes of Paduan's triumphant Roman past and a conception of music as science.

[50]"Sicut dicit Philosophus in principio Phisicorum: Cognicio nostra incipitur a notioribus" (Debenedetti 1906-1907, 79).

[51]"Testante Philosopho in Dyalectica, scientia est de universalibus et finites" (Debenedetti 1906-1907, 80).

[52]"...cuius verba volunt esse de villanelles, de floribus, arbustis, sertis, utere et similibus, dummodo sit bon sentencia, loquela et sermo" (Debenedetti 1906-1907, 80).

Chapter 3

The Extant Secular Repertory and the Flourishing of an Italian Musical Pre-humanist Tradition

The composer Jacopo da Bologna, who spent many years in the service of Veneto aristocrats, speaks of Marchetto in his madrigal *Oselleto salvazo* of circa 1340:

A wood bird in season sings sweet verses in elegant style: But such and such squawk so loud I cannot praise them.	Oselleto salvazo per stasone dolci versiti canta cum bel modo: tal e tal grida forte, ch' i' no l'odo.
By squawking loudly one cannot sing well, but with sweet and charming melody one can make a beautiful song, and this requires mastery.	Per gridar forte non se canta bene, ma con suave, dolce melodia se fa bel canto zò vol maistria.
Few possess it, yet all claim to be masters, composing ballads, madrigals and motets: they are all Florians, Filippottos and Marchettos.	Pochi l'hano e tuti se fa magistri, fa ballate, matrical e muteti, tut'en Fioran, Filipoti e Marcheti.

The land is so filled with little masters
that there is no room for disciples.[1]

Sì è piena la terra de magistroli,
che loco più non trovano i discipuli (42).

According to Jacopo, Marchetto is a master of singing in the correct manner, sweetly and without shouting. Jacopo laments that many are practitioners, yet few are masters like Marchetto. In addressing correct singing practice, Jacopo recalls Marchetto's final cause, or objective, of his *Pomerium*: to *teach* singers how to practice their vocation properly. The scholastic view that music be understood as a science, diffused by Marchetto and Pietro, may be perceived in the madrigal *O tu, cara scienzia mia, musica* by Giovanni da Cascia, who also spent years in northern Italy composing motets for aristocratic families:

O Music, dear science of mine,
O sweet melody which, through lovely songs,
makes lovers renew again their love.

O tu, cara scienzia mia, musica,
O dolce melodia con vaghi canti,
che fa' rinovellar tuttor gli amanti,

And I who, as a string in your consonance,
used to recreate your beautiful inventiveness:
Am now your proxy and your advocate.

e io son corda di tuo consonanzia,
che imaginar solea tuo bel trovato,
or son procuratore ed avocato.

That's why I return to you, dear Music,
because every fine deed of love
is learned from you.[2]

Però ritorno a te, musica cara,
ch'ogni atto bel d'amor da te s'apar (18).

Marchetto's name was also remembered in the works of Nicolò de Rossi, Franco Sacchetti, Jacopo da Montepulciano, and even in France in a ballade by Guido (Gallo 1985, 56). As we have seen, scholastic interest in nature among the intellectual circles came by way of Paris, where Pietro and playwright Albertino Mussato had first studied and taught.[3] In this chapter, I will examine the flourishing of Trecento repertory through the revivalist lens mapped out in chapters 1 and 2: the reclaiming of Greek and Roman

[1]Translation in CD jacket, *The Music of the Fourteenth Century: Two Gentlemen of Verona* (MoveRecords MD3091, 1987). This piece has two versions: one a three-part caccia, and one a two-part madrigal. Madrigal texts and page numbers in this chapter are from Corsi (1970) unless otherwise specified. Translations are by the author unless otherwise specified.

[2]Translation in CD jacket, *The Music of the Fourteenth Century: Two Gentlemen of Verona* (MoveRecords MD3091, 1987).

[3]Though it is not within the scope of this monograph, French scholasticism seems also to have influenced Padua's musical culture, and it will be left to other scholars to examine this phenomenon. For French musical theory, see Della Seta (1976), Page (1990), and Strohm (2001).

historical artifacts and the renaissance of classical political and philosophical ideals. The madrigal, caccia, and motet will be the primary focus of this investigation into secular music.

The earliest sources of indigenous Italian secular music in the Trecento are the Rossi Codex (Vatican City, Biblioteca Apostolica Vaticana, Rossi 215 *Rvat*) and the Ostiglia fragment (Ostiglia, Opera Pia G. Greggiati, Biblioteca Musicale, s.s.*Os*), a grouping of folios that together belong to one original source (Pirrotta 1992, 92). The music in this collection originated between 1330 and 1340, and geographical references in the texts and the use of local dialects place the contents of the manuscript in the Veneto region, between Verona and Padua, perhaps including Ferrara and the Po delta (Pirrotta 1992, 94). In his introduction to the facsimile edition, Nino Pirrotta notes that scholars delimited the manuscript's origin to the west by Lake Garda and Mantua; by Lake Garda, Verona, and Padua to the north; and by Mantua and Ferrara to the south (Pirrotta 1992, 92). All compositions in this collection are anonymous, though concordances determine that two are by Maestro Piero and two by Giovanni da Cascia.

Little is known about these composers. The earliest composer in the Italian Trecento, Maestro Piero, worked primarily in courts of northern Italy, namely, for the Visconti in Milan and the Scaligeri in Verona. Eight works by Piero survive, six of which may be classified as madrigals, although they share canonic qualities with caccias. One of his madrigals, *All'ombra d'un perlaro,* contains the name Anna, common throughout this early repertory, including in the madrigals of Giovanni da Cascia and Jacopo da Bologna.

Giovanni da Cascia, also known as Giovanni da Firenze, flourished in northern Italy in the mid-Trecento. He is linked with the composer Jacopo da Bologna at the court of Mastino II della Scala in Verona in 1351. Filippo Villani, in the second edition of *De origine civitatis Florentie et de eiusdem famosis civibus* (1385-1397), writes: "Giovanni da Cascia frequented the court of the tyrant Mastino della Scala in search of his fortune. And so he came to take part in a contest for excellence in art with Jacopo of Bologna, a highly skilled musician, the tyrant egging them on with offers of gifts. In that contest, he composed madrigals and many songs, in which his great skill was wonderfully displayed."[4] The composer of sixteen madrigals and three caccias, Giovanni is regarded as a consolidator of the madrigal style,

[4]Translated in Weiss and Taruskin 1984, 74. The passage originates from the chapter decicated to Francesco Landini. "Iohannes de Cascia, cum Mastini Della Scala tiranni veronensis atria questus gratia frequentaret et cum magistro Iacobo bononiensi artis musice peritissimo de artis excellentia contenderet, tiranno eos muneribus irritante, mandrialia plura sonosque multos et ballatas intoniut mire dulcedinis et artificiosissime melodie, in quibus quam magne, quam suavis doctrine fuerit in arte manifestavit" (Villani 1997, 408).

as Vivaldi consolidated the solo concerto in the eighteenth century. In Giovanni's hands, the madrigal began to exhibit essential characteristics, such as the melisma on the first and penultimate syllables of a line and the syllabic declaration of texts within the line. Giovanni's madrigals *O perlaro gentil* and *Appress'un fiume chiaro* also contain the name Anna, opening an interesting avenue of investigation which I will pursue in the latter part of this chapter.

The two fragments combined contain thirty-seven pieces between them: *Rvat* contains twenty-nine and *Os*, eight. Of the twenty-nine pieces in *Rvat*, twenty-one are madrigals, two are caccias, one is a rondello, and five are monophonic ballatas. *Os* contains eight madrigals. Madrigals clearly outnumber the other genres in the collection. While madrigals constitute the earliest form of indigenous Italian secular music, their past is rather murky. Unlike the other contemporary genres, such as the ballata, whose strict rhyming formula is shared by the French virelai (it consists of AbbaA), the madrigal (and by extension the caccia, a hunting song that owes much of its structure to the madrigal and the French chace) is a newly invented type of piece not found in earlier troubadour repertories or French fixed forms. Furthermore, in contrast to the French *formes fixes* – the ballade, rondeau, and virelai – the madrigal does not exhibit a connection to a dance form. Indeed, it is not particularly fixed at all, but instead follows the composer's whim. The piece consists of two-, three-, or four-line stanzas followed by a refrain. Pirrotta notes that "taken as a whole the madrigals suggest a practice that took a variety of forms, thus deserving the definition the genre had been given by Francesco da Barberino of a 'rudium inordinatum concinium,' in the sense that there are evidently no rules that establish a definitive form" (Pirrotta 1992, 100).[5]

The anonymous author of a short treatise, *Capitulum de vocibus applicatis verbis*, written between 1315 and 1320 and originating in the Veneto region, sheds light on the nature of this enigmatic genre. As I noted in the previous chapter, the author begins his discussion with a nod to Aristotle's *Physica* ("ut earum sentencia intellectu pleno et ordinate sit studentis, sicut dicit Philosophus in principio"), thus firmly placing his musical discussion within a scientific framework.[6] In describing the madrigal, the author observes that "madrigals are texts applied to several voices" ("mandrigalia sunt verba applicata pluribus cantibus"). This phrase suggests that madrigals were originally intended to be polyphonic compositions, very different

[5]The complete Barberino passage from *Documenti d'amore* translates as "the spontaneous singing is a disorderly ensemble of harsh rural harmonies, such as found in the madrigal and similar pieces" ("voluntarium est rudium inordinatum concinium, ut matricale et simili" 1912, 263).

[6]Debenedetti 1906-1907, 80.

from the evolution of the ballata, which, as we know from the examples in Rossi 215, began as a monophonic piece. In addition, the author states that the voices in the madrigal "should be entirely of longs and this is called the tenor, the other or others should be entirely of the shortest notes."[7] This description of the madrigal is reminiscent of the motet, whose tenor was most often borrowed from other sources and presented in longer note values. Unlike the motet, however, whose texts could be about any subject (most often they were linked to serious ceremonial events), the subjects of early madrigal texts are quite specific:

> The texts of madrigals should be about shepherdesses, flowers, orchards, garlands, fields, and the like, but in good subject matter, language, and expression.[8]

The origin of the word *madrigal* has also been much debated. It is found in various forms in the early literature, including *madriale, matricale, madregal*, and *marigalis.* Antonio da Tempo, a Paduan lawyer and man of letters, described the etymology in his *Summa artis rithimici vulgaris dictaminis* of 1332 as originating from *mandriale* or *mandria* (herd). He stressed the pastoral nature of the madrigal's subject matter: sheep and shepherds in the field. Scardeone notes in his description of Antonio da Tempo's career that he was highly regarded at the height of the Renaissance for his contributions, alongside Brandino Padovano, to the foundation of a Paduan literary tradition. Scardeone notes that Antonio lived during the time of Dante (before Petrarch), and hypothesizes that the younger Antonio learned from him.[9] Scardeone mentions that Antonio da Tempo composed two major treatises, one in Italian, the *Sull'arte ritmica,* dedicated to Antonio Scaligero, Veronese prince and generous merchant; and one in Latin, the above-mentioned *Summa*, also dedicated to the Veronese prince and which Scardeone observes was printed and widely distributed.[10] Scardeone

[7]The translation is in Gallo 1985, 121. "...quorum unus debet esse de puris longis et hic appellatur tenor, alter vel alii volunt esse de puris minimis..." (Debenedetti 1906-1907, 80).

[8]"...cuius verba volunt esse de villanellis, de floribus, arbustis, sertis, utere [*sic*] et similibus, dummodo sit bona sentencia, loquela et sermo" (Debenedetti 1906-1907, 80).

[9]"Floruit enim Antonius iste, Dantis Aldigerii temporibus, sed paulo anterior aetate Francisco Petrarca" (Scardeone 1979, 287).

[10]"Scripsit ergo Antonius Tempus De arte rhythmica opus insigne, et subtiliter omnes adinvenit modos, in quibus diversitas Italicorum metrorum consistit: ita ut probe nosse iam quisque valeat, Hetruscos, sive Italos poetas, in varietate metrica, et in numeris et concentibus nec Graecis, nec Latinis palmam ulla prorsus ratione concedere. Dicavit autem opus hoc Antonio Scaligero, prinicipi Venonensi, moecenati liberalissimo. Scripserat autem haec Latine quidem, sed minus eleganter: tum quod illa aetas, tum quod id dictionis genus minime ferret: tum etiam quod argumentum ipsum ex natura sua nec cultum, nec eloquentiam ullam Latini sermonis admitteret. Titulus autem operis

also points out that this treatise in Latin is not as elegantly written as the *Sull'arte.* With regard to Antonio's biography, Scardeone informs the reader that after taking the side of Frederick the Emperor against the state and making propaganda in defense of the Pope in Rome, Antonio saw his family's wealth confiscated, and the family was exiled. "I have read that this Da Tempo spread his family and flourished in Verona: there existed another Antonio Tempo, a great man who wrote in the vulgate."[11]

Antonio da Tempo devotes a lengthy section of his *Summa* to the madrigal, emphasizing the earthy nature of its texts:

> It is called madrigal because the words describe a herd of animals and shepherds and because for the first time we learn about this manner of singing from the shepherds. As a matter of fact, the shepherds, being rural and rough men, at first began to compose coarse words about the loves of Venus (namely, her earthly loves) and to sing and play them with their flutes in a rough manner, but nonetheless in a natural manner. Today madrigals of this genre are written by musicians in a more refined and beautiful way. The madrigal should be composed of popular and comprehensible words, with rugged inflections and earthy expressions. So the fact that madrigal texts are altogether different from other popular compositions is perhaps the reason why it is not easy to find other texts that are written specifically to describe the love of the land.[12]

Antonio then describes the quality of the madrigal music:

> The madrigal's (from *mandria,* or *pastorale*) accompanying music, according to modern musicians, must be elegant and rustic in some

est: Summa artis rhythmicae vulgaris dictaminis, ab Antonio Tempo iudice cive Paduano. Anno Domini M. CCC. XXXII. Quod opus nunc impressum et divulgatum, ubique circumfertur" (Scardeone 1979, 287).

[11]"Legimus huius familiam, quia aliquando adversus Rempublicam pro Federico Imperatore aperte, palamque suaderet defectionem a Pontifice Romano, fuisse proscriptis bonis in exilium relegatam. Audio tamen huius sobolem de Tempo propagatam, florere Veronae: atque alterum quoque Antonium Tempum, virum insignem, et in hac vulgari lingua..." (Scardeone 1979, 287).

[12]"Dicitur autem mandrialis a mandra pecudum et pastorum, quia primo modum illum rithimandi et cantandi habimus ab ovium pastoribus. Nam pastores tanquam rustici et homines grossi primo coeperunt amoris venerei circa compilare verba grossa et ipsa cantare et in suis tibiis sonare modo grosso, sed tamen naturaliter, licet hodie subtilius et pulchrius per rithimatores mandriales huiusmodi compilentur. Mandrialis namque in rithimus debet constare ex verbis valde vulgaribus et intelligibilibus et rudibus quasi cum prolationibus et idiomatibus rusticalibus: ita quod verba mandrialis sint quasi omnino diversa ab aliis verbis et modis vulgaribus rithimandi, quod forte non est ita facile invenire quemadmodum alia verba quae amoris venerei causa compilantur pro cantu" (Da Tempo 1977, 70-71).

> of its parts so that the music fits the words. And in order that it have a pleasant sound, the madrigal should be written for at least two harmonious voices. It may also be sung by more than two voices, as we see today, or by only one. But the madrigal does not resonate in the ear of the listerner when it is composed for only one voice, as it does when composed for more voices.[13]

Others have noted the connection between the words *madrigal* and *madre* (mother) and view the madrigal as a musical manifestation of the "mother" tongue since, unlike the motet, the madrigal is in the vernacular. Nino Pirrotta (1946-1947) has hypothesized a derivation from the word *materialis* (as opposed to *formalis*), implying that a madrigal is a poem without rules and without a specified form.

I propose a new source for the word and the genre of music: the landscape in and around the city of Padua. As we have seen in chapter 1, Padua was long known as one of the centers for the export of wool on the Italian peninsula. As far back as the Roman period, Paduan wools were cherished by diplomats, and in the later Middle Ages, the trade was resurrected and encouraged by the Scaligeri family. The Paduan countryside offered a unique breeding area for sheep. Just to the southeast of the city, about twenty kilometers away, rise the enigmatic hills called Colli Euganei from the flat landscape of the Po River delta. Here shepherds brought their flocks in the summer to graze on the mountain grasses. The Colli provide a perfect pastoral setting for poets. After a short trip from the center of town into the countryside, the city-dweller (Petrarch made his home in Arquà in his latter years) could find limpid streams, green pastures, and respite from the travails of the city. Pastoral scenery of the Euganean hills was a reality for the Paduans, and as we shall see, the Euganei are the subject of madrigals in the Rossi Codex.

Completing this pastoral picture, just two or three kilometers to the southeast of town on the way to Abano Terme (the hometown of the distinguished Pietro) was, and still exists, the town of Mandria. Could the madrigal have some connection to the name of the town, as the tarantella does to Taranto?

Several facts make this hypothesis a tantalizing probability. First, Mandria was at that time a well-established agricultural center dating back to Roman times. Second, Antonio da Tempo acknowledges that the word for

---

[13]"Sonus vero marigalis secundum modernum cantum debet esse pulcher et in cantu habere aliquas partes rusticales sive mandriales, ut cantus consonet cum verbis. Et ad hoc, ut habeat pulchram sonoritatem, expedit ipsum cantari per duos ad minus in diversis vocibus concordantibus. Potest etiam per plures cantari, secundum quod quotidie videmus, et etiam per unum; sed non ita bene sonat auribus audientium quando per unum cantatur sicuti quando per plures" (Da Tempo 1977, 70-71).

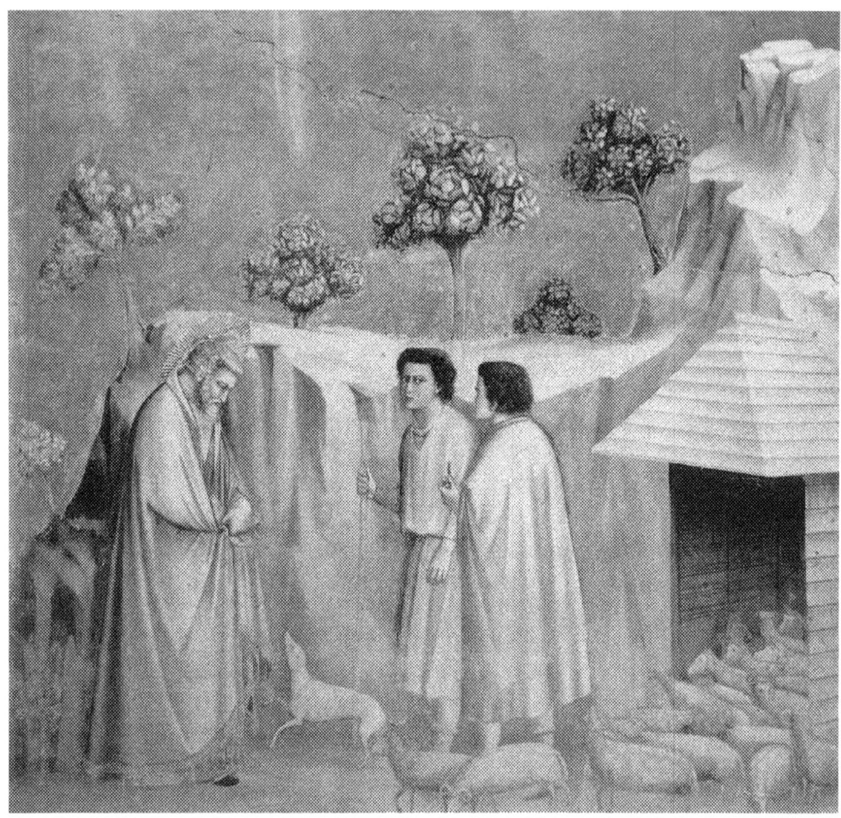

Figure 3.1: ***Joachim among the Shepherds***

this genre of music was *mandriale*, from *mandria*. Third, the wool trade was significant in early Trecento Padua, as illustrated by Giotto in the first frescoes of his Scrovegni Chapel cycle. Three of these frescoes – *Joachim among the Shepherds* (Fig.3.1), *Joachim's Sacrifice* (Fig.3.2), and the *Dream of Joachim* (Fig.3.3) – contain exquisitely detailed representations of a shepherd with his flock, representing scenes from the life of Joachim. Each fresco contains an image of a flock of goats or sheep accompanied by a vigilant dog. Giotto, known for his preference for painting "from nature," may have himself gone into the Paduan countryside to view the scene. The preeminence of the wool trade and the culture of the shepherds around Padua also help to explain the prominent presence of the seated woman spinning yarn in an alcove of the *Annunciation to Saint Anne* (Fig.3.4).

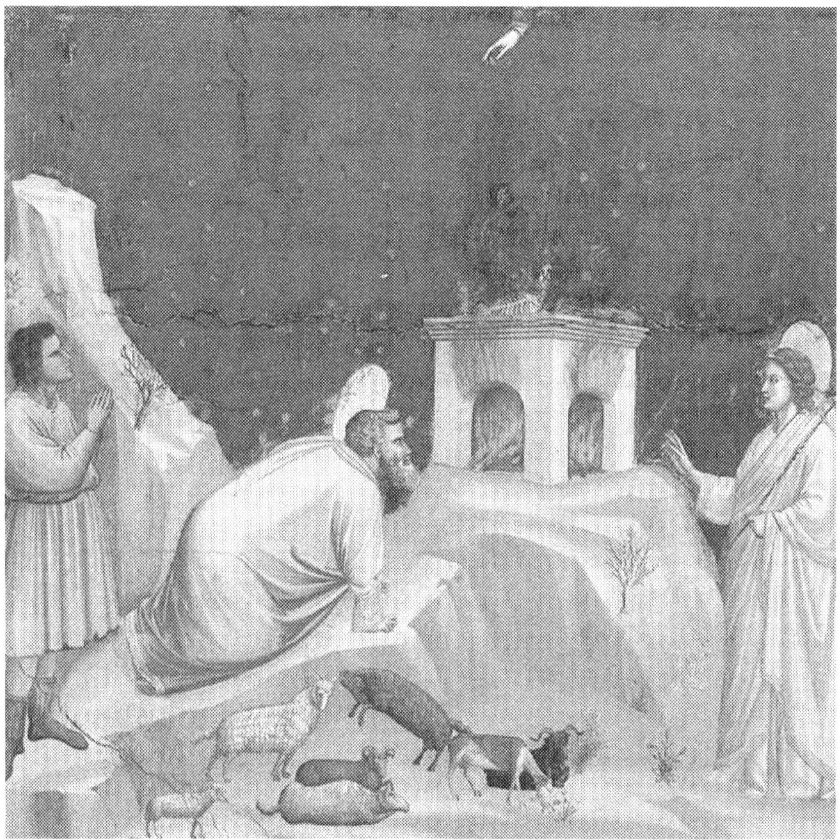

Figure 3.2: ***Joachim's Sacrifice***

The madrigal texts, and their accompanying music, realistically describe the culture of these small Veneto towns.

In addition, the textual style of the madrigals displays aspects of a courtly tradition, with echoes of the *dolce stil nuovo* of Dante and Petrarch as well as a simpler vernacular, popular style. Pirrotta (1992, 9) suggests that this repertory originated in an "open-minded environment, a circle that was not too 'courtly' in the strict sense of the term, but was nevertheless cultured and furthermore delighted in humor of a popular nature." The sophisticated textual style is demonstrated in the bilingual alternation of lines in madrigals *Ogni diletto* and *L'antico dio Biber.* More mundane e-xamples appear in *Quando i oselli canta.* As a whole, the madrigals display

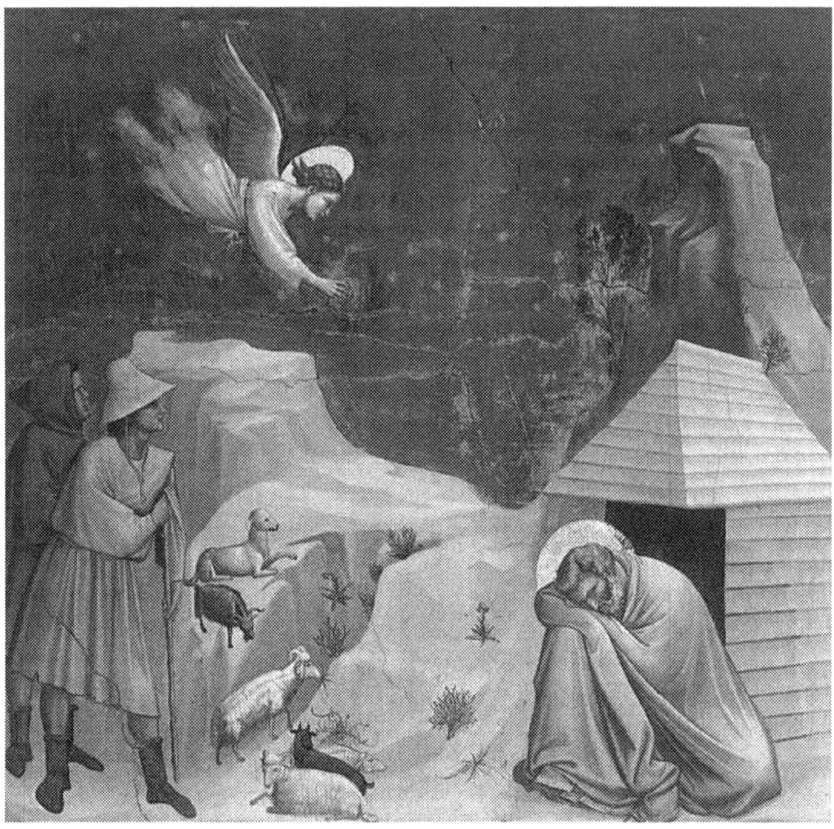

Figure 3.3: ***Dream of Joachim***

an uncanny faithfulness to visual detail. The level of detail rivals that found in Giotto's fresco painting.

This reflection of textual detail in the art of the period begins with Giotto (to be discussed in chapters 4 and 5), whose painting faithfully reproduces nature, people, and architectural structures. By the beginning of the fourteenth century, a movement spearheaded by Giotto and Duccio transformed art from medieval symbolic rendering into a new proto-Renaissance realism.[14] Birds, animals, and plants were painted with a freshness as if they had been drawn directly from nature. Trees were crafted in such detail that their genus could be identified. Later in the Trecento and continuing

[14]On realism and Giotto, see Mellini 2000, 72-86.

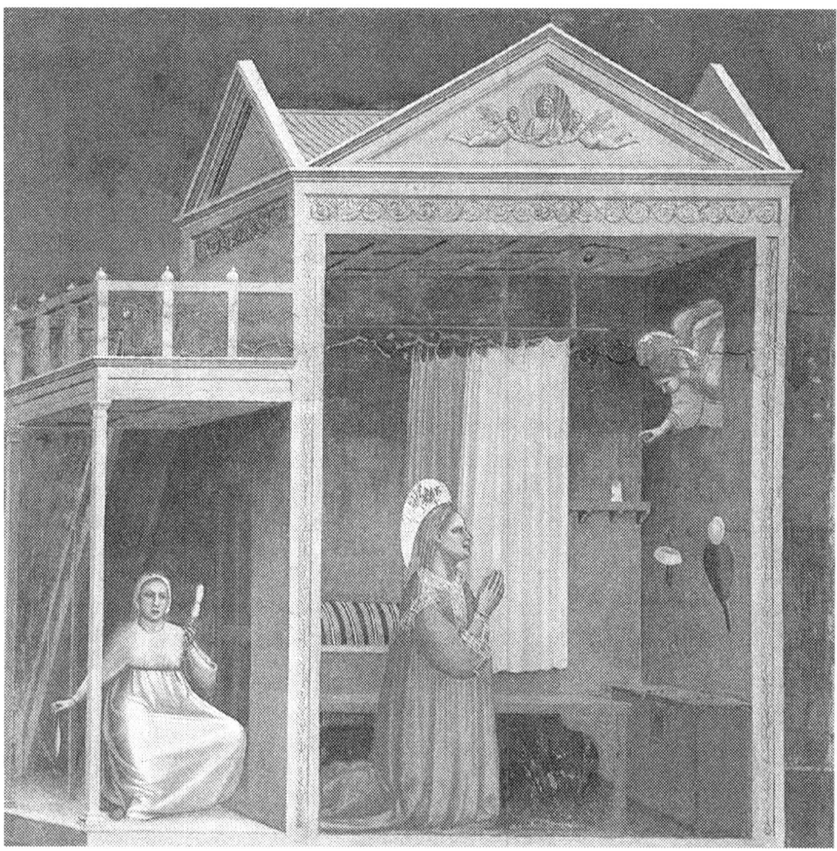

Figure 3.4: ***Annunciation to Saint Anne***

into the next century, illuminators from the Milanese and Veronese courts of Giovannino de' Grassi and Belbello da Pavia produced bestiaries cataloguing exotic birds and beasts of prey. Because of the geographical proximity and political connections to France – a nation with a highly developed tradition of illumination – Milan became the center for the production of manuscripts.

Madrigal poetry of the period followed a similar evolutionary path toward the depiction of realistic scenes. Like the medieval bestiary, madrigals often listed a multitude of birds such as falcons, peacocks, crows, parrots, and turtledoves, and animals such as leopards, rabbits, and serpents.

The locale of the poems also became more realistic, gradually transformed from the rugged terrain of an idealized countryside to the actual gardens of wealthy aristocrats. The gardens, located on the grounds of opulent villas and near cool streams, often contained a formalized section with a fountain and plants, where a lady could be seen. In certain cases the poets went to great lengths to specify the types of trees planted in the garden including, for example, the *perlaro*.

To return to a discussion of the origin of the madrigal, in *Expositio problematum Aristotelis*, particula 19, problem 6, Pietro describes comedy as follows:

> Comedy is a type of song from the country regarding rural subject matter and humble people. It is so named from the farmhouse; according to some it is of great merit: it deals with a world in the Greek style, and the song is mundane and popular. It concerns banal and unrefined affairs or the chatter of everyday life. Also of things that are said while eating dinner. Indeed, men went to listen to comedy after eating.[15]

Pietro's language is strikingly similar to the descriptions of madrigal texts. Both the madrigal and the songs that Pietro calls "comedy" describe the countryside and activities in the mundane world.

In the *Expositio*, Pietro appears to be describing the type of music that accompanied theatrical events. Indeed, theater was a flourishing form of expression in Padua, particularly in the work of the Paduan Albertino Mussato. Certainly music accompanied Mussato's plays, which were written in imitation of Seneca.[16] It seems most likely that the madrigal had some connection to the theater of the period. Madrigals may have initially functioned as inter-act music in the manner of the *intermedio*, popular in later centuries. Madrigals provide a reprieve from the serious world of tragedy and a break from long spans of narration. We know that many madrigals of the period shared common subjects, such as the love poems for Anna or Margherita. Perhaps they were performed during theatrical events over the course of an evening.

In proposing this new reading of the original use of the madrigal, we must keep in mind that the genre went through a particularly significant shift from its humble, mundane beginnings in the fields to a more serious function as a

[15]"Est autem comedia canticum agreste que res privatarum et humilium personarum comprehendit. Et dicitur a cosmos que est villa vel laus secundum aliquos: grece tamen mundus: et odi cantus quasi mundanus et vulgarus cantus de rebus enis vulgaribus tractat et affinibus et quotidiane locutioni vel dicitur comestione post cibum enim homines solebant ad eam audiendam convenire" (D'Abano 1475, 190v).

[16]On early Italian theater, see Alessandro d'Ancona 1891 and Megas 1969.

kind of commemorative piece in such later examples as Jacopo da Bologna's *Lo lume vostro* and Bartolino da Padova's *Imperial sedendo.* Through the course of the fourteenth century, the madrigal moved further and further away from light-hearted entertainment toward serious and highly stylized and intellectual forms of entertainment, even taking on characteristics of the motet, such as the isorhythm found in Lorenzo Masini's *Povero zappator.*

The evolution of the madrigal in the Trecento mirrors the evolution of music in the Paduan Renaissance. As has been noted, the madrigal began in the Virgilian pastoral tradition, as Antonio da Tempo elegantly describes in his *Summa.* In the middle of the fourteenth century, the madrigal crossed paths with the traditionally ceremonial motet and as a result began to shed its rustic traditions for a grounding in contemporary events. Instead of describing the anonymous woman in the fields, the madrigal documents such occurrences as a birth or a military victory. The individual person now emerges from the typology of the aristocrat, and individual emotions and biographies are brought to the forefront.

The Trecento madrigal chronicles the activities of bellicose families of northern Italy. The Della Scala family of Verona was the foremost rival of the Visconti in northern Italy. During the early part of the fourteenth century, under the rule of Cangrande I, the Della Scala family controlled the majority of northern territories, including Parma, Lucca, and Padua. In 1339, Cangrande transferred his power to his nephews Alberto and Mastino because he had no legitimate heir. Mastino and Alberto became the wealthiest noblemen in Italy – controlling an enormous section, including as many as thirteen cities – and were poised to attack Florence. In 1336 they began a conflict with Venice that would mark the beginning of their demise. In 1337 Venice, Florence, and Milan grouped together against Verona, and by 1340 Verona had lost all its territory except Vicenza. After 1340 the Scaligeri signed a treatise with the Visconti, and the two families continued to co-exist in relative peace. In his *Annali della città di Padova*, Giuseppe Gennari connects the Scaligeri, Visconti, and Carrara families through blood relationships: "I note only that through Taddea, daughter of Jacopo the Great of Padua, wife of Mastino della Scala, mother of Beatrice, called Queen, who married Bernabò Visconti, from whom was born Verde, consort of Leopold of Austria, the blood of the Carrara branched into the principal leaders of Europe."[17]

[17]"... noterò solamente, che per Taddea figliuola di Iacopo il Grande, moglie di Mastino della Scala, e madre di Beatrice detta Regina maritata con Bernabò Visconti, da cui nacque Verde consorte di Leopoldo d'Austria, il sangue Carrarese s' è diramato ne' principali Sovrani d'Europa" (Gennari 1804, 216).

The Carrara family dominated Trecento Padua beginning in 1318, when the city entrusted them with political and military governance.[18] Giacomo I (1264-1324) was assigned the name "protector, governor and ruler of Padua and the Paduan people," establishing the *Signoria*, which was consolidated by Ubertino (d.1345). The *Signoria* was extinguished during the first decades of the fifteenth century. The most prominent members of the family were Giacomo II (d.1350), friend of Petrarch, and Francesco il Vecchio (1325-1393), the must illustrative of all, who ruled for thirty-eight years between 1350 and 1388. It was during his reign that Padua reached its greatest military might and greatest splendor. His son Francesco Novello (1359-1406), following his father's will to create a potent state in the *Padana* region, joined forces with Venice and defeated Padua, which was incorporated into Venetian territory in 1405. Years later, Francesco and his sons Giacomo and Francesco were strangled in a Venetian jail (Semenzato 1987, 32).

The history of these families and the events in their lives became the inspiration for many madrigal texts during the course of the Trecento. Of the total 190 or so Trecento madrigals, 30 contain specific images or references to northern Italian personalities and territories, such as Padua, Verona, and Milan. These references are of three types: (1) political, (2) geographical, and (3) senhal. The first group of madrigals consists of references to events involving the ruling class or references to their emblems. For examiple, in the poem *Lo lume vostro*, set by Jacopo da Bologna, the first letters of each line form the name Luchinus, referring to Lucchino Visconti of Milan. Jacopo's *O in Italia felice Liguria* describes a baptism in the Visconti family. The Scaligeri ladder of Verona appears in the anonymous *La nobil scala che 'l signor lombardo.*

The second group contains madrigals with specific geographical references. Padua is recalled in an early piece from the Rossi Codex, *Pianze la bella Iguana*, in which we find a reference to the Euganei, women who roamed the Euganean hills outside of the city:

Fair Euganea weeps	Pianze la bella Iguana
if she sees not her lover.	se'l suo amor non vede;
She holds a golden thread in her hands	fil d'oro ten in mano
and hopes to draw recompense from it.	spera di mercede.
Nobly was I captured,	Zentil furto mi prese
for her fair eyes did wish it so.	che da i bei iochi scese.

[18]For a history of the Carrara family, see Kohl 1998.

Sweetly she sighs, for she sees not the sun, and ever, as all women do, she demands what she desires. She decks herself in humble scorn, and her serene beauty is restored.	Scese dolci sospiri poi che non ride el sole, e sempre, come donna, vol pur quel che la vole. L'umel sdegno l'adorna ch'a bella pace torna.
But happiness is put to flight, for Love is crossed, he that doth let this Euganea go gather nectar from another flower. Alas, how my heart breaks when her fair eyes weep.[19]	Torna il piacer a danno, ch'el se coruza Amore, che lassa questa Euguana per star con altre fiore. Oimè, co'l cor me franze quando i bei iochi pianze! (362)

As we recall from chapter 1, the Euganei first inhabited the hills southwest of Padua before the arrival of the Trojan Antenor. Significantly, instead of an imagined bucolic backdrop for the poem, with its stock of pastoral elements, the poet needed only to go into the Euganean hills, rich and fertile, for his Arcadian landscape. Like Giotto, the Paduan writer looked to imitate reality in his poetry. This writer is reminded of Shakespeare, who relies on the New World as inspiration for a distant culture in *The Tempest.*

Nascoso el viso, by Giovanni da Cascia, also includes a reference to the Euganei. Poets active in an around Padua favored the mythical Euganei over traditional nymphs:

I stood in a beautiful garden, the foliage hid my face, looking across a nearby spring where folk used to fish.	Nascoso el viso, stava fra le fronde d'un bel zardino; appresso a mi guardava sopra una fonte dove se pescava;
And I saw blonde and rosy-cheeked women lissome as were Euganeas, the nymphs once found in woods or sometimes in streams.	E vedea donne vermigliete e bionde lizadre al modo che solea le Euguane trovarse al boscho e quando a le fontane.
Some were barefoot, and some as they were born. I am unwilling to say more of how that day delighted me.	Qual era scalza, qual com'ela nacque: più non vol dir quanto quel dì me piaque (15).

This poem contains more formal elements than the previous one. In this instance the Euganean woman appear within a modern garden near a spring, where people used to fish. This idea is very different from Pirrotta's notion (1992, 92) that Euganeas are "mythical fairies or nymphs of the Euganean hills near Padua." These were historical figures transplanted

[19]Translation in CD jacket, *D'Amor Cantando* (OPS 30-141, 1995), 20.

into a pastoral landscape. The Euganean women carry out the stock role of nymphs in the forest bathing in a spring. Once again we see the poet borrowing Paduan history and the actual fecund landscape of the Euganean hills for his pastoral scene. The impetus here is proto-Renaissance, and one can see it play itself out even further in the fifteenth-century placement of the Madonna in modern Renaissance chambers with elegant views of aristocratic land holdings in the background.

Piero and Jacopo da Bologna, perhaps as part of a competition, set the same text, *Si come al canto de la bella Iguana/ obliò suo camin più tempo el greco*, to music. In this poem a Euganean woman sings, and Pirrotta (1992, 92) comments on her "evident allusion to Circe and Ulysses." Again the poet blends actual Paduan history with pastoral tradition to produce a Paduan myth. The poem reads:

As, enthralled by the beautiful Euganea's song, the Greek forgot his journey for a long time, taking his pleasure with the nymph in her human form,	Sì come al canto de la bella Iguana obliò suo cammin più tempo el greco, prendendo suo piacer con forma umana,
In your case also, O woman. turned away from every other Pleasure, if your pleasure were simply to be with me.	così, per esser, donna, sempre teco, faresti la mia voglia esser lontana ogn' altro piacer, sendo'l tuo meco;
Being endowed with every virtue, you are a perfect gemstone, Margherita.	però che se' d'ogni virtute unita, tu se' perfecta gemma margherita (8).

Geographical landmarks associated with Verona also appear in the madrigal repertory. The Adige River winds around the pastoral gardens in Jacopo da Bologna's *Nel ziardino che l'Atice cenge.* In addition to the reference to a castle built by the Scaligeri on the shores of Lake Garda in *Dal bel castel se parte de Peschiera*, the line "dove'l Po fa rivera" seems to refer to the region where the Po River empties into the Adriatic Sea.[20] Pirrotta (1992, 93) believes that the madrigal concerns Mastino II della Scala, who left from the castle of Peschiera to be with his older brother Alberto, even though Alberto usually sojourned in Padua, which is not on the Po River. Giuseppe Corsi, on the other hand, argues that the madrigal's protagonists are Niccolò II, who became signore of Ferrara and Modena, and Verde della Scala, daughter of Mastino II, who married Niccolò II in 1362. However, it seems a bit too late in history for these two to be the subject of the anonymous poem.

[20]The topography of this poem has been a subject of contradictory interpretations. For the debate, see Pirrotta 1992, 92-93.

The third group (senhal) consists of poems that contain names or family emblems embedded within the text. This last category will serve to link several poems and the warring families together. The name Margherita is present in several of the madrigals believed to have originated in the northern courts. We have already seen the name in Jacopo's *Si com'al canto della bella Iguana* as well as in his *Lucida petra, o margherita cara.* Other Trecento poems contain the name Anna in their texts, including Giovanni da Cascia's *Donna già fui leggiard'ANNAmorata.*[21] Still another group makes mention of the Visconti family symbol, the *biscia* (water snake), such as Jacopo da Bologna's *Nel bel ziardino che l'Atice cenge, Posando sopra un'aqua vidi,* and *Soto l'imperio.* While madrigals began in the comic vein of the pastoral, I believe that these poems recount actual events in the interconnected lives of the Visconti and Scaligeri families and, in the new spirit of individuality, demonstrate the burgeoning Renaissance realism in poetry set to music. I will develop a link between the poems concerning the deeds of Luchino Visconti, his wife Isabella, their sons Luchino and Giovanni, his lover Margherita Pusterla, and other members of the Lombard and Veronese families.

Composed by Jacopo da Bologna, the madrigal *O in Italia felice Liguria* was probably commissioned by Luchino to commemorate the birth of his twin sons Luca and Giovanni in 1346. At that time Milan, under the rule of Luchino, experienced a period of considerable territorial expansion, moving as far south as Lucca. Liguria, on the west coast of Italy, was under continual attack from the Lombards during the early part of the fourteenth century. The fact that the children were baptized in Liguria confirms that the Milanese rulers had captured the territory by 1346. The setting also alludes to the beautiful and skillful Isabella di Carlo Fieschi, Luchino's third wife, who was of Ligurian descent.

O in Italy, happy Liguria and
especially you, Milan, God praise
and glorify the birth of the
two lords heaven predicted for you.

O in Italia felice Liguria,
e proprio tu, Milan, Dio lauda e gloria
de' due nati segnor, che'l cel t'aguria.

They were born on
a Friday between the
sixth and third hours.

Segno fo ben, che fo de gran vittoria,
ch'un'aquila li trasse a cristianesimo
e Parma a lor donò da po' el batesmo.

It was indeed a sign, a sign of great
victory when an eagle carried them to

Un venere fra sesta [e] terza naquero
Luca e Zuane a chi lor nomi piaquero.

[21] Pirrotta (1963) includes senhals in his editions of the song texts.

christianity and to Parma. Thereafter
Luca and Giovanni, to whom their names
were pleasing, baptized them.

Quaranta sei un emme cum tri ci
corea e fo d'agosto al quarto dì (41).

Forty-six, an M and with three Cs,
and it was on the third day of August.[22]

The *aquila* (eagle) in this poem suggests several possible interpretations. First, the bird is a well-known reference to military strength often associated with the power of the Holy Roman Empire. More particularly, the eagle alludes to the bird that formed part of the Visconti seal; and specifically, the bird can be traced to the shield of Obizzo da Ferrara, who, along with Ugolino d'Este, attended the twins' baptism and donated the city of Parma to the Visconti (Carducci 1973, 392). The image of Venus is also significant. According to Millard Meiss, the Lombard rulers believed that they were the natural descendants of Venus and Anchises. This would account for the auspicious eagle in the poem as well as, perhaps, the numerous references to Venus and her son Aeneas in madrigal poetry, a point to which we will return later.

The madrigal *Lo lume vostro* by Jacopo da Bologna also concerns the deeds of Luchino Visconti. Various alternative meanings have been posited for this poem, which contains an acrostic of Luchino's name, a device reminiscent of Marchetto's motet *Ave regina celorum.* Pirrotta suggests that the madrigal makes reference to the banishment of Luchino's three nephews, Bernabò, Galeazzo II, and Matteo, in 1436 for their part in a conspiracy to defraud Luchino's family (Pirrotta 1963, IX). The conspiracy, however, appears to have been masterminded by Francesco Pusterla, a close and trusted confidant of Luchino's father, Azzone, who along with other ministers became rich and powerful on the coattails of the Visconti. Upon gaining power, Luchino began insulting these ministers in public, swearing to retake what was rightfully his. Francesco Pusterla, angered by Luchino's behavior, vowed revenge and formed a conspiracy. Margherita, Francesco's wife and a distant relative of the Visconti, did nothing to dissuade her husband; rather, she stirred his anger by engaging in an illicit affair with Luchino. When Luchino discovered the conspiracy he sent Francesco, Margherita, and their children to jail, where they spent the rest of their days (Litta 1819-1883, tome 9, table 2).

The language of *Lo lume vostro* is permeated with light, a symbol of justice and virtue. Light shines on law-abiding citizens and is denied to

[22]Translation in CD jacket, *Suso in Italia Bella* (Arcana A38, 1995), 38.

delinquents, who are locked up in a dark cell:

Your light, my dear sir, is decorated by virtue so perfect it does not give light to delinquents, but is always warm to good people.	Lo lume vostro, dolce mio segnore, *Virtute sic perfecta est ornatum,* Ch'a' rei non luce, a' boni sempr' è chiaro.
This is so noted and now well known in those who have tasted bitterness for having secretly erred.	*Hoc est notum et [iam] satis probatum* In quegli c'han sentito il gusto amaro Nascosamente per comporre errore.
A woman reigns who is called Isabella; there is no brighter star in the sky.	Una vi regge ch' è si bella: Sul ciel no è posta più lucente stella (37).

The fact that the poem speaks of light and absence of light suggests that the poet may be referring to the punishment dealt to the Pusterlas, rather than the banishment of the nephews, an action that occurred years later and does not, on the surface, involve a loss of light. In addition, the text enigmatically alternates between Italian and Latin, which can also be seen in the troubadour convention found in the poetry of the Genovese Raimbaut de Vaqueiras.[23] The bilingual nature of the poetry indicates the madrigal's close evolutionary association with the motet, a fourteenth-century musical form with text usually composed in Latin, or containing an amalgam of languages. In subject matter, this ceremonial madrigal also echoes the function of the motet in the later Renaissance, when it was used to commemorate official matters, such as the completion of Brunelleschi's dome in Florence, related in Dufay's motet *Nuper rosarum flores* and sung entirely in Latin to the same text.

Luchino's love for Margherita was certainly no secret to Lombard society. In fact, the name Margherita is present in several of Jacopo's madrigals. Even as late as the 1840s, Cesare Cantù wrote a historical novel entitled *Margherita Pusterla*, chronicling her tempestuous affair with the Lombard ruler. The word *Margherita* has several significations. For one, Margherita is the name of a simple country flower – the daisy. Second, the word derives from the Latin meaning "pearl," a reference found in Jacopo's madrigal *Lucida petra*, which describes a shiny stone. Third, the story of Santa Margherita seems particularly appropriate for a madrigal text. As a young girl, Margherita embraced Christianity and consecrated her virginity to God. For this reason, she was disowned by her family and ended up watching sheep in the countryside, where one day a lustful Roman, attracted by her great beauty, demanded that she be his mistress. After repeated refusals and because of her Christian faith, she was brought to Antioch to

[23] Another later example is Nicola de Preposti's *La fiera testa che d'uman si ciba.*

stand trial. There she was burned and thrown into a cauldron. Having miraculously survived these attacks, she was finally beheaded. The story of Santa Margherita seems ideally suited for madrigal poetry because of the pastoral setting and the repeated refusals of the Roman.

Like Isabella and Margherita, Anna makes numerous appearances in madrigal poetry, traditionally believed to have originated in northern Italian courts. The name appears in different guises, from its compilation of several words, such as "A NNAscere nel suo vis' el parecchio" in Maestro Piero's *All'ombra d'un perlaro*, to a portion of a word, such as *ANNAmorata* in Giovanni da Cascia's *Donna già fui leggiard'ANNAmorata.* Moreover, Anna appears in Piero's *Sovra un fiume regale*, in which the ritornello reads, "Anna, mio cor, Anna la vita mia."

Although scholars believe that *Anna* refers to a member of the Veronese circle – because of the appearance of the *perlaro*, a distinctly Veronese tree, and because of Veronese dialect exhibited in the poems – the inclusion of the word *biscia*, a water snake and emblem of the Visconti family, in connection with her name may indicate an allusion to the Visconti. In Giovanni da Cascia's *Donna già fui leggiard'ANNAmorata,* a beautiful woman transforms herself into a horrible *biscia* in order to kill her false lover. She asks how he could have made her suffer for so long, and states that she will not turn back into a woman until she has finished tormenting him.

I was once a beautiful woman in love, showing this love to my beloved; now I am transformed into a horrible serpent	Donna già fui leggiardra innamorata, faccendo al servo mio dolce sembiante; or sono in biscia orribil tramutata
to kill this false lover. How could he have made me suffer so, saying villainous things instead of loving me.	sol per uccider questo falso amante: non so come 'l suo cor mai lo sofferse, ch'a dirmi villania se discoperse.
When I am satisfied in tormenting him, I will become a woman again.	Com'io di tormentarlo sia ben sazia, tornerò donna, renderogli grazia (13).

Pirrotta has hypothesized that this poem – in addition to the other seven "Anna" poems – was probably composed between 1349 and 1352, after the death of Luchino and before the deaths of Mastino and Alberto (Pirrotta 1963, II). Isabella Fieschi, Luchino's forlorn wife, is the woman who best fits the description of a devoted wife to a Visconti who, it was said, poisoned her husband. Isabella may have been tormented by her husband's overt affair with Margherita Pusterla, and she is believed to have taken up with another man. As proposed in Pompeo Litta's genealogy of Italian families, she may have taken a fancy to Ugolino Gonzaga on the occasion of the baptism of her two boys in 1346, recounted in Jacopo's *O, in Italia, felice liguria* (Litta 1819-1883, tome 9, table 3). Litta mentions that the following year, on her way to Venice, Isabella stopped in Mantua to meet Ugolino and the two continued the journey with great pomp. Upon receiving word of the scandal from none other than Mastino della Scala, Luchino swore revenge. Before he could act, Isabella poisoned him.

Litta conjectures that Isabella may not have been guilty of the murder, but rather that she was the victim of an elaborate plot to divest her sons of their natural inheritance. In addition to the rumor of the poisoning, Archbishop Giovanni, who succeeded Luchino as the ruler of Milan, spread the word that the twins of 1346 were illegitimate, born of a union between Galeazzo II and Isabella (Carducci 1973, 392). Isabella publicly confessed to attempting to pass the boys as legitimate. They were stripped of their rights to succeed their father as rulers of Milan.

All three poems containing the *biscia* speak of a beautiful woman who transforms herself into a venomous snake to kill her false lover. A fourth poem, *Soto l'imperio del posente prince* by Jacopo da Bologna, also contains a reference to the *biscia*; in this case, however, the woman does not reside in a garden but rather under the rule of the prince "in whose name are found golden wings" ("che nel so nom' à le dorate ale"). The prince was probably Luchino's successor, Galeazzo II, since his name contains the letters *ale*. Isabella in fact did live in Milan after the death of her husband. Furthermore, *Soto l'imperio del posente prince* shares some key images with the earlier *Lo Lume*. In the ritornello of *Lo Lume*, the poet chooses the verb *regna* (rule) to describe Isabella's power: "a woman rules you who is very beautiful" ("una donna vi regna ch' E SI BELLA"). *Soto l'imperio* makes use of the same metaphor in the third line, referring again to a Visconti figure: "the *biscia* whose bite conquers me" ("regna la bias el cui morso me vince"). Additionally, both poems use a similar light image in the ritornello. *Lo lume* explains that there is no brighter star than Isabella in the sky ("sul ciel no è posta più lucente stella"), while *Soto l'imperio* tells of the woman " who shines on me more than the sun; the more I remember, her the more she pains me" ("custei me fe' zà lume più che'l sole;/ cum più zò me recordo, più me dole."). In short, one could argue that these two poems concern Isabella. *Lo lume* describes her before, and *Soto l'imperio* after, she poisoned her husband.

The Anna poems share the same setting with the *biscia* poems: a shady area beside a cool river. The scenes are rendered realistically, recalling the proto-Renaissance inclination toward capturing as accurately as possible what is in nature. The most distinct constituent of these vistas is the *perlaro*. The *Grande dizionario* traces the *perlaro*, a tree common in the Veneto region of Italy, to the vulgar names of two different species of trees,

Melia azedarach – the china-tree, or china-berry – and *Celtis astralis* – the nettle-tree (Battaglia 1986, 53).[24] The *perlaro* is also called the *bagolaro* and the *olmo*, a tree found commonly lining Italian motorways. The earliest usage of the word *perlaro* appears in the Trecento madrigal, and the editors of the *Grande dizionario* cite the various Anna poems mentioned in this chapter.

Like the birds and animals in poetic texts, trees were infused with symbolic meaning. According to Carducci (1973, 358), the *perlaro* had two significations: it was known as the "albero della pazienza," and the "albero dei paternostri di San Domenico." This latter significance remains unclear, although it seems that the *perlaro* did have a sacred connotation, given that, as Carducci (1973, 358) relates, it was brought to Italy during the crusades. Another possible significance of *perlaro* (which has yet to be discussed in the literature) is its relation to the name Margherita. *Margherita* is derived from the Latin *perla*, or precious stone. The *perlaro*, in fact, may have gotten its name from the small berries that grow from its leaves. L. H. Bailey (in his horticulture book) describes the tree as follows: "one of the most desirable shade trees, both from the bright green tint of the foliage, which is retained until late in the autumn, and also from the fragrance of the numerous lilac-colored flowers which are produced in April. These are succeeded by an abundant crop of berries, of a yellowish translucent color" (Bailey 1929, 2024). The choice of *perlaro* in the Trecento repertory, as opposed to the similar "bagolaro, olmo o giracolo," is significant if one reads the tree to be symbolic of Margherita, a beautiful maiden. For Anna, another maiden, was often in its shadow, the shadow of Luchino's mistress Margherita Pusterla.

The *perlaro*, in fact, appears in six of the eight Anna poems: Giovanni's *Apress' un fiume chiaro* and *O perlaro gentil;* Maestro Piero's *All'ombra d'un bel perlaro* and *Sovra un fiume regale;* and Jacopo's *O dolze, apres'un bel perlaro fiume* and *Un bel perlaro vive sulla riva.* All six poems describe an idyllic setting, with maidens dancing around trees and making garlands, or a lover contemplating the pain he is suffering because of his adoration for Anna. The remaining poems, both written by Giovanni da Cascia, *Donna già fui leggiard'ANNAmorata* and *Più non mi curo de la tua rampogna,* exhibit a completely different tone, that of the jilted lover. These poems are not written from the perspective of the male in love with a beautiful lady, but rather from the point of view of a woman reacting to her partner's

[24]L.H. Bailey (1929, 2024) describes the*melia azedarach* as a tree native of the Himalayan region, as well as the Southern United States. The same dictionary provides the following description of the celtis australis: "The nettle-trees are valuable as shade trees or as single specimens on a lawn, mostly with wide spreading head and green foliage. They generally flourish in the Mediterranean region to Persia" (710).

infidelity. The anger at infidelity is similar to that found in the *biscia* poems discussed earlier. In summary, the *Lo lume* and *Soto l'imperio*, the Anna poems and the three *biscia* poems appear to be interrelated. The Anna poems describe a man's love for a beautiful woman, while the three *biscia* poems describe her disdain for his infidelity.

Scholars agree that the Anna poems were most likely performed in Verona under the auspices of Mastino della Scala, based on the preponderance of the *perlaro*, references to the Adige River, and the interrelated texts on the theme of Anna (Pirrotta 1963, I-II). Jacopo, Giovanni, and Piero are known to have competed together at the court of Mastino before 1351, and scholars believe that they may have exhibited their skills as poets and musicians by setting the same texts (Pirrotta 1963, I-II). An examination of the Visconti *biscia* and other ceremonial madrigals has demonstrated that the poets were inspired to a great degree by contemporary events. Whether it was the baptism of two sons, the rooting out of a conspiracy, a poisoning, or an illicit love affair, madrigal poets, like the painters of the time, were bringing together elements of pastoral poetry and the portrayal of real events and personages.

Bartolino da Padova, who lived in Padua and Florence c.1365-1405, incorporated the emblem of the Carrara family in his madrigal *Imperial sedendo fra più stelle:*

Like an emperor seated among more stars than there are in heaven, a chariot worthy of honor descended beneath a lord more benevolent than any other.	Imperial sedendo fra più stelle dal ciel desese un carro d'onor degno soto signor d'ogni altro ma' benegno.
Its wheels were driven by four ladies: Justice and Temperance and Courage And one by Prudence, among such nobility.	Le rote soi guidavan quatro done, Iusticia e Temperancia con Forteza ed an' Prudenza tra cotanta alteza.
In the middle was a Saracen with gold wings who figured as the maker of this treasure.[25]	Nel mezo un Saracin con l'ale d'ore tene' 'l fabricator del so tesoro (241).

In this madrigal Bartolino also mentions four virtues, all of whom are found in Giotto's Scrovegni Chapel frescoes. Justice is of paramount importance, and justice's connection to music will be further illuminated in the following chapter.

The image of peace as a bird in a garden appears in Bartolino's madrigal *Alba Colomba*:

[25]Translastion in CD jacket, *D'Amor cantando* (OPS 30-141, 1995), 39.

The white dove with her green branch, nourished in a noble garden, rose up on wing, announcing peace.	Alba colomba con sua verde rama in nobile giardino nutricata, pax pax nunziando su l' al' è montata.
She landed on a green branch To rest a bit and looking upward decided to fly higher still.	Posò suo volo suso in verde scoglio per riposarsi e, rimirando in giuso, prese argomento di volar più suso,
For she was already tasting the good odors that were up there among the boughs and other flowers.[26]	perché gustava già i boni odori ch'eran lassù tra frondi ed altri fiori (239).

Another of Bartolino's madrigals, *Quel sole che nutrica'l gentil fiore,* praises the Sun and its effect on the earth:

That Sun which nourishes the gentle flower, sometimes descends to see what he thinks is more beautiful than himself.	Quel sole che nutrical 'l gentil fiore, discende talor giù per veder quello ch'a lui di lui par esser più bello.
Then after he has looked around a while by himself, he goes back up and tells the gods about her marvelous beauty.	Poi ch'alquanto seco ha contemplato, ritorna su e riferisce a li dei la mirabil belleza di costei.
And now, only high in heaven, of your beauty the angels are praising its supreme purity.	Or sol in alto ciel di tuo biltate laudan gli angioli la somm'onestate (243).

In addition, Bartolino composed *Se premio de virtù è sol onore*, a madrigal lauding virtue:

If sound alone is the prize of virtue, it is highly erroneous of anyone to think he can achieve fame without it.	Se premio de virtù è sol onore, molt'è fallace de zascun la brama che senza lei se crede aquistar fama,
Therefore the superficial mind is without and is far from wisdom,	sì ch'ela è priva e for d'ogni sienzia seguendo l'ombra e non la vera esenzia,
following the appearance and not the true substance, with passionate desire it pays attention to what it can see.	unde a la vista e al parer attende voltando sempre col disio fervente da l'eser proprio la volubel mente.

[26]Translation in CD jacket, *Il Solazzo: Music for a Medieval Banquet* (HMU 907038, 1993), 34.

Deserving praise brings glory as in the desire of an ambitious mind, it acquires value and it accomplishes its effect,	Ma se pur gloria al mondo è digna laude, ch'era l'disio nel vano intelletto, vertute aquista e giungine a l'efetto,
It is both the cause and the prize of such an aspiration whose fulfillment gives pleasure and makes one happy.	perché lei è lo frutto e la radice di cotal sper'e con piacer felice (243-244).

Paduan pride in its ancient heritage forms the backdrop for the subject of this poem, just as the ancestral wool trade is represented in Giotto's painting of the pregnant Anna, or the building of bridges in the image of remains of ancient ruins. In these examples we find the two principal themes that underlie the early madrigal repertory: the careful description of nature, and the allusion to an ancient past.[27]

Continuing this thread, we find that several madrigals from the Rossi Codex make obvious references to astrological symbols. Astrology as practiced by Pietro, and represented on the walls of the Salone della Ragione in Padua, was to be viewed and practiced as a natural science, a reflection of the natural influences the planets exerted on the earth and its inhabitants. In addition, the mention of astrology carries with it a strong allusion to a Roman past, whose influence was felt in everyday life, as in the adoption of names of the planets for names of the week. In the following Rossi examples of madrigals with astrological themes, therefore, we may once again witness the confluence of nature and the Renaissance in the genre of the madrigal.

To begin, each mention of *lucente stella* is a reference to Venus, also known as Lucifer, because it is the brightest star in the firmament. Venus had enormous influence on, among other things, love and music. It therefore provides an appropriate backdrop for Trecento poetry. *Lucente stella* begins:

Shining star, you who destroy my heart, turn on me a new gaze inspired by love, have pity on him who languishes for you.[28]	Lucente stella, ch'el mio cor desfai con novo guardo che move d'amore, azi pietà de quel che per ti more (353).

We find the same visual backdrop in Giovanni da Cascia's madrigal *La bella stella*:

[27] In addition, while the *raison d'etre* of the madrigal has often been perplexing for this reader – since the piece is not allied to dancing – reading these texts as examples of a kind of dark humor or a comedic interjection at the expense of a hapless hero provides the text with more credibility and allows for a fuller appreciation.

[28] Translation in CD jacket, Microgologus, *D'Amor Cantando* (OPS 30-141, 1995), 22.

The beautiful star whose flame lasts always alights in my mind. Come out, shiny and brilliant, from behind a mountain.[29]	La bella stella, che sua fiamma tene accesa sempre ne la menta mia, lucida, chiara già del monte uscia (14).

The planet of love is alluded to in the madrigal *Quando l'aire comenza a farse bruno*:

When the air begins to darken and the first star appears I see a very beautiful woman.	Quando l'aire comenza a farse bruno e a parer la stella, aparveme una donna molto bella (7).

Padua is alluded to as a "shining star" in this chapter's final example, Johannes Ciconia's ceremonial motet *O Padua, sidus preclarum.* Believed to have been composed in 1405-1406, the motet praises the grandeur of Padua and its citizens:

Padua, shining star resplendent like a bright, flowering garland, a model of virtuous living.	[O] Padua, sidus preclarum hocce nissa fulgido regula virtutum morum serto refulgens florido!
Legal sternness! Praises thee as do philosophic truth, artistic fellowship, and poetic majesty.	Te laudat juris sanctio, philosophie veritas, et artistarum concio, poematum sublimitas.
Thou did uphold the start of Antenor's race whence thy people enjoy an exemplary sort of benefaction.	Tu Antenoris generis regis sumpsisti exordium, quo proles tua muneris genus habet egregium.
A fullness of fruits and wealth a fruitfulness and playfulness that comes from the expanse of thy land, all stand freely at thy disposal.	Frugum, opum fecunditas, telluris orta spacio tibi servit jocunditas, fertilitas ocio.
Mountains and swelling rivers, fields and flowery courts, church spires, houses, bridges and baths grace thee.	Te plena monte flumina, te castra jura florea decorant, templi culmina, edes et pontes, balnea.

[29]Translation in CD jacket, *The Music of the Fourteenth Century: Two Gentlemen of Verona* (MoveRecords MD3091, 1987).

Fame recounts throughout the world the tidings of thy praise and Johannes Ciconia echoes it with faithful song.[30]	Tue laudis preconia per orbem fama memorat, quem Johannes Ciconia canore fido resonat.

With its evocative nod to Antenor, its pastoral descriptions of ancient Padua, and its praise for the contributions of its philosophers and artists, Ciconia's text epitomizes several newly investigated influences on the secular music of northern Italy: madrigal texts reflected both an honoring of ancient memories and a celebration of the new interest in nature and science that we have seen in chapters 1 and 2. These seemingly contradictory forces formed the foundation of a uniquely north-Italian musical aesthetic and set the scene for the development of musical style in the rest of Italy.

Ciconia's poem also eulogizes Padua's commitment to virtuous living and the rule of law. The concept of justice is the central subject of the next chapter, focusing on Giotto, music, and the Scrovegni Chapel frescoes.

[30] Translation and edition is found in Bent and Hallmark 1985, 220-221.

Chapter 4

Music and Justice in Giotto's Scrovegni Chapel Frescoes

Forming part of a series of fourteen frescoes painted by Giotto, *Justice* and *Injustice* are at eye level, below the expansive narrative cycle of the lives of Mary and Jesus, in the Scrovegni Chapel in Padua (Fig. 4.1). The Virtues appear on the sides beneath *Heaven* and the *Last Judgment*, while the Vices are on the side flanking *Hell*. The images are paired off so that the Virtues and Vices are seen directly across from one another in the Chapel. Reading from the entrance toward the altar, one finds *Hope/Despair, Charity/Envy, Faith/Idolatry, Justice/Injustice, Temperance/Anger, Fortitude/Inconstancy*, and *Prudence/Folly*. *Justice* and *Injustice*, located at the center point of the series of Virtues and Vices, are the only two figures complemented by tiny scenes beneath them. The central placement of *Justice* and *Injustice* among the Virtues and Vices is unusual in literary and figurative history: most cycles feature charity or humility as the primary virtue, with avarice and pride as the most loathsome vices.[1] Giotto painted a relief-like space under *Justice*, imitating the texture of marble in its gray tones. In this niche, he placed a musical scene consisting of three dancing women (Fig. 4.2).

One holds a tambourine while the other two strike poses. They are most likely performing a carole or another type of dance song. Dance songs, popular in the early Trecento, were monophonic pieces usually performed

[1] Pfeiffenberger 1966, V:20.

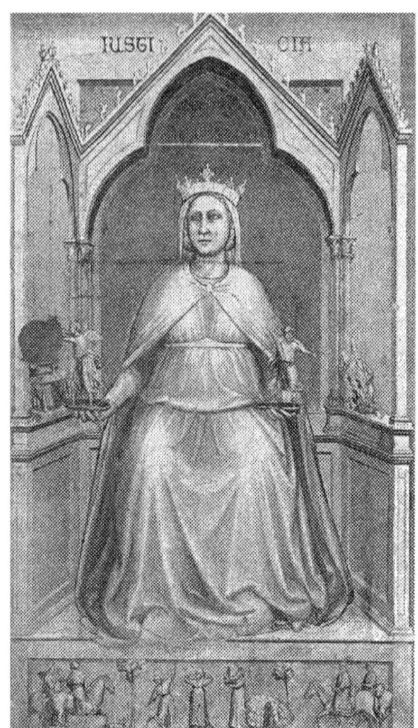

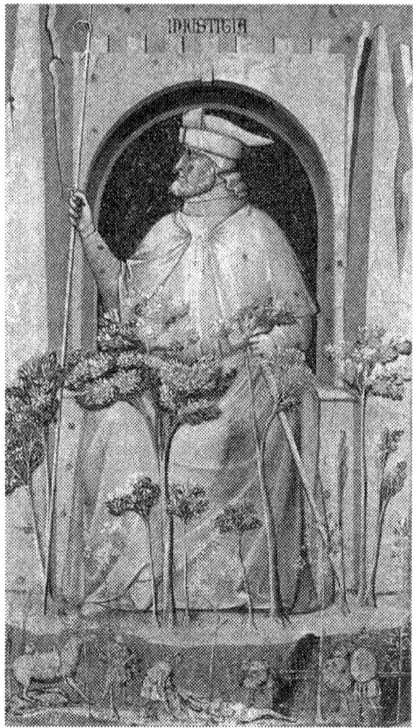

Figure 4.1: ***Justice* and *Injustice***

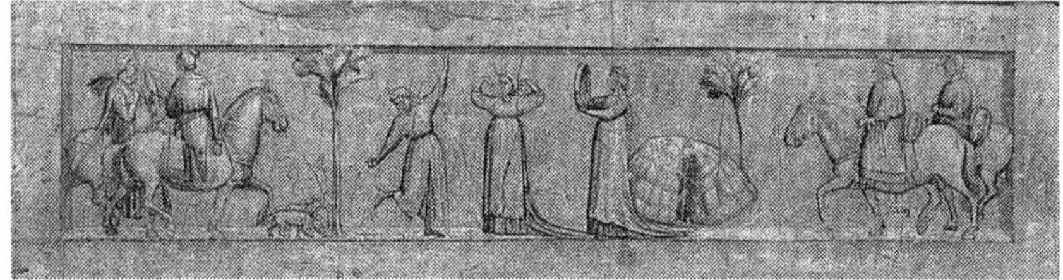

Figure 4.2: ***Justice*. Detail, dancing figures.**

by one person to the sound of a tambourine, lute, or vielle. The three figures are framed by two sets of men on horseback, who move toward them. Giotto's image captures the blissful life one can enjoy when justice prevails in society.[2] Importantly, in a just world there is music. Giotto's is

[2]The text under *Justice* reads: "Equa lance cuncta librat/ Perfect Iusticia:/ Cornado

a pastoral scene, a tradition revived, as we have seen in chapter 3, in the early madrigal and ballata texts found in the Rossi Codex.

The nature of justice, thoroughly contemplated by Greek and Roman writers, was also foremost in the minds of the Paduan citizenry in the late Middle Ages. Speeches delivered by Paduan statesmen often began with an appeal to justice. Ironically, the tyrant Ezzelino Romano, in a 1236 speech delivered at Monselice after he took the reins of power, was reported to have opened with "O gloriosa Iustina, civitatis Padue Regina."[3] Justice was of particular importance to the Paduans during the reign of the Carrara family after 1318. Writing about the events of 1324, Galeazzo and Bartolomeo Gattai mention the newly instituted rule of Marsilio da Carrara:

> And his governance was so good that he was beloved by all the citizenry because justice, faith, hope, charity, and strength were a part of him, the last of which he always needed in battles with the de la Scala.[4]

Justice was closely allied with public good. Giuseppe Gennari recounts that in 1277, the *comune* was interested chiefly in "promoting public good in and out of the city."[5] The ancient Roman roads, such as the "strada Vicentina," were restored. The new large edifices reflected Paduan knowledge and pride in their, for the most part buried, Roman past. Decrees were introduced to promote and maintain a tranquil city life. For example, Gennari informs us that only chess and other table games (cards were not included since they were not yet invented) were permitted in public (1804, 24). The number of people accompanying a nuptial ceremony was regulated to twenty per side, to lessen the chaos and noise that often accompanied such celebrations. Giotto's Scrovegni Chapel frescoes include a *Wedding Procession* with an appropriately small group of celebrants and musicians.

Accompanying Giotto's visual ode to justice and harmony in the Scrovegni Chapel is a reminder of life under the rule of injustice. Underneath the male *Injustice*, nature is depicted as chaotic and music does not exist (Fig. 4.3).

---

bonos vibrat/ Ensem contra vicia/ Cuncta quadent liberate/ Ipse si regnaverit/ Agit cum iocunditate/ Quousque que volverit/ Miles probus tunc venatur/ Mercator it..." The final part of the subscription is illegible. ("It [*Justice*] balances everything with an equanimous spear. It vibrates its sword against vices. The whole world feels free under its rule. It acts joyfully wherever it turns, the honest soldier in his hunting, the merchant goes...") For more about the subscription, see I. B. Supino 1920, 147-148.

[3]Guglielmo Cortusi 1941, 3.

[4]"E in questa suo signoria portossi sí bene, che venne in amore e in benivolenza di tuto il popolo, perché sempre in lui fu justizia e fede e speranza e charittà e forteza; la quale sempre gli fu di bisogno contra ala guerra, ch'egli e 'l comune di Pado aveva con

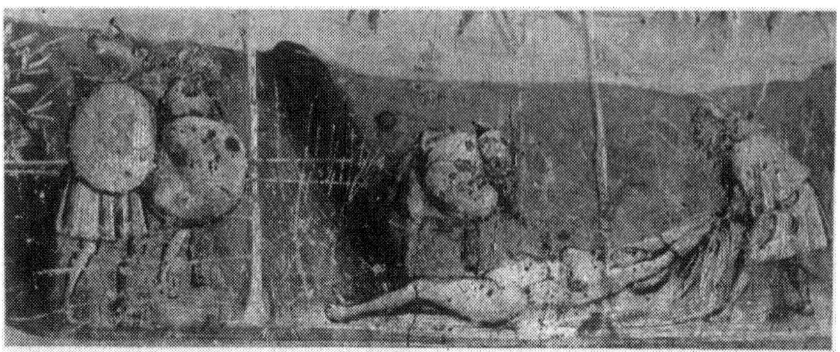

Figure 4.3: ***Injustice*. Detail, dancing figures attacked.**

Music is also absent in Dante's *Inferno* and in Giotto's *Hell* in the Scrovegni Chapel's *Last Judgment.* Below *Injustice*, Giotto again included small figures but has omitted the frame separating the figures from the Vice above them. Furthermore, the neat trees underneath *Justice* grow wildly upward into the area occupied by the bearded *Injustice.* Men with shields and staves assault the peaceful party, knocking a man off his horse and dragging a nude woman. The scene behind the figures is rough and jagged, while that beneath *Justice* is smooth and orderly. Balance is the rule under *Justice*: two men on horseback to the left and right flank the three women. Beneath *Injustice,* the figures scatter.

Scholars have yet to examine thoroughly the traditions underlying the enigmatic representations of music-making beneath the figure of *Justice* and the disruption of music-making beneath *Injustice* in the Scrovegni Chapel frescoes. Jonathan Riess establishes a parallel between *Justice* and the figure of the Christ-Judge in the *Last Judgment*, citing Aquinas's writings on Virtues and Vices as one of his philosophical underpinnings.[6] He describes the tiny scene as "evocative of the Golden Age that was believed to have existed when Justice lived among men, an Earthly paradise that was described by Virgil" (1984, 242). Riess also explores the themes of good government and common good in Giotto's *Justice.*

Bruce Cole (1996, 362) writes that a connection exists between the Virtues and Vices and the narrative scenes described above. With regard to

---

misser Can da la Scalla" (Gatari 1931, 13).

[5]"... promuovere dentro e fuori della Città il pubblico bene" (Gennari 1804, 24).

[6]Studies on Giotto's Virtues and Vices include Cole 1996, Riess 1984, and Pfeiffenberger 1966. For Virtues and Vices in art, see Ludovico Zdekauer 1913.

Justice he notes, "Interestingly enough, the throne type, pose and gesture of God the Father are related to the *Justice* on the basement level" [of the Scrovegni Chapel]. Cole asks, "Does this mean that *Justice*, who occupies the central space on the right-hand basement level, was considered a very important and sacred Virtue, and that her pose was derived from that of God the Father? I do not know but it is possible."

Selma Pfeiffenberger suggests that Cicero's *De Officis* is the source of Giotto's crowned female *Justice* "because he is the only writer to term Justice 'queen' of the Virtues."[7] Other scholars, including Cesira Gasparotto and Nicolai Rubenstein, view Giotto's images of music-making as representing the burgeoning civic pride most often associated with Tuscany. In "Il buono e il cattivo Governo," Gasparotto (1966) argues that the scenes below *Justice* and *Injustice* represent the effects of good and bad government, and that Giotto's *Justice* and her musical counterparts provide antecedents and inspiration for the representation of harmony and justice in Ambrogio Lorenzetti's fresco the *Effects of Good Government in the City* in Siena. In Lorenzetti's image, nine dancing women and one tambourine player appear in the central piazza in *Good Government*, while in the *Mal Governo*, the women are assaulted.[8] In all of these interpretations, the scholars do not provide theories regarding the presence and meaning of music in these scenes. Giotto's extraordinary *Justice* is an anomalous creation. In *Recht und Gerechtigkeit im Spiegel der europäischen Kunst*, a history of justice's iconography, Wolfgang Pleister (1988) has not uncovered a single precedent for the combination of music and justice. Justice is pictured traditionally holding scales and a sword. In the iconography of the Virtues and Vices, music is most traditionally found accompanying temperance or prudence, as we see in Giovanni Bellini's *Allegory of Prudence* (Fig. 4.4).

What is the literary or figurative source for Giotto's linking of justice and music? In unraveling the meaning of the juxtaposition of justice and music, a rich interdisciplinary tableau of philosophical and historical antecedents comes to light. Two primary and heretofore unexamined influences on Giotto's representation of *Justice* and *Injustice* will be explored in this chapter, beginning with the astrological writing of Pietro and his contemporaries Ristoro d'Arezzo and Cecco d'Ascoli. It will be argued that *Justice* and *Injustice* display astrological undertones and can be read as idealizations of Venus and Mars. The astrological references in Giotto's conception of *Justice* and *Injustice* are more convincing when one takes into account that Pietro wrote about a branch of science called "judicial astrology," or

[7]While Pfeiffenberger (1966, V:20) does note Cicero's influence on the seated *Justice*, she does not take into consideration the meaning of music in the scene.

[8]For more, see Rubenstein 1958, 183.

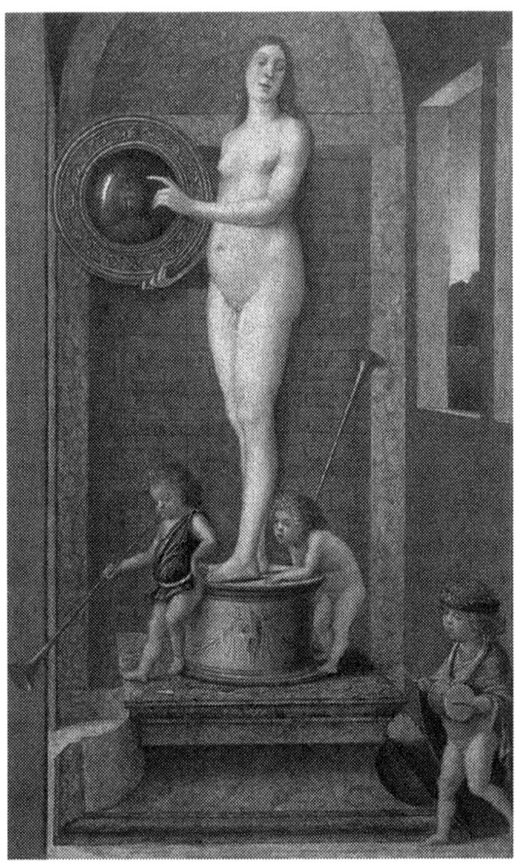

Figure 4.4: **Giovanni Bellini, *Allegory of Prudence***

what we modernly understand as astrology. While scholars have examined the *Last Judgment* and its connection to *Justice*, the judicial aspects associated with astrology are yet to be researched. A second influence is that of Cicero, namely, his *De Republica*, as transmitted by Augustine and Aquinas. In the *De Republica*, Cicero makes a clear connection between peace and music in a just society. It will be seen that his *De Officiis* is also an important literary precursor of Giotto's *Justice*. An examination of these antecedent traditions provides an understanding of the anomalous placement of music underneath *Justice* and strengthens Bruce Cole's assertion that Giotto was an "auditory painter."

Enrico Scrovegni, whose father, Reginaldo, was immortalized by Dante in the seventh circle of his *Inferno*, probably completed the family chapel in 1303.[9] The Scrovegni were moneylenders, and Reginaldo their infamous usurer. Indeed, it is believed that Reginaldo was so corrupt and avaricious that even while on his deathbed, he asked Enrico to hide the key to his safe. Witnesses to his death say that when he breathed his last breath, a long, infernal laugh was heard, with the smell of sulfur, a sign that Beelzebub had come to take him to Hell (Selvatico 1870, 9). The chroniclers tell us that Enrico built the chapel, called Santa Maria Annunziata, in honor of Mary. He did this in hopes of replacing the dark shadow cast by his treacherous family with the light of good deeds and, indeed, the light of the Redeemer (Selvatico 1870, 12). This chapel is situated in the old Arena, or forum, of Padua, next to what was once the Scrovegni Palace. The church was dedicated to Santa Maria della Carità, appropriate for a donor looking to atone for his family's sins. In March of 1304, Pope Benedict XI granted indulgences to those who visited the "Santa Maria della Carità de Arena" in Padua (Stubblebine 1969, 105). The chapel was formally consecrated on March 25, 1305, on the Feast Day of the Annunciation.

Perhaps after a visit to Rome, where he undoubtedly saw Giotto's work, Scrovegni enlisted the services of the young Giotto to decorate the inside of his newly erected chapel. Francesca Flores d'Arcais advances the notion that Giotto was first summoned to Padua by the Church of the Santo's Franciscan monks, who wanted a "modern" master to paint the Santo's Chapter House, and that he was in Padua between 1302 and 1305 (Flores d'Arcais 1995, 128). Flores d'Arcais suggests that Scrovegni met Giotto while he was working on the Santo's frescoes. While there exists no primary evidence for Flores d'Arcais's argument that Giotto was in Padua prior to working in the Scrovegni Chapel, evidence does indicate that he and his studio were involved with the painting of the Santo's Chapter House frescoes and of the frescoes (now destroyed) in the Salone della Ragione (Dornpacher 1951).

Giotto's work in the Salone della Ragione is crucial to establishing a connection between Pietro – and by extension, astrology – and the Scrovegni Chapel frescoes. It is known that Pietro provided the program for the Salone della Ragione astrological frescoes, and two contemporary chroniclers confirm Giotto's authorship. Giovanni da Nono mentions the Tuscan painter in his *Visio Egidij Regis Patavie*, written c.1325:

> The twelve signs of the Zodiac and the seven planets with their influences shine in this magnificent covering worked on by Giotto, the

[9] For more on the Scrovegni family, see Bellinati 1974, 23-30.

> greatest painter; other golden stars with windows and other figures similarly shine from the inside.[10]

Circa 1446 Michele Savonarola noted that the artists who repainted the Salone della Ragione frescoes followed the original program of the Paduan professor:

> Magnificent and unique pictures circle the walls in the upper portion in which are represented the heavenly bodies and in a marvelous manner, images of actions to which men are naturally inclined; the author of this group is our writer of the *Conciliator* [Pietro d'Abano].[11]

Giotto's name has also been linked to Pietro in other ways. Indeed, the earliest literary document preserving Giotto's name is Pietro's *Expositio problematum Aristotelis* of around 1310 – preceding the famous examples from Dante and Barberino by half a decade (Thomann 1991, 239-240).[12]

The reference to Giotto appears in Pietro's discussion of Aristotle's question: "Why do [men] make images of the face? Either because this [i.e., the face] shows what kind of people they are, or because these images allow us to recognize them best" (Thomann 1991, 241). In his commentary on Aristotle's answer, we note that Pietro's argument is strikingly similar to one made by Marchetto in his *Pomerium*, insisting that notation capture sounds as if recorded from nature. Marchetto wrote: "Art imitates nature as far as it can (as Aristotle said in book II of the *Physica*.) I shall prove this with an example: he who paints a lily or a horse strives as far as he can to paint it so as to resemble a horse or a lily in nature."[13] Pietro also believed that painting should capture the nature of the object or person it depicts, and it is in this explanation, in the *Expositio* 36.1, that we find the reference to Giotto:

> He gives two solutions, saying first: the reason is that by means of images of the face is represented the kind of constitutional arrangement of that person whose image it is, and most of all (1) when it is

[10]"Duedecim celestia signa et septem planete cum suis proprietatibus in hac cohopertura fulgebunt, a Zotho summo pictorum mirifice laborata, et alia sidera aurea cum speculis et alie figurationes similiter fulgebunt interius" (Da Nono 1934-1939, 20).

[11]"Nam ea in parte quedam singulares et egregie picture illud' circuunt, quibus corpora planetarum, et ad que opera peragenda magis homines ab eis inclinantur, mirum in modum etiam per figuras demonstrantur. Huius autem ordinis institutor noster gloriosus Conciliator existitit" (Savonarola 1902, 47-48).

[12]Thomann argues that Pietro's mention of Giotto predates that of Dante in the *Purgatorio*, Francesco da Barberino in *Liber documentorum amoris*, and Riccobaldo da Ferrara in *Compilatio chronologica*.

[13]This translation is in Gallo 1985, 115-116. For more about Marchetto and Giotto, see Beck 1999, 4-24.

> painted by a painter capable of producing a likeness in all respects – for example, by Giotto – so that we reach by means of this [i.e., the image] the knowledge of him [i.e., of whom the image is made] in such a way that if he met [us] he would be recognized through it [i.e., the painted image].[14]

Giotto's connection to Pietro is even more intriguing if we consider the astrological implications of the images. Not yet discussed in the literature on Giotto's Virtues and Vices, astrological formulas linking them with the seven planets may open another avenue of investigation, explaining the significance of the dancing figures below the seated *Justice*. Could Pietro's knowledge of astrology have influenced the conception of the Virtues and Vices in the Scrovegni Chapel, as it did in the astrological figures in the Salone della Ragione? Giotto did paint the twelve astrological images in Padua, as has been noted above by Giovanni da Nono. Furthermore, scholars believe that Pietro, the foremost intellectual to write on the subject of astrology in Padua, advised Giotto on the representation of the comet in the Scrovegni Chapel's *Adoration of the Magi* (Bellinati 1997, 15).

Pietro's primary work in the science of astrology appears in three treatises: the *Imagines, Lucidator dubitabilium astronomiae*, and the *De motus octave sphere.* In addition, astrology is mentioned in his encyclopedic tomes, including the *Conciliator, Expositio*, and *Decisiones physionomiae.* Lynn Thorndike, in his *History of Magic and Experimental Science*, writes that by Pietro's time *astronomy* and *astrology* took on meanings that we have gone to great lengths to show as being derived from similar Greek words, *nomos* and *logos* (Thorndike 1923, 890-891).[15] Furthermore, Graziella Federici Vescovini (1988, 64), in her edition of the *Lucidator*, argues that *astronomy* and *astrology* were used interchangeably in the work. Both scholars make a distinction between the science of motion and the effect of this motion on the earth under the rubric of astrology and astronomy, respectively. Pietro argued persuasively that both astronomy and the related astrology are sciences, and he relied on book 2 of Aristotle's *Physica* to make his case in the *Lucidator dubitabilium astronomiae* (Vescovini 1988, 110). While it is not within the scope of this study to find the etymology of the words, it is noteworthy that Pietro's and Marchetto's treatises on astrology and music share similarly uncommon titles, *Lucidator* and *Lucidarium.*

Pietro also discussed justice apart from its astrological connotations in

[14]"Solvit dupliciter dicens primo causam esse quia per imagines faciei representatur qualis fuerit dispositio ipsius cuius est imago, et maxime cum fuerit depicta pictore sciente per omnia assimilare, puta Zoto, ut ea deveniamus in cognitionem illius ita..." (Thomann 1991, 241).

[15]For Pietro's etymology of astronomy and astrology, see Vescovini 1988, 108-109.

his *Expositio*. Four *particulae*, or chapters, treat aspects of human behavior. The chapters appear sandwiched between his discussions of air and wind (natural phenomena) and sight and hearing (human bodily functions). Their inclusion in the scientific *Expositio* suggests that he regarded behavior as part of human physiology, making action a subject that can be scientifically studied. Pietro begins these chapters with fear and fortitude (*particula* 27), followed by temperance and intemperance (*particula* 28); justice and injustice (*particula* 29); and prudence, intellect, and knowledge ("prudentia et intellectus et sapientia") in *particula* 30. Temperance and intemperance, justice and injustice are paired Virtues and Vices, reminiscent of what we find in the Scrovegni Chapel. Pietro believed that justice was the noblest of the virtues, borrowing the three-part definition of it as "natural and positive, distributive and commutative." Briefly, when comparing Pietro's Virtues and Vices to those depicted by Giotto, one notes that both include temperance, justice, and fortitude. While Giotto also appeals to the more religious of the virtues, such as hope, faith, and charity, Pietro is drawn to knowledge and intellect. The selection of Virtues and Vices reflects the contexts in which they exist: for Giotto, in a chapel, for Pietro, in a scientific treatise. Their representations in different contexts signal that their meanings were fluid and that they could serve the purposes of both sacred and secular arguments. Interestingly, in the *Expositio*, Pietro does not include music in his treatment of justice, and we will need to dig further into his astrological tracts for this connection.

It is in his *Lucidator* that astrology (in this context meaning both the modern astronomy and astrology) has adjudicatory implications. In explaining the scientific virtue of astrology, Pietro divides astrology into two branches: one investigates the motions of the planets, the other, the effects of these motions. Pietro denotes this second branch of the influence of the planets as "judicial astrology" (Vescovini 1988, 115). This judicial astrology is further subdivided into an introductory division concerned with prejudgments, and a practical part that concerns itself with the making of judgments (Vescovini 1988, 115). This last subdivision is divided into four parts: revolutions, nativities, interrogations, and elections. Thorndike (1923, 890-891) notes that this division is traditional and that the last part includes the science of images.[16]

Evidence suggesting a link between Giotto's *Justice* and the representation of music may also be found by piecing together astrological passages

[16]"But he [Pietro] accepts the division of the science of the heavens into two parts, one descriptive and dealing with the measurement and motion of the stars, the other judicial and studying their effects. The latter is subdivided as usual into the branches of revolutions, nativities, interrogations, and elections, which last includes the science of images."

from Pietro's *Conciliator, Expositio*, and *Decisiones physionomiae*. Each of these three tomes investigates in scholastic, Aristotelian terms the nature of all properties known to man. In piecing together the antecedents of Giotto's musical *Justice*, we find that Venus is the missing link in the enigmatic relationship between *Justice* and music. In the *Decisiones physionomiae* we find that Pietro aligned Venus with music.[17] The fifth *decisio*, concerning the nature of those born under the influence of Venus, reads, "Those born under the sign of Venus delight in singing and playing music."[18] The description reads, "Venus resembles Zeus but in a wider and gentler form, with flesh of pure whiteness, especially in the case of an oriental, round, fleshy face. Her eyes are beautiful, almost like blades, with contiguous eyebrows, thin lips, and a well-formed neck and beautiful small breasts, a narrow waist, and wavy hair." With regard to her attributes, he continues: "She should walk according to her spirit, be affable in speaking. She is inclined to loose appearance and ornaments, and takes great pleasure in games, banquets, drunkenness, in songs and musical instruments."[19]

Ristoro d'Arezzo, in his treatise entitled *Della composizione del mondo*, amplifies on Venus's fair and impartial attributes. Written in 1282, this treatise consists, like Brunetto Latini's *Tesoretto*, of a compendium of facts concerning the formation of the physical world. However, unlike Latini, Ristoro's discussion relies heavily on astrological considerations. The treatise was quite influential during the Trecento – it was probably the foundation for Cecco d'Ascoli's *L'Acerba* – because it incorporated the writings of Arabic astronomers and translated their findings into the vernacular. Ristoro's text makes a striking connection between the figure of Venus and the virtue of justice. This is extraordinary because it suggests the connection between music and justice, since Venus is traditionally depicted as the planet influencing music. In his chapter "Of the seven spheres, with their stars, which are called planets and their significance," Ristoro begins by noting the luminosity of Venus, which is surpassed only by the sun:

> And later we find another heaven (the third) in which there is only

[17]In the *Decisiones physonomiae*, a treatise well known in the fourteenth and fifteenth centuries, Pietro develops a doctrine of the influence of the planets on earth (Vescovini 1986, 60).

[18]"Et omnino voluptatum sibi appetitus existit cantu et in instrumentis musicis delectatur" (D'Abano 1548, 33).

[19]"Venus Iovi assimilatur spetiosior tamen et blandior existit et denotat similiter carnosum album albedine pura praecipue si fuerit orientalis faciei rotundae multae carnis oculi eius sunt pulchri superciliis vinctis subnigri labia tenuia collun vividum et formosum pectus angustum breves costae capilli ad crispitudinem tendentes, secundum quidem animam ambulans est suaviter locutionis affabilis apparitioni et ornatui plurimum intentus mulierum amator ludorum epulationum ebrietatum et omnino voluptatum sibi appetitus existit cantu et in instrumentis musicis delectatur" (D'Abano 1548, 33).

> one large, clear, splendid star, which is called Venus. It reflects light on the earth and creates shadows; there it passes with its rays, almost sparkling, and it is the most delightful star that humans can see, and it seems the largest, besides the sun.[20]

In order to explain Venus's relation to justice, Ristoro first underscores Venus's light, since light is traditionally the image that represents justice. Light shines on the just and is denied to the unjust. Indeed, astrologers usually bestow the attribute of justice to the realm of the Sun in the sign of Leo.

The relationship between justice, light, and harmony is typical of Trecento musical texts. In the motet *Lux purpurata / Diligite iustitiam* by Jacopo da Bologna, the duplum reads, "Honor justice, you who administer states," and ends with "let concern for his subjects be uppermost in a ruler, that his people may live in harmony and peace."[21]

In a later motet, *Imperial sedendo* by Bartolino da Padova, describing the rule of the Carrara family, we find the family's virtues extolled in a symbol, the chariot: "Its wheels were driven by four ladies: Justice and Temperance and Courage and by Prudence, among such nobility" ("Le rote soi guidavan quatro done, Iusticia e Temperancia con Forteza/ Ed an' Prudenza tra cotanta alteza").[22]

In describing Venus, Ristoro argues that she has two sides to her nature: one is in the house of Taurus, which influences luxury, music, and games, and the second is in Libra, which evinces justice and the common good.[23]

Describing the first, he cites the wisdom of the savi, who claim that Venus signifies beauty, adornments, pleasantries, games, "love songs" ("canti d'amore"), "all types of instrumental sounds" ("tutte le generazioni de'suoni delli stormenti"), and later "singers of love and players of love" ("cantatori d'amore e suonatori d'amore").[24] Later in book 3, chapter 5, subtitled "Of Venus, her signs, significance, effects, orbits, and motives" ("Di Venus, e de' suoi segni, e delle sue significazioni, e de' suoi effetti, e degli orbi suoi, e delle sue cagioni"), Ristoro expounds on the second aspect of Venus, which

---

[20]"E dopo questo troviamo uno altro cielo (lo terzo), nel quale è posta una stella sola, grossa chiarissima, lucente, la quale è chiamata Venus, e rende lume sopra la terra, e fae ombra alle cose che stanno erte, là ov'ella fiede colli suoi raggi, quasi scintillare e vagheggiare, ed è la più dilettevole stella vedere al viso umano che sia, e pare la più grossa istella che sia da indi in su, four del sole:" (D'Arezzo 1864, 32-33). Jacopo Alighieri (son of Dante) also wrote a comprehensive treatise, probably in Verona, in the 1340s. It is entitled *Il Dottrinale* (1895), and chapter 42 relates justice to concord.

[21]Translation in CD jacket, *Suso in Italia Bella* (Arcana A38, 1995), 38.

[22]Corsi 1970, 241.

[23]For more on depictions of music in the Salone della Ragione frescoes, see Beck 1999, 68-84.

[24]D'Arezzo 1864, 32-33 and 110-111.

influences justice because the planet also has its house in the sign of Libra. Libra is symbolized by scales, and "it seems that Venus was justice and loved justice, and this sign is called Libra."[25] He confirms that the wise men believed that

> she signified delight, love and justice; and was averse to lechery, discord, fighting, war, and all that was not just.[26]

The two sides of Venus, music and justice (Taurus and Libra), suggest a fascinating new reading of Giotto's two-tiered *Justice* in the Scrovegni Chapel. The crowned figure represents the influence of Venus in Libra (justice), while the predella figures account for the influence of Venus in Taurus (music).

If this is the case, then it follows that *Injustice* was also inspired by an astrological figure. Mars is by far the most belligerent planet. Finding its houses in both Aries and Scorpio, Mars is the planet of warriors, battles, and aggression. Ristoro explains that it is the nature of Mars (in Scorpio) to harm people for no reason:

> And Mars with his people seasonally kills and harms without reason and without fault in order to dominate and instill fear in people.[27]

The figures beneath Giotto's *Injustice* do appear to be victims of random violence. Men come upon three women and attack them. Mars is by nature prone to brutality. Ristoro explains: "he is wicked, and because of his bad tendency to kill and to spread blood, and start fires, his nature is to voluntarily perform evil deeds."[28] In addition, the claws that grow from *Injustice*'s fingers recall attributes of the deceptive Scorpio. In the *Decisiones physionomaie*, Mars is described by Pietro as follows:

> A long nose like a woodpecker, long teeth, prominent chest, reddish hair, an insipid beard of few sparse hairs; he resembles a eunuch. As for his nature, he is impetuous, strong, audacious, a virtuous warrior who spreads blood, litigious, he spurs men to fight, blasphemous, foolish, inclined to perversity of all kinds, of sturdy walk, capable of

[25] "...pare che Venus fosse giustizia ed amasse giustizia, e questo segno è chiamato libra" (D'Arezzo 1864, 111).

[26] "E puosero ch'ella avia a sigificare dilezione, ed amore e giustizia; e questo può essere: imperciò che la lussuria e la generazione è impedita per la discordia, e per la lite, e per la guerra, e per la non giustizia" (D'Arezzo 1864, 111).

[27] "E Mars con questa sua gente per stagione uccidono e fanno male fuor di ragione e senza colpa, per signoreggiare ed essere temuti dalla gente" (D'Arezzo 1864, 100).

[28] "...e per lo malo usamento e per mal' usanza e'z costuma d'uccidere, e di spandere lo sangue, e di mettere fuoco, è convertito in natura di fare volentieri male" (D'Arezzo 1864, 100).

> injurious machinations; he speaks badly of everybody, spreads dishonest gossip. He is satisfied with what he does and of its opposite.[29]

In the Salone della Ragione frescoes, Mars is the only planet represented with a musical instrument. He is shown blowing into two horns, announcing the coming of blustery spring weather. The horns may also be understood as representing belligerent behavior. Horns are blown in Trecento manuscript illuminations to denote warring factions. For example, there is a prominent horn player in the *Cronaca figurata di Giovanni Villani*, "Come i genovesi fecero grande danno a' pisani, che tornavano di Sardegna." (Rome, Biblioteca Apostolica Vaticana, Codex Chigiano L. VII, 296, f. 224). Giotto includes a man blowing a horn in a crowd of men with raised sticks and clubs, while Judas kisses Christ in the foreground in the *Capture of Christ*.

In addition to the astrological works, classical and scholastic treatises elaborating on the nature of justice are important sources of its iconography. Jonathan Riess (1984, 75), who argues that Giotto's portrayal of *Justice* is unheralded in medieval Italy, suggests a reading of the figure as "the benevolent power within the community that generates wealth, that directs it into useful or socially fruitful areas." Furthermore, Riess notes that the predella figures beneath the seated figure represent "the Common Good that Aquinas [*Summa theologica* question 58, articles 5 and 6] describes as the chief consequence of the pursuit of political justice." The figures beneath *Injustice* "indicate the social disorder that arises when, as Aquinas described it, individuals pursue selfish ends" (Riess 1984, 73).

Aquinas devotes several chapters to questions concerning justice in his *Summa theologica* 2.2.57-62. In question 58, article 2, he notes the communal quality of justice, stating: "On the other hand, there is Cicero holding that the purpose of justice is to hold men together in companionable living in common. This implies a social relationship. Therefore justice is occupied only with our dealings with others." Quoting Cicero once more, Aquinas notes that "justice is the most resplendent of the virtues, and gives its name to an upright man" (Aquinas 1975, 51). In Giotto's painting we note that compositionally *Justice* is also the most resplendent and complex of the images.

Though the frescoes certainly betray Thomistic influence, Riess's reading omits the striking allusion to music that Giotto makes in this fresco.

[29] "Nasus magnus est et picus dentes longos habens et pectus acutum capilli ruffedini attingentes barba ircina paucorum pillorum spadoni enim similatur. Quantum quidem ad animam est impetuosus fortis audax et bellicosus victoriosus sanguinis effusor litigiosus suscitans homines ad riam discordiam feminando turpium verborum effusor stultus periurus receptionis plurimae longus incessus ingeniosus cogitationis iniquae semper malaloquitur et inhonesta plurima que ostendens quae perpetrarae intendat, nullus quex ipso contentatur et e contra" (D'Abano 1548, 32).

In researching Aquinas's philosophy of justice, I have not found one mention of music. Indeed, when Aquinas speaks in depth about music and the seven virtues, it is in relation to temperance.[30] For Aquinas and the Dominicans, the tempered participation in earthly music was a means toward their ultimate goal, the contemplation of God. In the *Summa theologica*, Aquinas devotes question 141 to temperance, and asserts that "the pleasures of the other senses play a different part in man and in other animals," implying that humans can find pleasure in the senses apart from the sense of touch. Aquinas writes,

> Thus the lion is pleased to see the stag, or to hear its voice, in relation to his food. On the other hand, man derives pleasure from the other senses, not only for this reason, but also on account of the becomingness of the sensible object.

With regard to sound he explains,

> Wherefore temperance is about the pleasures of the other senses, in relation to pleasures of touch, not principally but consequently: while in so far as the sensible objects of the other senses are pleasant on account of their becomingness, as when a man is pleased at a well-harmonized sound, this pleasure has nothing to do with the preservation of nature.

Aquinas views temperance as a measure of good behavior; and the enjoyment of music may be measured in the same fashion. If Giotto had looked to Aquinas for a template for the portrayals of virtues and vices, it seems more probable that he would have decorated *Temperance* and not *Justice* with a musical predella. Conversely, *Anger, Temperance's* paired Vice in the Scrovegni Chapel, also does not have a musical equivalent in philosophy. Instead, I argue that a reading of Cicero rather than Aquinas best contributes to an understanding of Giotto's enigmatic, musical *Justice*. A more appropriate source for the depiction of the singing and dancing women below *Justice* is to be found in Roman theories of government. It will be shown that Cicero's writings contain a blueprint for Scrovegni and his family to elevate themselves in the estimation of Paduan citizenry, and that Cicero's *De Republica* contains an irrefutable passage linking music to justice.

Let us begin with Cicero's treatise *De Officiis*, which contains his most detailed treatment of the uses of justice. This work was certainly known in the late Middle Ages, as attested to by the works of Aquina mentioned above. *De Officiis* reads in part as a manual for the citizen of means to

[30] For more on Aquinas and music, see Beck 1992-1995, 123-138.

live a pleasant life by comporting himself justly. Just as the iconography of Giotto's chapel suggests, justice and charity are closely allied. Completing the passage by Aquinas discussed earlier concerning resplendent justice, Cicero insists:

> Of this again there are two divisions – justice, in which is the crowning glory of the virtues and on the basis of which men are called 'good men' and, closely akin to justice, charity, which may also be called kindness or generosity (Cicero 1913, 1.7.20).

The connection is further amplified:

> The first office of justice is to keep one man from doing harm to another unless provoked by wrong; and the next is to lead men to use common possessions for the common interests, private property for their own (Cicero 1913, 1.7.20).

These passages can be read as a manual for Enrico Scrovegni, a roadmap to rid himself and his family of their past and to reinvent himself as a virtuous man. Cicero maintains, for instance, that justice is the best way to achieve popularity. In 2.10.37, he observes:

> But when men, with a spirit great and exalted, can look down upon such outward circumstances, whether prosperous or adverse, and when some noble and virtuous purpose, presented to their minds, converts them wholly to itself and carries them away in its pursuit, who then could fail to admire in them the splendor and beauty of virtue?

In presenting oneself as a virtuous man, Cicero argues, a citizen must first and foremost exhibit a strong sense of justice:

> As, then, this superiority of mind to such externals inspires great admiration, so justice, above all, on the basis of which alone men are called 'good men,' seems to people generally a quite marvelous virtue – and not without good reason; for no one can be just who fears death or pain or exile or poverty, or who values their opposites above equity. And people admire especially the man who is uninfluenced by money; and if a man has proved himself in this direction, they think him tried as by fire (Cicero 1913, 2.11.38).

Cicero views justice as a sign of community, later writing that justice is essential to having the reputation of a just person:

> . . . every walk and vocation in life calls for human co-operation – first and above all, in order that one may have friends with whom to enjoy social intercourse. And this is not easy, unless one is looked upon as a good man (Cicero 1913. 2.11.39).

Ultimately, Cicero notes the connection of justice to good faith, and it is here that we can align pagan ideology with Giotto's Christian iconography in the meaning of the *Last Judgment*:

> The foundation of justice, moreover, is good faith – that is, truth and fidelity to promises and agreements (Cicero 1913, 1.7.23).

Furthermore, musical metaphors linked to justice appear in the *De Officis.* For example, flagrant instances of bad breeding are noted (Cicero 1913, 1.40.145): "like singing in the streets or any other gross misconduct." Cicero compares good behavior to the tuning of an instrument: "However slightly out of tune a harp or flute may be, the fault is still detected by a connoisseur; so we must be on the watch lest haply something in our life be out of tune." The tuning is then viewed as an example of community: "Far greater is the need for painstaking harmony, inasmuch as harmony of actions is far better and far more important than harmony of sounds" (Cicero 1913, 1.40.145). Cicero also stresses that the ability to hear musical tones and the ability to judge character are related: "As, therefore, a musical ear detects even the slightest falsity of tone in a harp, so we, if we wish to be keen and careful observers of moral faults, shall often draw important conclusions from trifles" (Cicero 1913, 1.40.146). Cicero cogently compares the concord of a well-knit community to the harmony of music in his *De Republica.*[31] This notion was transmitted to later writers, as attested to in a famous passage in the chapter of *City of God* entitled "Cicero's Opinion of the Roman Government." Quoting Scipio from the *De Republica,* Augustine writes in book 2.22:

> At the end of the second book, Scipio says: "As, when lyres or flutes accompany the voices of singers, a kind of harmony should be maintained out of separate sounds, and the trained ear cannot endure any false note or disagreement, and such harmony, concordant and exact, may be produced by the regulation even of voices most unlike...."

Cicero explains that different types of music work together to create harmony. The three types of music are for strings, winds, and the voice. This conceptual division is important to underscore because it corresponds to the same three-part division found later in the writing of Augustine, and attributed by Pietro and Marchetto to Augustine in the early fourteenth century. Both Paduan authors divided sound into organic (for the voice), harmonic (produced by air, but not sung), and rhythmic (without air). Two of the musical subdivisions are also mirrored in Giotto's fresco: one woman

[31]Cicero's treatise was known to Paduan intellectials in the early Trecento. Albertino Mussato owned a copy of the treatise (Billanovich 1942-1955).

sings (vocal music) and one beats the tambourine or plays percussively. As in Cicero's description, Giotto's musical dancers are restrained in their music-making, for restraint softens the disharmony between voices.

Cicero extends the musical metaphor to social divisions and notes that the different sounds correspond to the high, middle, and low strata of the citizenry:

> "... so by combining the highest, lowest and between them the middle class of society, as if they were tones of a different pitch, provided they are regulated by due proportion, the state may produce unision by agreement of elements quite unlike. The agreement of this musicians call harmony in singing is known as concord in the body politic. This is the tightest best rope of safety in every state, and it cannot exist at all without justice."[32]

Here we uncover the crucial philosophical antecedent of Giotto's *Justice*. Justice ensures harmony and concord within a community, as represented in the harmony of music. Giotto's figure translates this statement directly into visual form. Under *Justice* concord exists, under *Injustice* this world is disrupted. The architectural spaces painted by Giotto in these panels demonstrate his affinity for classical styles. *Justice* sits in a niche surrounded by classical and Gothic decorations. Behind her the space drifts off into a distant blue tinge framed by an arch and Gothic embellishments. On the other hand, a medieval arch with ramparts reminiscent of a fortress frames *Injustice*. In front of him, the walls are cracked and the trees are overgrown. He resembles a judge in contemporary costume seated before the ruins of a town wall. He does not face the viewer; one arm holds a sword while the other clings firmly to a crooked staff, both symbolizing the avarice and corruption that recall his rule (Wieruszowski 1944, 23).

Classical balance is also maintained in the tiny scene below the seated *Justice*. Two horsemen approach the dancing ladies on either side. They occupy the center of the scene between two trees. The entire vignette is neatly contained within a proscenium-like border. In contrast, the balance is completely disrupted under *Injustice*, where only one horse appears on the left, while on the right men with shields stand watching the assault. In addition, the border is omitted and the scene blends directly into the space of the seated *Injustice*. In a just world, harmony and balance reign; in an unjust world, there are no boundaries, and discordance is the rule. Through rational restraint, a concept particularly emphasized in the writing of Aquinas and later adopted by Boccaccio in his *Decameron*, the classes come together in harmony. Cicero makes the equation: harmony in music

[32]Cicero in Augustine 1957, 2.21.

results in concord in a community. Concord is the most potent bond in a community and ensures security.

A knowledge of Augustine is particularly important in the reading of music and *Justice* in the Scrovegni Chapel because Augustine's theories of music as pronounced in his *De Musica* also link justice to charity – with a musical accompaniment. Augustine wrote extensively on the subject of music, and his theories appear dispersed throughout treatises on the Psalms.[33] Augustine's most comprehensive treatment of music appears in his *De Musica,* a treatise written as part of a series of works, never completed, on the liberal arts, well known in the medieval period and by medieval musicians. Historians have noted its wide influence on the history of notational practice. William Waite (1954, 29) specifically discusses its relationship to the Notre Dame repertory of the twelfth century and writes: "It is this work [*De Musica*], I suggest, that provided the Notre Dame composers with the necessary system for the re-establishment of precise rhythmic values." Waite stresses that the treatise is devoted not to metrics but rather to rhythm with regard to music and words. He writes, "There can be no doubt that Augustine himself intended this work to be a treatise on rhythm as a part of music and not a treatise on metrics" (Waite 1954, 30). Waite documents the influence of Augustine on later medieval music treatises, especially Roger Bacon's *Opus Tertium* (1267). Bacon wrote that for the interpretation of Scripture "it is necessary that one should thoroughly understand the laws of meters and rhythms and it is impossible to comprehend these unless one knows the five books of Augustine's *De Musica*" (Waite 1954, 36).

Augustine's writings about music further illuminate the meaning of the small scene beneath Giotto's *Justice.*[34] In book 1, chapter 12, of the *De Musica,* Augustine notes harmony's relation to the number three: "Therefore, this great harmony is in the first three numbers. For we say one and two, and three, and nothing can be put between. But one and two themselves are three" (Augustine 1947, 198-199). Augustine also discusses music's relation to dance in this treatise, noting in book 1, chapter 12, that dancing is a representation of rhythm:

> And suppose an instrument struck in rhythm, with one sound a time's

[33]For a bibliography of music and Augustine, see McKinnon 2001, 174. For Augustine and music in the Trecento, see Brown 1984, 25-65.

[34]Giotto was already familiar with the character of Augustine, who is seen in his painting of the vault and intrados in the fourth bay of the Upper Basilica of Saint Francis of Assisi (1297-1300). Here he completed portraits of the doctors of the Church and of saints. Augustine is seated among books and dictates his words to a scribe. Though Augustine is most notably represented in iconography with books, several later portraits of him appear with music in the work of Guariento, and, in the fifteenth and sixteenth centuries, in the work of Carpaccio and Raphael.

> length and the next double repeatedly and connectedly, to make what are called iambic feet, and suppose someone dancing to it moving his limbs in time. Then could you not give the time's measure, explain the movement's intervals alternating as one to two, either in beats heard or the dancing seen?

This is striking because one often thinks of dancing as an accompaniment to rhythm, but Augustine notes that like instruments or the voice, dance may also present mercurial rhythm. Likewise, as noted by Cicero earlier, music and dance must be enjoyed in a tempered fashion because many things in singing and dancing are reprehensible, and, if we take meter from it, the most divine art becomes degraded.

The relationship between music and justice is also found in Augustine's commentaries on the Psalms. The commentary to Psalm 32 contains a long digression on the subject of justice and its relation to the Ten Commandments: "The Justice I speak of, what is she like? Who is to describe her? All things that delight the eyes derive their beauty from her; if we are to behold and embrace her, we must cleanse our hearts. We acknowledge ourselves her lovers." At the end of this long passage he exhorts the reader: "Think well on all I say and 'Give praise to the Lord on the harp, men upright of ear, sing to Him with the psaltery, the instrument of ten strings' " (Augustine 1947, 110-111).

Most relevant to Giotto's *Justice* is Augustine's complex argument relating musical properties to charity and justice. In book 6, chapter 15, and in subsequent chapters of his *De Musica*, Augustine turns to a discussion of the virtues and their relation to moderating the body's propensity for sin. Augustine notes fortitude, prudence, temperance, and justice in his discussion of how to mollify the needs of the flesh. He argues that these virtues must concern themselves with music because "these numbers [as represented by music] are pre-eminent by virtue of the beauty of their ratio" (Augustine 1947, 365).[35] One cannot avoid them because "by moving bodies they produce the sensible beauties of time" (356).[36] Interestingly, Augustine argues that the numbers of the universe are represented in bodily movements when we walk or sing, "even though they pass through us unnoticed" (370-371). Through a virtuous life of contemplation, one can learn the properties of music and other pleasurable actions without overstepping the boundaries of what is reasonable. Ultimately, though, Augustine believes that charity

[35]Augustine (1947, 172) relates number to music in his famous dictum, "Music is the science of measuring well [modulandi]."

[36]That Augustine's views about music were known in Padua at the time of Giotto can be attested to by Marchetto's quotation in his *Lucidarium*. Marchetto quotes Augustine:"Symphony, as Augustine says, 'is that concord of notes in which there is not an irrational or dissonant pitch' " (Marchetto 1985, 205).

is the strongest virtue: "For they [the people] are purified, not by flashing human reason, but by the effective and burning fire of charity" (378). In conclusion then, while Augustine does clearly relate music and the virtues, he does not specifically use music as a metaphor for community under the rule of justice.

The passages from Cicero and Augustine are salient because they clearly iterate the relation between music and justice. The direct allusion of justice to music does not appear in the writings of Aristotle, on whose philosophy Aquinas would have most relied. While the Philosopher certainly recognized the importance of a musical education in his *Politics*, music does not appear in his description of justice. Rather, Cicero's musical metaphor demonstrates Platonic influence. One of the crucial questions asked in the *Republic* is "What does Justice mean, and how can it be realized in human society?" (Plato 1941, 1) In answering the question, Plato writes repeatedly about the uses of music – specifically in relation to education.[37]

In chapter 9.4, entitled "The Aim of Education in Poetry and Music," we read that the moral qualities of good and bad may be measured in musical terms: "And absence of grace, rhythm, harmony is nearly allied to baseness of thought and expression and baseness of character; whereas their presence goes with that moral excellence and self-mastery of which they are the embodiment" (Plato 1941, 89-90). Plato then notes that music will aid a citizen in his judgment, a point reiterated by Aristotle in his *Politics*: "rhythm and harmony sink deep into the recesses of the soul and take the strongest hold there, bringing that grace of body and mind which is only to be found in one who is brought up in the right way. Moreover, a proper training in this kind makes a man quick to perceive any defect or ugliness in art or in nature" (Plato 1941, 90). A young man would therefore be better able to naturally perceive good from bad, even though reason may not yet dictate his judgment:

> Approving all that is lovely, he will welcome it home with joy into his soul and, nourished thereby, form into a man of noble spirit. All that is ugly and disgraceful he will rightly condemn and abhor while he is still too young to understand the reason; and when reason comes, he will greet her as a friend with whom his education has made him long familiar (Plato 1941, 90).

Plato relates the just person to harmony of spirit in a way that reminds us of Cicero's musical metaphor. Unlike Cicero, however, Plato focuses his comments on character: "But in reality justice, though evidently analogous to this principle, is not a matter of external behavior, but of the inward self

[37]See also Aristotle, *Politics*, book 8.

and of attending to all that is, in the fullest sense, a man's proper concern" (Plato 1941, 141-142). He follows this assertion with a musical example:

> The just man does not allow the several elements in his soul to usurp one another's functions; he is indeed one who sets his house in order, by self-mastery and discipline coming to be at peace with himself, and bringing into tune those three parts, like the terms in the proportion of a musical scale, the highest and lowest notes and the mean between them, with all the intermediate intervals (Plato 1941, 142).

Only when these parts are linked together in harmony does a person have the free will to "go about whatever he may have to do" (Plato 1941, 142). And finally, "Justice is produced in the soul, like health in the body, by establishing the elements concerned in their natural relations of control and subordination, whereas injustice is like disease and means that this natural order is inverted" (Plato 1941, 143). Here one can see the classical linkage between the two attributes as they battle one another.[38]

The three-part division espoused by Plato recalls the same in Cicero and may have influenced Giotto's choice of three dancers. The architecture bearing the figures of *Justice* and *Injustice* also supports the idea that Giotto specifically wished to emulate a classical source rather than a medieval one. His preference for the classical has been pointed out by his characterization of *Justice* as sitting on a throne with fine Gothic arches, whereas *Injustice* stands before the ramparts of a cracked and decrepit medieval castle.

Not only do classical philosophical texts, such as Cicero's, seem to be reflected in Giotto's *Justice*, but obvious precursors to the Virtues and Vices also exist in Roman art. Alistair Smart (1983, 97) notes that "Giotto's knowledge of ancient art is nowhere more apparent than in the *grisaille* frescoes of the Virtues and Vices (the themes of which go back to the *Psychomachia* of the Latin poet Prudentius)," and furthermore, that "the heroic Virtues of the Scrovegni Chapel would scarcely be conceivable without the example of Roman statuary."[39]

[38]Perhaps of some interest to the previous chapter, we note that Plato in chapter 9.3 – almost in passing – mentions the best instruments required for performance: "Our songs and airs, then, will not need instruments of large compass capable of modulation into all the modes, and we shall not maintain craftsmen to make then, in particular the flute, which has the largest compass of all. That leaves the lyre and the cithara for use in the town; and in the country the herdsmen many have some sort of pipe" (1941, 87). This is interesting because it brings to light the idea that the grouping of instruments in Giotto's *Wedding Procession* makes little sense. In Plato's description the stringed instrument is for the city and the pipes represent the shepherds.

[39]The influence of the classical style on Giotto's Scrovegni Chapel frescoes has been noted by other scholars. See, for example, Flores d'Arcais (2002, 18):"The Roman world is a fundamental constant in the Paduan cycle, and does not appear sporadically as it does

With regard to *Justice*, Smart quotes Panofsky concerning the tiny human figures standing in her scales imitating a diminutive Victory. Smart (1983, 98) argues: "That at least the Victory was derived directly from an ancient prototype seems certain: a similar image appears, for example, on the silver cup of Boscoreale as an attribute of the Emperor Augustus." As noted earlier, Giotto spent time in Rome before arriving in Padua, probably between 1285 and 1288 in the workshop of his teacher Cimabue (Flores d'Arcais 2002, 13). He was a young man at the time and greatly influenced by the classical style to which he was introduced in Rome, where he likely completed a crucifix in the Church of Aracoeli and frescoes in Santa Maria Maggiore.

Giotto raised the figure of *Justice* to a level of complexity never before seen, instilling in her a new civic sense (Zdekauer 1913, 400). Giotto's *Justice* is "queen of the virtues" in Ciceronian terms and is the only figurative example of this Virtue to wear a crown. She embodies the philosophical and intellectual pursuits that were popular in Padua during the first two decades of the fourteenth century, reflecting the scientific study of the adjudicary properties of astrology found in the work of Pietro, and representing the confidence and pride with which Padua was reviving its Roman past.

---

at Assisi.... A flowering of classical reminiscences constitutes the principal ornament of the painted architecture."

Chapter 5

Paduan Pre-humanist Influences on Giotto's Depictions of Music

In addition to the small musical scenes below *Justice* and *Injustice*, representations of music-making appear in Giotto's *Annunciation, Last Judgment, Wedding Procession*, and *Kiss of Judas* in the Scrovegni Chapel. The preponderance of musical angels and musicians in the narrative scenes has prompted Bruce Cole to call Giotto an "auditory painter" (Cole 1996, 345). What is the nature of Giotto's musical representations in the Scrovegni Chapel and in other works? This chapter will examine Giotto's representations of music-making in his frescoes and in his wood panel painting. It will be argued that Giotto may have collaborated with Marchetto in his representation of musical figures in the Scrovegni Chapel and that Marchetto's motet *Ave regina celorum* may be linked to Giotto's frescoes both in music and in text. Furthermore, it will be argued that, like contemporary Paduan pre-humanist intellectuals Pietro d'Abano and Marchetto da Padova, Giotto was influenced by Roman antecedents, in Giotto's case by vestiges of Roman architecture and musical instruments. Unlike his predecessor Cimabue, Giotto sought to replicate the actual instruments in his painting instead of painting stylized versions. Giotto's representations of music-making and the instruments themselves achieve a new degree of realism, and he infuses layers of complexity and meaning into the iconography of his musical representation.

Marchetto flourished in Padua in the years 1305-1319, and evidence suggests that he might have worked as a teacher at the Cathedral of Padua between 1305 and 1308. He completed the treatises *Lucidarium*, a survey of *musica plana* in which he divided the whole tone into five equal parts, in 1317 or 1318, and the *Pomerium*, the earliest major work to systematically consider triple and duple meters, before 1319.[1] Both treatises contributed to the establishment of the Italian notational system in the Trecento, and both were influential into the late Renaissance, prompting scholars to consider Marchetto the most important theorist between Guido of Arezzo and Tinctoris.[2]

He also composed motets, including *Ave regina celorum/ Mater innocencie/ [Ite missa est]*, which contains an acrostic of his name, MARCUM PADVANUM. F. Alberto Gallo (1985, 54) has suggested that this motet was played during the festivities for the opening of the completed Scrovegni Chapel in 1305. A second motet, *Ave corpus sanctum*, has also been attributed to Marchetto, based on its similarity in style to *Ave regina celorum.*

Scardeone's biography of Marchetto in his *Historiae de urbis Patavii* is remarkably rich and divulges heretofore unconsidered information about the composer's life and work. Scardeone notes that Marchetto was so well known and conversant in music during his time that he became the great friend of Robert of Anjou, King of Sicily (1275-1334).[3]

In the following passage we learn about Marchetto's journey to Robert's court in Naples – a new detail in Marchetto's otherwise rather obscure biography:

> It was said that he [Marchetto] was the first to provide the general principles concerning how to use tones in modulation which I understand are called enharmonics. Since he was considered learned by everyone in this field, he was invited by Robert, famous King of Sicily, who patronized all the most learned men of the time. Marchetto went to the court of Naples and there was given many praises.[4]

Furthermore, Scardeone provides an approximate time for this visit:

---

[1]Oliver Strunk (1950) amplifies on the chronology of these treatises. Marchetto's third treatise, the *Brevis compilatio,* was completed after 1318.

[2]For more on Marchetto's influence, see Gallo 1966 and Herlinger 2001.

[3]For music in the Neapolitan court in the fifteenth century, see Atlas 1985.

[4]"...qui sua aetate de Musica primus, in co modulandi genere, quod Enharmanium dici audio, praecepta generalia dedisse perhibetur. Quare cum illis temporibus magni nominis esset, et doctissimus in ea re a cunctis haberetur, invitatus a Ruberto, inclyto Sicilae rege, qui doctissimos quosque ea tempestate fovebat, Neapolim profectus est, ibidemque in eius aula multa cum laude versatus" (Scardeone 1979, 297).

> In the meantime he wrote the book "On the precepts of the art of measured music," which he named the *Pomerium*.[5]

This places Marchetto's trip to Naples before 1319, the latest possible year the *Pomerium* is believed to have been completed. In addition, it illuminates the reason – which had previously been a mystery – for the dedication of the *Pomerium* to Robert. Scardeone notes the dedication as follows:

> At the outset of the *Pomerium* we read: "to the Prince, Lord Robert by the grace of God, King of Jerusalem and of Sicily, Marchetto da Padova dedicates this humble work."

Scardeone writes that Marchetto "was, therefore, close to Robert at one time, as Timothy was close to Alexander; Marchetto had learned how to calm and excite the sentiments of the king to the point that Robert liked to vary the sound and rhythm of songs."[6] His association with the king of Sicily places Marchetto in the artistic milieu of the most famous artists and writers of Italy – among them Boccaccio and Petrarch. Both Marchetto and Giotto were favorites of the king.[7]

Archival documents from Naples provide evidence that Giotto received payments from the king between 1328 and 1333. One such document, dated January 20, 1330, includes Robert's decree that Giotto is a "painter familiar and faithful to ourselves." Flores d'Arcais (1995, 348) suggests that Giotto may have been summoned to Naples to decorate the Church of Santa Chiara, though only a few fragments of his works in Naples have survived.

Comments in his *Lucidarium* attest to the notion that Marchetto was familiar with the latest developments in painting. He cites book 2 of Aristotle's *Physica* in explaining that art should imitate nature as closely as possible, that the painter should strive to paint a horse or a lily so that it resembles the object "in nature."[8] Marchetto's use of the phrase "in nature" is significant because it epitomizes the "new" painting style that flourished

---

[5]"Scripsit iaterim De praeceptis artis Musice mensuratae librum, quem Pomarium nominavit" (Scardeone 1979, 297).

[6]"Fuit is igitur apud Rubertum, ut Timotheus olim apud Alexandrum: qui remittere et excitare norat regis affectus, prout variare cantum, vocisque modos sibi placebat" (Scardeone 1979, 297).

[7]Robert of Anjou's connection to music is further illuminated by a dedication to him in a musical manuscript from Prato. For more on the manuscript, see Pescerelli 1991, 173-179. Robert placed a high priority on justice during his reign, citing Aristotle frequently in his sermons. On Robert and the arts, see Kelly 2003, 133-192.

[8]This passage is translated in Gallo 1985, 115-116. "... ars imitatur naturam in quantum potest (per Phylosophum, secundo Physicorum). Probatio per exemplum: nam qui depingit lilium vel equum, nititur ipsa depingere in quantum potest ad similitudinem equi seu lilii naturalis" (Da Padova 1961, 50).

during the first decades of the fourteenth century. Painters began to depict real objects from nature as opposed to stylized versions. Trees, birds, and animals were painted with a freshness that imitated their appearance in the countryside.

The Florentine Giotto was the greatest practitioner of this style.[9] Giotto's fame in this regard was already widespread in the Trecento, as confirmed by the following excerpt from Boccaccio's *Decameron* (1348-1350):

> Giotto was a man of such outstanding genius that there was nothing in the whole of creation that he could not depict with his stylus, pen, or brush. And so faithful did he remain to Nature (who is the mother and the motive force of all created things, via the constant rotation of the heavens), that whatever he depicted had the appearance, not of a reproduction, but of the thing itself, so that one very often finds, with the works of Giotto, that people's eyes are deceived and they mistake the picture for the real thing (Boccaccio 1972, 494).

The new notational system outlined by Marchetto in his *Lucidarium* and *Pomerium*, in which duple meter is given the same importance as triple, with "tails" added to notes in order for the written notation to best imitate sound, is groundbreaking and quintessential to the understanding of Marchetto and his connection to a similar trend in painting. Prior to the developments of the Ars Nova in Paris and in Padua, the Franconian system was employed. Because of notational limitations, however, this system could not capture the subtleties of newer metric division. While the Franconian system influenced Marchetto, he went much further, describing perfect and imperfect time and demonstrating that the breve could be divided into two to twelve semibreves in perfect time and into two to eight semibreves in imperfect time (Herlinger 2001, 827).

Marchetto's notational theories allowed the composer to capture the sounds on paper more exactly, as a more accurate reflection of nature. He did this by introducing "tails" to notes to differentiate them in length.[10]

Marchetto's knowledge of the development of realism in art and his parallel contribution to this trend in his own notational theory suggest a connection to Giotto, who was the foremost practitioner of this new art and in Padua when Marchetto was active. Furthermore, Marchetto's motet *Ave regina celorum/ Mater innocencie* displays compositional links to Giotto's

[9] For Giotto's attention to nature, see Stubblebine 1985, 89-90, and Oertel 1966, 86-89.

[10] "Cum igitur ipsae notae scriptae ad artem musicae pertineant, licet ipsa musica de se sit accepta scientia, oportuit ergo quod proprietates additae notis ipsis, scriptis propter necessitatem modi tradendi, adderentur eisdem secundum perfectiones repertas ab ipso homine, qui instituit talem artem. In homine autem primo et principaliter invenitur dextrum et sinistrum" (Da Padova 1961, 14).

frescoes.[11] Marchetto's knowledge of these frescoes is significant because if we accept Gallo's dating of the *Ave regina celorum* motet (1305), Marchetto's text would be the earliest description of Giotto's painting in history.[12]

Furthermore, it will be argued that Marchetto may have played a role in the *pentimento*, or over-painting, in the representation of music in the fresco *Wedding Procession*. A discussion of Marchetto's reliance on classical writing about music, as confirmed in his *Lucidarium* and *Pomerium*, will serve as a bridge between the frescoes and earlier medieval views on the role of music.

The exploration of these connections between artist and composer illuminates a new musical chapter in the already rich cultural legacy of Padua. Marchetto will be viewed not only as an influential theorist and composer but as a philosopher in step with the latest developments in pre-humanist thought in Padua as exemplified by his contemporaries, the distinguished Paduan poet and friend of Dante, Lovato Lovati, and the playwright and statesman Alessandro Mussato.[13] Marchetto's reliance on Aristotle's *Physica* in his musical theory is part of the tapestry of classical influences found in Padua at the turn of the Trecento. These classical influences are found in Giotto's painting, as argued by Alistair Smart (1983, 96), and may explain why Giotto was the first painter to include secular musicians as decorative motifs in his fresco painting.

Giotto's Scrovegni Chapel frescoes represent the pinnacle of his achievements and are arguably the most important series of paintings in the history of the pre-Renaissance.[14] They consist of scenes dedicated to the story of Joachim and Anna, the life of the Virgin, the life of Christ, the Passion, and the Last Judgment; fourteen personifications of Virtues and Vices placed within imitation polished marble niches below the lowest register of frescoes on the side walls of the Chapel; decorative medallions; and border pictures.

[11] F. Alberto Gallo (1974) has hypothesized that the theorist wrote the motet *Ave Maria celorum/ Mater innocentia* for the opening ceremonies of the chapel in 1305. He proposed this because of the acrostic of Marchetto's name in the duplum of the piece and the anacrostic of Gabriel's announcement to the Virgin, *Ave Maria, grazia plena*, in the *triplum*.

[12] The earliest known literary reference to Giotto's frescoes in the Scrovegni Chapel appear in Francesco da Barberino's *Documenti d'Amore* (c. 1308-1312), which mentions the figure of Envy: "Inimica: inimicatur enim patientibus eam unde Invidiosus invidia comburitur intus et extra hanc padue in arena optime pinsit Giottus" (Barberino 1912, 165). ("Animosity: it suffers this, indeed, with endurance, as where Envy is consumed inside and out with enviousness – this painted excellently in the Scrovegni at Padua"). Translation found in Stubblebine 1969, 109.

[13] For an overview of early humanism in Trecento Padua, see Hyde 1966, 283-311.

[14] For the history of and commentary on the Scrovegni Chapel, see Salvini 1953 and Basile 1993.

The principal narrative scenes concern the Virgin and are distributed in three rows on each side of the chapel (Fig. 5.1).

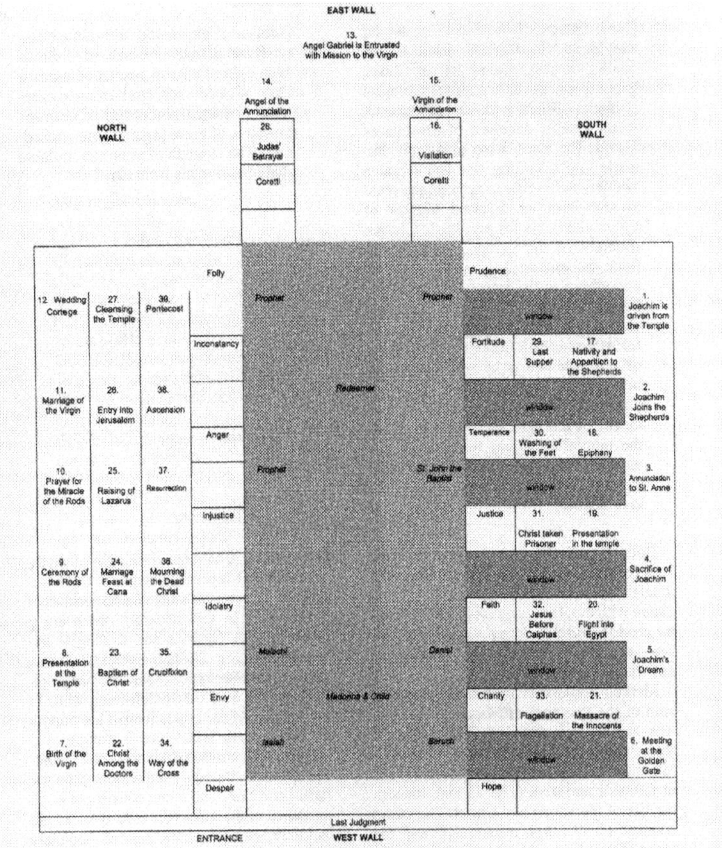

Figure 5.1: **Diagram of Giotto's frescos in the Scrovegni Chapel**

The left wall (north side) contains three rows of six scenes each, while the right wall (south side) contains two groups of five scenes and one of six scenes. Five scenes are painted on the back wall (east side), among them the *Annunciation*, the most prominent of all and the namesake of the chapel. The total number of frescoes that concern the principal biblical narrative of the three walls – north, east, and south – is thirty-nine. These scenes are easily counted because each is contained within a border of geometrically painted frames. The *Annunciation* on the back wall is the only scene that breaks this tightly knit compartmentalization in that it covers the entire arched surface of the back wall and is divided into an upper and lower portion (Baccheschi 1966, 100-101).

That the asymmetrical number of scenes shifts between six and five is unusual and is a direct result of the architecture of the building. Six windows line the south side, while none exist on the opposite side. The southern light furnishes the best light for the illumination of the frescoes, and it seems that Giotto himself may have designed the architecture of the chapel to ensure the optimum surfaces for his paintings. In addition, the bare nature of the inside, which Stubblebine has called "a skin of blank walls" and lacks columns, pilasters, niches, and other architectural embellishments, is particularly suited to frescoes, creating a kind of "viewing box" (Stubblebine 1969,74).

Significant similarities arise when comparing the structure of Marchetto's motet *Ave regina celorum* and the numerical framework of Giotto's frescoes (Fig. 5.2).

Marchetto's motet makes allusions to the 39 scenes that directly concern the life of the Virgin as represented in Giotto's narrative. Strikingly, Marchetto's motet consists of 39 *longa* measures.[15] In addition, the tenor of the piece, which seems to be newly composed, displays a curious juxtaposition of the numbers 6 and 5. The talia of the tenor measures 6 and consists of 5 pitches.[16] In the facsimile we note that there are 5 pitches – three in ligature and two *longa* – between rests. The grouping in the chapel is the same: Giotto has painted 3 groups of 6 scenes on the left hand wall, and on the opposite wall, another top row of 6 scenes beneath which are 2 groups consisting of 5 pictures each. As noted earlier, this curious juxtaposition of numbers is necessitated by the windows on the left-hand side. The motet consists of 6 x 6 measures of the talia (the color consists of 18 measures) resulting in the number 36. Marchetto then concludes the piece with 3 measures whose tenor contains a kind of cadence and whose upper voices slow down in time, adopting the slower movement of the tenor.

How de we account for the last 3 extra measures? There are several explanations. Marchetto needed the musical time for practical reasons; namely, to finish setting the text of his poem – a subject to be investigated in more detail – which contains the acrostic of his name in the duplum. Perhaps these measures allude directly to the scene of the *Annunciation* on the rear wall. Although Giotto created a space for five scenes, only three actual narratives have been painted. These are the *Annunciation, Judas's*

[15]For Gallo (1974, 48) the count is 39.

[16]For a discussion of the structure, a facsimile, and an edition of Marchetto's motet, see Gallo 1974, 48-49 and 54-56.

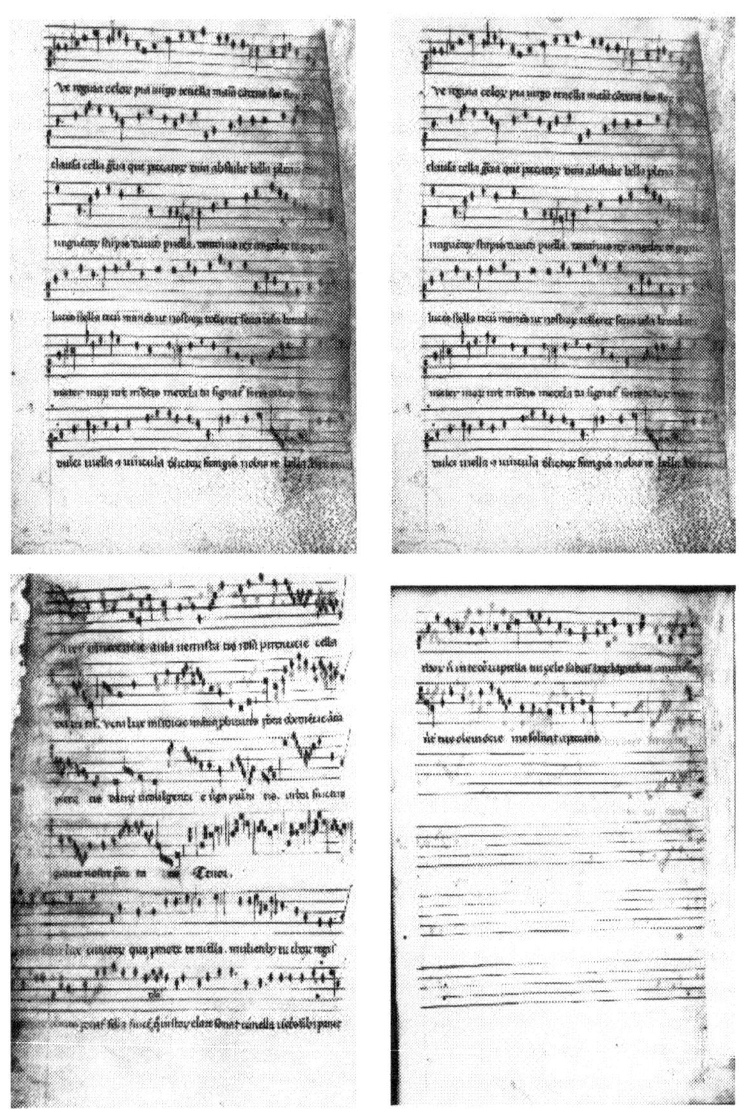

Figure 5.2: **Marchetto da Padova, *Ave regina celorum/ Mater innoncenicie*: Oxford Bodleian Library, Ms. Canon. Class. Lat. 112, ff.61v, 62r, 62v.**

Betrayal, and the *Visitation.* The other two niches contain architectural spaces called coretti (concealed chapels). These have been described as "illusions of the transept that was never constructed" (Baccheschi 1966, 106).

Marchetto may have deemed these scenes to be unimportant and therefore not included them in his own count. The scenes included in our count (and Marchetto's 39) are those with which the viewer is directly confronted when entering the small chapel.

Marchetto's motivation for mirroring the fresco in his motet may be understood in the context of his concern – explained in the beginning of this chapter – for the reproduction of music as if captured from reality. In this case, Marchetto not only reproduces on paper the notes he wishes his musicians to sing, but in a visual-musical play, echoes Giotto's complex matrix of frescoes. Therefore, Marchetto's notation reproduces Giotto's frescoes as if from "nature." Indeed, this kind of interdisciplinary work is not unique in this time in Padua. Giotto's paintings inspired a miniaturist to decorate an antiphoner for the Cathedral of Padua. A musical manuscript dating from c. 1306 contains illuminations based on Giotto's frescoes.[17]

In addition, as has already been pointed out and despite the fact that the original frescoes no longer exist, it is believed that Giotto probably decorated the walls of the Salone della Ragione following the program of Pietro. The monumental impact of Giotto's frescoes was felt by generations of Paduan artists, who imitated the paintings in the Scrovegni Chapel, placing Padua at the forefront of Italian painting.

The influence of Giotto's images on Marchetto's composition are further demonstrated in the text of Marchetto's motet. The *triplum* and *duplum* read as follows:

> *Triplum*: Rejoice, Queen of the Heavens, tender and pious Virgin Mary, white flower among flowers, sealed celle of Christ, grace that relieved the sinners of cruel struggles. Filled with the perfume of sweet smells, daughter of the line of David. The Lord, King of Angels, has made you a shining star and remains within you in order to rip off the cruel arrows from us. Blessed Mother of virtue, medicine for our death. Chosen fountain of the garden, you sweetly have the manna. In you the light of everything is lit, from you I take the honey. For the women you lead the chorus with a suave *viella* [fiddle] and for us you break the rebellious chains of sins. Blessed is he who drinks the bile for us, sweet fruit with which it plays with clarity, *the cimella* [chalumeau] of the just. In you he prepares the nuptial bed, and there is no immorality. Of the love for you the small and humble some shall languish.

[17]For more, see Bellinati 1974, 23-30.

Duplum: Mother of innocence, hall of beauty. Rose of chastity, cell of divinity. True light of charity, manna of honesty. Door of obedience, ark [maybe tomb] of mercy. Bestower of indulgence, rod of chastity. Fruit tree of grace [against] our wickedness. The strength of your mercifulness shall absolve me from sins.

Triplum
AVE regina celorum,
pia virgo tenella.
MARIA candens flos florum,
Christi(que) clausa cella
GRACIA que peccatorum
dira abstulit bella.
PLENA odore unguentorum,
stirpis David puella.
DOMINUS, rex angelorum
Te gignit, lucens stella.
TECUM manens ut nostrorum
tolleret seva tela.
BENEDICTA mater morum,
nostre mortis medela.
TU signatus fons ortorum,
manna (das dulcinella,
IN te lucet) lux cunctorum
quo promo de te mella.
MULIERIBUS tu chorum
regis dulci viella,
ET vincula delictorum
frangis nobis rebella.
BENE(DICTUS futurorum
ob nos) potatus fella.
FRUCTUS dulcis quo iustorum
clare sonat cimella.
VENTRIS sibi parat thorum
nec in te corruptella.
TUI zelo febris horum
languescat animella.

Duplum (M)ater innocencie,
Aula venustatis,
Rosa pudicicie,
Cella deitatis.
Vera lux mundicie,
Manna probatis.
Porta obediencie,
Arca pietatis.
Datrix indulgencie,
Virga puritatis.
Arbor fructus gracie,
Nostre pravitatis.
Virtus tue clementie
Me solvat a peccatis.[18]

Marchetto lays claim to the composition of this piece by including his name in the first letters of each line of the *duplum*. The acrostic is the text's most striking characteristic. The *triplum* contains Gabriel's salutation to the Virgin Mary (Luke 1:28). Gallo has noted the theme of the *Annunciation* in this text and suggests that the motet was composed for the opening ceremonies of the chapel on March 25, 1305. This day marked the Feast Day of the Annunciation and was traditionally celebrated in the city of Padua with great pomp and circumstance. Paduans took to the streets for

[18]Note the acrostic of Marchetto's name in the first letters of each line.

a grand processional, and a dramatic office was held in the Virgin's honor.[19]

Selvatico writes that secular music was also heard on this day, with citizens coming to the Scrovegni to hear jongleurs and play games.[20] Yet to be discussed in the literature is the fact that the text includes another allusion to the Virgin, which links the motet directly to Giotto's frescoed walls. The *triplum*, which extols the virtues of the Virgin, contains several references to music, and I maintain that the text is an early musical/textual description of Giotto's painting the *Wedding Procession* (Fig. 5.3).

The *Wedding Procession* appears on the left-hand wall, on the top tier, just to the left of the *Annunciation*. Art historians have extolled the scene as a capolavoro, praising Giotto's representation of the calm and exquisite movements of the Virgin Mary (Gnudi 1959, 138). The scene is multidimensional in time. One action consists of Mary and her attending ladies coming upon a group of musicians. The second action depicts the musicians, who were playing their instruments before the women arrived.[21]

One man plays a vielle while two blow into wind instruments. The musicians are clad in classical garb, wearing short, draping tunics and wreaths on their heads. The upper part of the picture has been badly damaged, and what remains is a balcony with a large leafy branch, a sign of the Virgin's forthcoming pregnancy.[22]

The description of the wind players has been recently reevaluated after a restoration in the 1960s, when a cleaning revealed the outline of two long trumpets, the same kind of instruments that appear blown by angels in the figures surrounding God in the *Annunciation*, to which we will return.[23]

---

[19]The music and texts of the office are edited and printed in fascimile by Vecchi 1954. The date of the first celebration has been widely debated. Archival evidence notes that it took place as early as 1278 and continued until the 1600s. For documents concerning this debate, see Zannocco 1937, 370-373.

[20]". . . se simpegnava di render più splendida codesta festività coi canti dei trovatori, coi giuochi dei giullari, e con tutte quelle baldorie e gazzarre che più poteano a què dì riuscir, gradite alle moltitudini" (Selvatico 1870, 26).

[21]In the *Republic* 1941, 263, Plato describes the "nuptial number" derived from 33+43+53=216 or the gestation period of a human child. Add 3x4x5=60 for a nine-month-old child. These numbers are prominent in Giotto's scene: there are 3 musicians + Mary=4, and 3 musicians + 2 male onlookers=5; 7 Virgins are represented in the numbers 3+4.

[22]Baccheschi (1966, 100) lists two basic descriptions that have been given to the action: (1) Mary and the seven other virgins are escorted by temple servants to the high priest so that he may give them the precious materials used in making a new curtain for the temple. On the way the maidens encounter three musicians and pause to listen. (2) The scene is concerned with the newly married couple, Mary and Joseph, as they make their way to their new home escorted by serving maids and musicians. One plays the vielle while two appear to be blowing into small wind instruments.

[23]For more on the restoration of the frescoes, see Colabich, Prosdocimi, and Saccomani 1964.

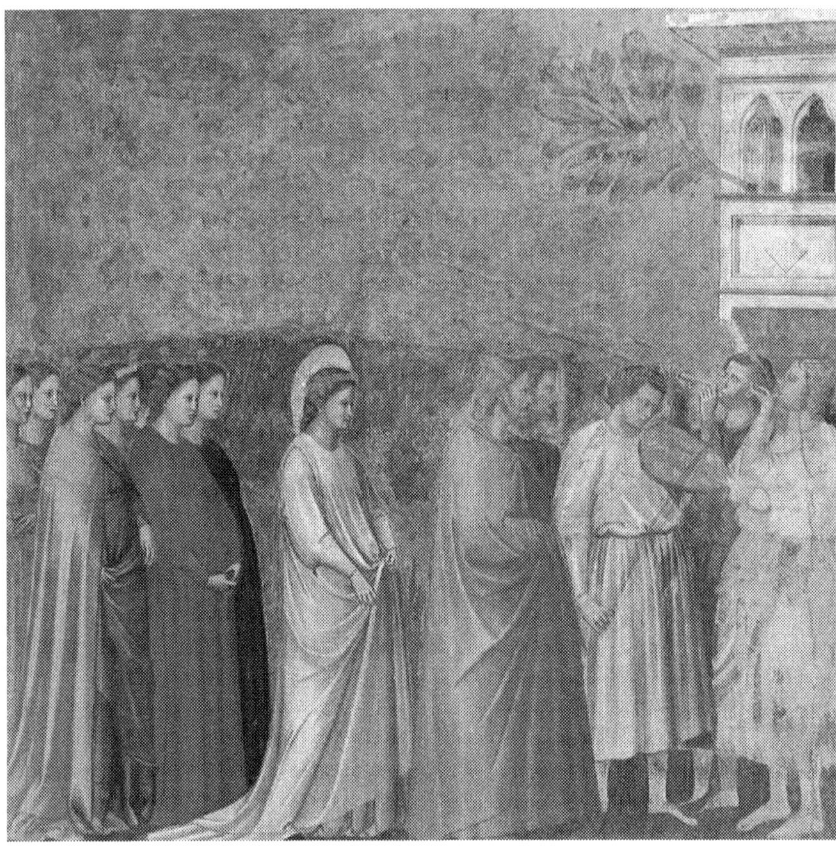

Figure 5.3: ***Wedding Procession.*** **Padua, Scrovegni Chapel.**

Note that the two players' heads are tilted upward. This indicates that Giotto first intended them to play trumpets, long instruments that were often tilted just past horizontal. Recorder, or shawm, players were more comfortably depicted with their heads tilted slightly downward. See, for example, Simone Martini's recorder player in the Assisi Chapel. At some point, Giotto made a change to more muted instruments. This *pentimento* by Giotto indicates that he may have wanted, in retrospect, to mirror in his choice of instruments Mary's supremely calm demeanor in the scene. The prominent vielle, or basso, instrument certainly suggests that he did.

Giotto made numerous changes to his Scrovegni Chapel frescoes. Tintori and Meiss (1962) document alterations, in among others, the *Expulsion of*

Joachim from the Temple, the *Nativity*, and the *Wedding Procession*. In addition, Giuseppe Basile (2002, 33) notes a *pentimento* associated with music in the painting of the two angel musicians in the right corner of the *Mission of the Annunciation to Mary*. It appears that originally Giotto had intended to depict an angel blowing into a long-barreled trumpet; one can see faint outlines of such a trumpet. The trumpet was replaced by an angel blowing more horizontally into a shortened instrument. The *pentimenti* were completed with the application of new plaster (*intonaco*), or they were added after the plaster had dried (*secco*).

At least one change in the *Wedding Procession* has been noted by Tintori and Meiss (1962, 165) in the clothing of the figure seen walking ahead of the Madonna. They note that Giotto wanted to maintain a sense of movement by making the lower hem of the figure's garments incline upward to the right, which he achieved by painting in background color and adding a flowing red line from the bottom left up to the knee level. Thus he turned a heavy cape into a light mantle. The same change to a lighter, airier, and more appropriate mood is achieved by painting higher wind instruments as opposed to long trumpets. The *secco* painting was done with water paints, which dissolve easily, accounting for the visible outlines of the trumpets once the fresco was cleaned.

Several reasons may be posited for Giotto's initial decision to represent trumpets. It is widely believed that the painter probably witnessed the famous Paduan festivities of the Feast Day of the Annunciation to the Virgin Mary.[24] This assumption is based on the fact that the fresco displays a compositional structure recalling the placement of the Virgin and the angel Gabriel in compartments from which they spoke the lines of the dramatic office. Trumpets were traditionally used in the processionals in Padua, as the following description indicates:

> The angel and Maria were placed on two chairs arranged for the purpose and were carried to the Scrovegni, preceded by the trumpeters of the commune and the Paduan clergy, and followed by the mayor with all the citizens and with the heads of the arts.... In the courtyard of the Scrovegni, the angel was to greet Maria with an angelic salutation. All of this without any expense whatsoever to the commune or the monks: on this day the trumpeters of the commune and the public servants were to play the trumpets and play accompaniment to the angel and Maria from the Palace to the Scrovegni without payment or reward of any sort....[25]

[24] Brunelli 1925, 100-109. Brunelli notes that the angel and Mary are placed in "luoghi deputati," or special theatrical chambers, used in Giotto's dramatic representation of the Annunciation in Padua.

[25] "...sopra due cattedre a ciò destinate, montavano l'angelo e Maria, e così veni-

Trumpets also signified announcements and were intended to elicit the attention of the crowd. A Paduan chronicle of 1293, for example, describes a *gonfalone*, each of whom had his own salaried trumpeter preceding him during processions or public outings.[26] We also note that it was traditional for trumpets to be sounded after the doctors of the university were awarded their degrees (Carpenter 1972, 37-38). These traditions could have inspired Giotto's choice of trumpets.

In addition to their visual signification, Giotto may have chosen the trumpets for a compositional reason: to establish a recurring motif. The long lines of the trumpets echo the lines in architecture that permeate the entire fresco cycle. Trumpets also appear in the *Annunciation* (where, interestingly, several also seem truncated) and in the *Last Judgment*, where they are played by angels. As we shall see in frescoes by Cimabue, angels playing trumpets were often included in Last Judgment scenes. Emanuel Winternitz (1967, 30) notes that musical angels, other than those found in apocalyptic scenes, became commonplace with the popularity of legends of the saints and stories of the Virgin, such as the Assumption and the Coronation, subjects that in the future will receive large ensembles of angel orchestras. In choosing to truncate the trumpets, not only in the *Wedding Procession* but also in the *Annunciation*, Giotto has softened the tone of the scene to better fit the solemnity of the depictions. Interestingly, and as an aside, noisy wedding celebrations were viewed as public nuisances in the late thirteenth century. Giuseppe Gennari recounts that a decree was made concerning the "accompagnamento delle spose novelle" (Gennari 1804, 24). He recounts that it was a very old tradition that parents and friends accompany the bride to the house of her husband. This was done with great festivity, with "suoni e di canti," but causing commotion and confusion among the citizenry and presenting a hazard for the public. Therefore, in 1277 it was ordained by law that no more than twenty people per side of the family were allowed to march in procession during such occasions. He comments that it was a "wise order" because "such large gatherings could be perceived as a threat to the state" ("Saggio ordinamento, perchè le adunanze troppo numerose potevano essere sospette di macchinazione contro lo stato," 24). Is it possible that Marchetto, the most prominent musician-composer of

---

vano portati fino all'Scrovegni, precedendo i tubatori del comune e il clero padovano, e seguendo il signor prodestà con tutti i cittadini e con i gastaldoni delle arti.... Nel cortile dell'Scrovegni l'angelo doveva salutare Maria con la salutazione angelica. Tutto ciò senza nessuna spesa del comune o dei' monaci: i tubatori del comune e i publici salariati dovevano in questo giorno suonare le trombe, e suonando accompagnare l'angelo e Maria dal palazzo all'Scrovegni senza paga ne premio di' sorta ec" (Dall'Acqua 1842, 104-105).

[26]"Ogni gonfalone aveva i suoi trombettieri salariati, che nelle processioni o nelle comparse pubbliche lo precedevano" (Gennari 1804, 70).

Padua, was witness to the completion of the frescoes and may have counseled Giotto against the trumpets, suggesting something softer, more civic minded?

A fascinating parallel example of truncated trumpets appears in the Barrile Chapel in the Church of San Lorenzo in Naples. In a fresco by the school of Giovanni Barrile, we find a scene of the *Wedding of the Virgin.* In the center Mary and Joseph are wed, witnessed by virgins and friends of the groom. They stand in front of two structures, one round and one square. Between the buildings and the couple are two figures blowing into trumpets. We can still discern the outline of the trumpets on the face of the rounded building. As noted, both Marchetto and Giotto were at one time in Naples. In both the Scrovegni Chapel and the Naples example, long-barrel trumpets do not seem appropriate for the scene.[27]

A comparison of Marchetto's *triplum* of *Ave regina celorum* and Giotto's *Wedding Procession* reveals some striking similarities not heretofore mentioned in the literature that shed light on the mystery. The text is a deeply felt laud of the Virgin Mary and speaks directly of the nuptial bed, placing it in the same part of the Virgin's narrative as in Giotto's fresco. Gallo (1974, 47) notes that the *triplum* is an amalgamation of two principal chants, the antiphons *Ave regina gratia plena* and *Benedicta tu in mulieribus.* As perplexing is Mary's direct association with musical attributes. First we note that in line 8 the author describes her as a direct descendant of the line of David.[28]

Marchetto takes this theme from Luke, where we read that Joseph is a direct descendant of the line of David. This lineage is significant because David is the leading musical figure in the Middle Ages, the one most abundantly represented with musical instruments. The figure of David playing stringed instruments was generated in the Middle Ages most predominantly in the Psalters and medieval Psalm commentaries. In early medieval illu-

[27]Taddeo Gaddi also included two long-barreled trumpets in his *Wedding of the Virgin* in the Baroncelli Chapel in Santa Croce in Florence c.1328-1330. Unlike Giotto's *Wedding Procession* in the Scrovegni Chapel, the two trumpets appear on the left side of the picture following the wedding party, accompanied by a bagpipe and portative organ. The placement of the trumpet also seems to have been changed: an outline of a longer second trumpet appears below the topmost trumpet. See also two trumpet players in the *Wedding of the Virgin,* dated 1375, a panel of a polyptych in the Collegiata di Santa Maria in Impruneta (with varying attributions to Niccolò di Pietro Gerini, Tommaso del Mazza, and Pietro Nelli) and in Agnolo Gaddi's *Wedding of the Virgin,* painted in 1392-1394, in the Cappella della Sacra Cintola in the Cathedral of Prato. Not all wedding scenes after Giotto include trumpets; for example, we see a woman playing a psaltery in the Rinuccini Chapel of Santa Croce in Florence c. 1365.

[28]In Luke 1:26-27 we read, "In the sixth month the angel Gabriel was sent from God to a city of Galille named Nazareth, to a virgin bethrothed to a man whose name was Joseph, of the house of David: and the virgin's name was Mary."

mination we find examples of David playing his psaltery surrounded by musicians. For instance, in the *Vespasian Psalter* – the older surviving copy of the so-called Roman version of the Psalms, dated from the second quarter of the eighth century – David sits on a throne with four trumpet players at his feet.[29] This motif may be seen as a precursor to the many musical coronation scenes found much later. Augustine, of whom we will say more later, was particularly responsible for dispersing images of music in the Psalms through his extensive and beautiful discussions of the allegorical meanings of each instrument. The choice of David rather than another descendant seems particularly relevant here as a measure of Mary's musical lineage.

Lines 19-20 of Marchetto's *triplum* are particularly eye-opening. We read: "MULIERIBUS tu chorum regis dulci viella." The mention of the *viella* is particularly significant since this identical instrument appears in the Giotto painting. In addition, Marchetto mentions that the vielle leads a chorus of women, which parallels Giotto's Mary leading a chorus of virgins. Though Mary does not actually do the playing (she is never portrayed playing musical instruments in her iconography), she appears as a conduit, so to speak, for the harmony of the music played by the instrumentalists. It is through Mary that the virgins hear the music of the vielle and are ruled by its strains. This interpretation is further clarified by Mary's placement in the center of the scene as an intermediary between the players and the chorus of virgins. She guides them by the metaphor of her implied music, just as it is through her that the good qualities extolled in Marchetto's poem are experienced on earth. This may account for her placid demeanor, which has traditionally been viewed as musical by Gnudi (1959, 142). Music has traditionally been allied with virginity in the medieval period. Revelations 14:1-5 provides the Christian source for this belief. In a description of the Lamb on Mount Sion, the Bible reads:

> And I heard a voice from heaven like the sound of many waters and like the sound of loud thunder; the voice I heard was like the sound of harpers playing on their harps, and they sing a new song before the throne and before the four living creatures and before the elders. No one could learn that song except the hundred and forty-four thousand who had been redeemed from the earth. It is these who have not defiled themselves with women, for they are chaste; it is these who follow the Lamb wherever he goes.

Two pertinent images relating to Giotto's fresco appear in this passage. First, the chaste followers who can hear the song of God are reminiscent

[29] Backhouse 1997, 15. The illumination originates from England, Canterbury, Cotton MS Vespasian A. i, f.30b.

of the group of virgins following Mary in the *Wedding Procession.* Thomas Connolly has noted that the virgins sing a kind of "inner" song, one that is not heard. Quoting the *Passio* of the Roman virgin Saint Cecilia, we find that she "sang in her heart to God alone."[30] The "new song" will help to clarify why it is not Mary who plays the vielle in Giotto's fresco and why she nevertheless leads the choir of virgins with the *viella* in Marchetto's poem.

The notion of the "new song" versus the "old song" originates from the Psalms. Numerous lines contain an exhortation for the believers to sing a new song. For example, in Psalm 32 (the Hebrew/Reformed Psalm 33) we read, "Praise the Lord on the cithara, sing to him with the psaltery of ten strings! Sing to him a new song, sing to him well" (lines 2-3). Christian commentators on the Psalms, most notably Augustine, have devised intricate allegorical interpretations of the music in these poems and have translated the presence of singing and musical instruments into Christian doctrine. Therefore we read Augustine's explanation of Psalm 33: "Divest yourself of what is old; you have learnt a new song. A new man, a new testament, a new song."[31] The "new song" becomes linked with celestial melody, while the old is linked with melodies of the flesh (Robertson 1963, 127-132). In addition, Psalm illuminators included images of the difference between the old and new song in their texts. Raucous musicians in unsavory demeanors with tumbling dancing figures were shown with the old, and calm, serious, and pious demeanors with the new.[32] In Giotto's fresco, then, we are reminded of the women's chastity and their keen connection to the music in heaven. With their calm demeanors they represent the "new song." In this light, however, though Mary is often depicted as the leader of the virginal choir, the mention of the *viella* is still unique and further solidifies the relationship between Marchetto's words and Giotto's picture.

Scholars have noted the connection between the vielle player and Christ. The stringed instrument has been linked to the lyre, the principal instrument of Apollo on Parnassus. Apollo is subsequently aligned with Christ because he "could well be employed [by Christians] as a personification of justice, both as god of music which, like justice, reduces strife and discord to harmony, and as the god of the sun," as Christ was the figure of light and healing (Edwards 1988, 22).[33] The notion of justice and music continues in

[30]Connolly 1980, 19. Connolly (1983, 129) notes that Saint Cecilia, the famous virgin of Rome, was depicted with instruments beginning in the fourteenth century with a statue by the Master of Saint Anastasia (c. 1325) in the Museo Castelvecchio of Verona.

[31]Translation of commentary and text of Psalm 32 in Cattin 1984, 162-163.

[32]See, for example, the Psalter from the Abbey of Saint Remigius, Reims (12 c.). Cambridge. Saint John's College, MS B 18, fols. I, 182, reproduced in Robertson 1963 plate 29, 30.

[33]The allusion to Giotto's viellist and Christ, however, could just as easily be made if

the musical reference in lines 25-26, "FRUCTUS dulcis quo iustorum clare sonat cimella," where the *cimella* represents the "just." As we have seen, justice is one of the central themes of the Chapel frescoes: it is central to the painting of the *Last Judgment* on the back wall, in which trumpeting angels border the seated Christ in Judgment. In unprecedented iconography, Giotto painted the seated *Justice* above a marble-like predella containing three women: one plays the tambourine, one sings, while a third dances. The link between music and justice is clear in Giotto's fresco. Could Marchetto's motet be further evidence of this connection?

Verses 25-26 of Marchetto's *Ave regina celorum* contain a second interesting allusion to Giotto. Marchetto mentions the *cimella* in Latin, which translates to *ciaramella* in Italian, "chalumeau" in English.[34] The instruments found in the *Wedding Procession* may be viewed as small, single-reed instruments, though certainly not bagpipes. Upon close scrutiny of the scene, one notes that the third musician does not have the instrument at his lips but seems poised to play, while his companions are playing. This may account for the singular *cimella* in the text. Notably, Marchetto does not mention trumpets at all, but rather the "new" instruments painted by Giotto in the fresco. In fact it is difficult to make out the smaller reed instruments. They seem to be an invention, to fit the existing outlines created by the shortened trumpets. This has interesting implications. It is certainly plausible that Marchetto, who enjoyed the distinguished reputation of philosopher and greatest musician in Padua, may have inspected the frescoes (or been asked for his opinion) and perhaps suggested to Giotto that the trumpets might not be appropriate for the scene. Tintori and Meiss confirm that Giotto painted in the traditional manner, from top to bottom, so the *Wedding Procession* would have certainly been completed during the earliest phase of painting,[35] early enough for Marchetto to suggest changes and write his motet text. Indeed, the artists Giotto and Marchetto are linked in history because of their contributions to the splendor of the Scrovegni Chapel, the former in painting, the latter in music. They must also both have been familiar with the Annunciation festivities that took place in Padua each March 25th, as was noted earlier.

Musical instruments are also present in Giotto's two-tiered *Annunciation* fresco. The scene is divided into two parts: the upper, which has also been called a "Heavenly Prologue," is a representation of Heaven and the Eternal

---

the figure is read as Orpheus, who was able, with the sound of his instrument, to resurrect the dead.

[34]On the chalumeau, see Shackleton 1980, 111.

[35]Tintori and Meiss (1962, 160) explain, "The overlapping of the patches of intonaco prove beyond any question that on both nave walls as well as on the triumphal arch Giotto worked in the normal and practical sequence from top to down."

Father, surrounded by legions of angels, decreeing that the event will take place, while the second level captures the occasion on earth (Baccheschi 1966, 100). In Giotto's sequence of frescoes, this scene occurs just after the *Wedding Procession.* The angel Gabriel appears kneeling with open mouth on the left, while Mary receives his words with closed lips on the right. God is surrounded by legions of angels, some of whom play instruments. Under closer consideration, we note that in the left background two angels play lute and tambourine, mirrored by two angels playing psaltery and cymbals in the right foreground. Others appear to be singing. In the right foreground, an angel plays a trumpet, also seemingly shortened as in the *Wedding Procession*, while a second angel plays what Howard Mayer Brown (1985, 214) has described as a double recorder. The choice of instruments reflects an array typical of medieval angel choirs. Marchetto acknowledges the image of the angel choir in the first part of his *Lucidarium* when he quotes Remigius as writing: "The vastness of music encompasses all that lives and all that does not live; thus the choir of all the angels, archangels, and saints sings without end, chanting 'Sanctus, Sanctus' before the eyes of God."[36]

Marchetto was familiar with the classification of sound into three general groups, all of which are represented in Giotto's picture. He describes them in book 1, chapters 7 and 13, of his *Lucidarium* as three "species of music" (Herlinger 1985, 89). The first is designated as "harmonic music," produced by the voice of human beings or animals. This music is created by the "sound of air set in vibration by the breath" (Herlinger 1985, 91). The second is "organic" music, which is produced not by the voice but by the breath of humans, as in "trumpets," and then he mentions the instruments "*cimellis*, pipes, organs and the like" (Herlinger 1985, 97). Note that here he cites the same instrument (*cimella*) that appears to be what Howard Mayer Brown has described as a "single-reed" instrument. The third and final category is "rhythmic" music, which he contends is all sound that is not practiced by the voice but by the "monochord, the psaltery, the bell and similar instruments" (Herlinger 1985, 101). This tripartite distinction in musical sound is found in Augustine's *De ordine*, and can be traced even further back to Cicero's *De Republica.*[37] Each of these types of musical sound is distinctly represented in Giotto's fresco. Furthermore, the representation of the Annunciation in two

[36]All translations of Marchetto's *Lucidarium*, as well as the Latin edition, are in Herlinger 1985. Herlinger (1985, 77) notes that this passage is not in Remigius but is approximated in Macrobius *Somnium Scipionis* 2.3.11. The Latin reads, "Magnitudo musice capit omne quod vivit et quod non vivit; hanc concentus angelorum, archangelorum, sanctorumque omnium ante conspectum Dei Sanctus, Sanctus dicentes since fine decantant."

[37]Augustine, *De ordine* 2.39 and Plato, *Republic* 2.41.

parts – unprecedented in the history of art – accentuates the musical quality, or motion, of the scene. In the midst of heavenly music, God transmits the knowledge of the Annunciation to the angel Gabriel, who in turn repeats it to a waiting Mary.[38] There is implied musical transmission in this scene, corresponding to the musical dramatic reenactment of the Annunciation practiced in Padua at this time.

The celebration went as follows: clerics dressed as Mary, Elizabeth, Joseph, and Joachim went in procession from the sacristy around the cathedral carrying silver books. A small boy-chorister dressed to represent Gabriel (sitting on a chair) was carried from the baptistery and taken into the church; the clerics stopped in the middle of the church to represent a choir. The subdeacon paused after the readings and the words *Et egressus angelus ad eam dixit* were spoken. At this point the boy dressed as Gabriel came forward, and kneeling with two fingers of his right hand lifted up, began the antiphon *Ave Maria grazia plena.* These are the words of Marchetto's acrostic, and perhaps the motet was sung at this point, to replace the singing of the antiphon. A connection to Giotto's fresco is further noted: in his painting Gabriel is kneeling with two fingers raised. While receiving the spirit (symbolized by a dove), Mary arises and sings the antiphon *Ecce ancilla.* Marchetto was quite familiar with this antiphon, as evidenced by the fact that he uses it in his *Lucidarium* as a musical example in the chapter "Formation of Modes" (Herlinger 1985, 489).[39] Thus the heavenly music is transmitted to earth through the figure of Mary, who in the earlier scene guides the chorus of believers with her vielle.

The movement in Giotto's fresco from heavenly to earthly music reflects a pervasive theme alluded to at the beginning of this chapter: the interest in the representation of earthly phenomena as experienced in nature. A similar progression appears in Marchetto's two theoretical treatises, and is pervasive throughout many medieval writings on the theory of music. Marchetto's *Lucidarium* begins with several chapters outlining the history of music and its meaning, while his second treatise, the *Pomerium*, appears to describe music as a strictly physical phenomenon.[40]

The *Pomerium* contains no eloquent allusions to past writers about music – Boethius, Cassiodorus, or Augustine – as are in the first treatise. Rather, when describing the properties of intervals, Marchetto chooses to quote the scientific Aristotle and his *Physica.* Another example of Marchetto's use of scientific language is Marchetto's choice of definition for the

---

[38]For a description of this scene, see Young 1933, 248-250, and Stevens 1986, 308-311.

[39]Laura Jacobus (1999, 93) discusses the implied musicality of the scene.

[40]Musical treatises from the late thirteenth and fourteenth centuries were often paired, as seen in the works of Garlandia, de Muris, and Philippe de Vitry. The first treatise concerns fundamentals, the second mensuration (Herlinger 1985, 5-6).

word *music*. In book 1, chapter 6, of the *Lucidarium*, he notes that "music derives from *moys*, which means 'water,' since music was discovered by the waters, as Remigius reports; for just as water cannot be touched without its being moved, so can there be no music without its being heard" (Herlinger 1985, 87).[41]

Other writers, such as Cassiodorus, expressed the relationship between music and the Muses in letters written about the liberal arts. Marchetto mentions that music "began with the Muses themselves," and that these Muses received their name from "the word *maso*, that is, 'to seek', since through their agency, according to the ancients, the power of song and the harmony of the voice were sought." In the Trecento, Boccaccio selected this second etymology of music from water in his *Commentary on the Divine Comedy*. For Boccaccio, music derives from the nine Muses and can be divided into nine parts – whereas Marchetto mentions only six: "the lungs, the throat, the palate, the tongue, the front teeth, and the lips" (Herlinger 1985, 91).[42] For Boccaccio the word originates in Parnassus, while for Marchetto it originates on earth.

Like Giotto, Marchetto investigates the properties of music as derived from nature. In his treatises Marchetto reproduces on paper the world around him (particularly the musical world) as faithfully as possible. In the *Pomerium* Marchetto argues that music is a science and since science is perfect, so music must be as well.[43] Notation is necessary to faithfully capture the intentions of the composer: "In order, however, that one may know what the wish of the composer is, when music is to be sung in perfect time and when in imperfect, we say that when they are combined some sign ought to be added at the beginning of the music so that by means of it the wish of the composer who arranged this varied music may be known."[44]

The shift toward realism is noted in the work of Giotto in Padua and in the notational practices of Marchetto. The affinity of the *Ave regina celorum* motet and the frescoes indicates that the two artists knew each other's works and collaborated to some degree in the decoration (musical and visual) of the Scrovegni Chapel, and both witnessed and participated in the city's celebration of the Feast of the Annunciation. Both lived in Padua during the so-called pre-humanist period, when educated laymen were writing poetry in Latin verse and extolling the Roman traditions on which Padua was founded. Both placed a portrait of themselves within their particular artistic contributions to the Chapel: Giotto's self portrait

[41]For the tradition of music deriving from the word *water*, see Swerdlow 1967 3-9.

[42]"Boccaccio writes that the voice is formed by four teeth, one tongue, two lips, one palate, and... one throat" (Beck 1998, 60).

[43]Augustine (1947, 172-173) made this argument in his *De Musica*.

[44]*Pomerium* translated by Strunk 1965, 163.

appears most probably in the Scrovegni Chapel, and Marchetto's name appears in the acrostic of the *duplum*; these self-referential gestures signify the beginning of the transition to the Renaissance (Gallo 1985, 70). To return to the discussion of musical instruments in Giotto's work, they can also be found in the *Last Judgment* in the Scrovegni Chapel frescoes. In the *Last Judgment*, Christ sits within an egg-shaped, multi-colored cornice bordered by ten angels, four of whom play long-barreled trumpets (Fig. 5.4).

The two uppermost angels blow vigorously into their instruments. These trumpets are the only two in the entire cycle that are completely pictured: bell and barrel. The remaining angels blow into incomplete instruments, and appear to have been truncated by the ravages of time. By including trumpets in the *Last Judgment* scene, Giotto follows a prescriptive tradition: his teacher Cimabue, as we shall see later in the chapter when we turn our attention to Giotto's musical representations in the Upper Church of Saint Francis of Assisi frescoes, also incorporated trumpet-playing angels in the *Last Judgment*. Yet while Cimabue's angels blow into decorative, stylized trumpets, Giotto's angels puff out their cheeks and hold their realistically rendered instruments like professional players.

In the *Coronation of the Virgin*, a fresco attributed to the "School of Giotto" in the Scrovegni Chapel, we see forty angels playing a wider array of instruments, including a tambourine, lute, shawm, and a stringed instrument, perhaps a gittern or a lute. The musical angels appear in the fourth row from the bottom and are at the eye level of the Virgin, who is receiving her crown with hands crossed in front of her chest. The *Coronation of the Virgin with Saints* was painted later (in the 1320s or 1330s) by Giotto, with the assistance of Taddeo Gaddi (Brown 1985, 234), as we shall describe later in the chapter.

We find that in Giotto's portrayal of music-making, the choice of musical instruments in a particular scene helps to accentuate the general mood of the image. Therefore, in contrast to the elegant and calm mood of the *Wedding Procession*, we find the clamor of the *Betrayal of Christ*, the only other image in the narrative series (not counting, of course, the *Annunciation*, the *Coronation*, and the *Last Judgment*) to include representations of musical instruments. In the midst of the chaotic scene of angry soldiers coming to arrest Christ, Giotto paints a man holding a horn with his left hand and blowing it in the direction of the heavens. The horn has numerous meanings in medieval painting. First, it signifies battle and military conflict. More broadly, it represents aggression and belligerence, as in the case of the horns at the mouth of the figure representing the month of March, who is ruled by the warrior Mars (this subject will be covered in chapter 6). A later

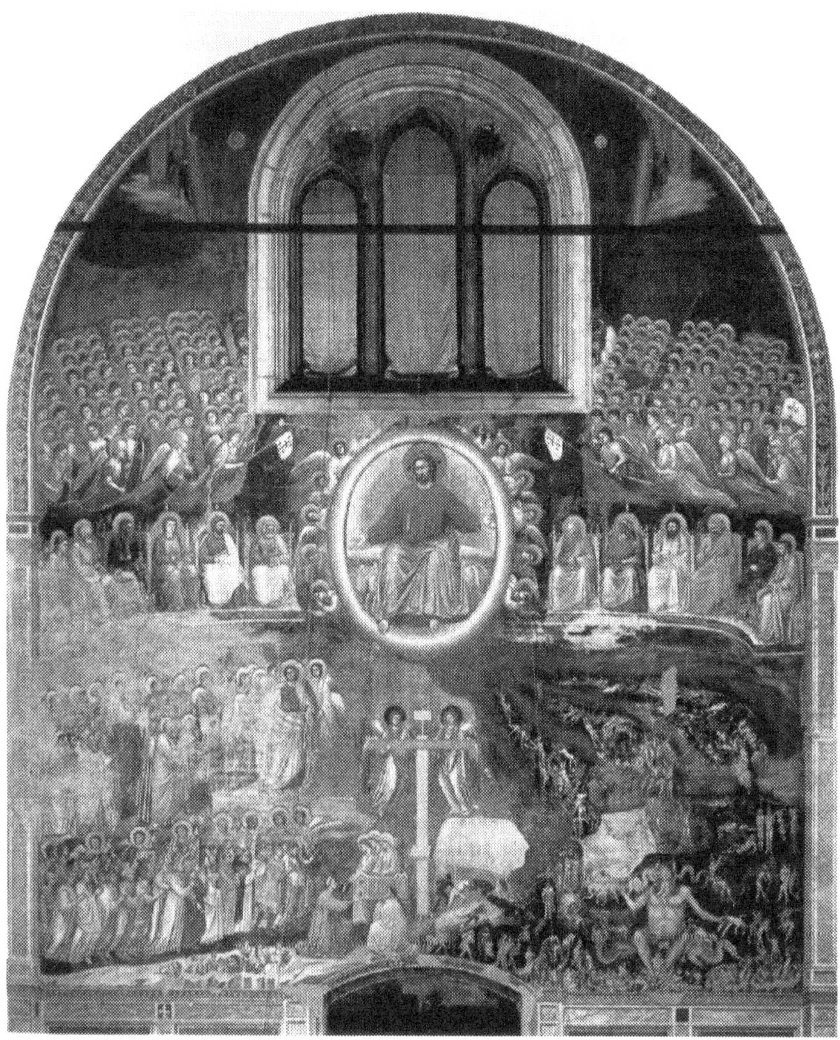

Figure 5.4: **Giotto, *Last Judgment.* Detail, Christ surrounded by musical angels. Padua, Scrovegni Chapel**

example of the horn as portrayer of military aggression is found in the Sercambi manuscript of the *Chronicles of Lucca.* Second, the horn signifies the hunt. It was believed that certain horn calls could lure particular types of wild animals to the hunter. The horn also signaled to rival hunters and their dogs that prey had been sighted. Many madrigals and caccias (or chase songs) written in the early fourteenth century capture the sounds and urgency of the chase. The two-fold metaphor of the horn helps to illuminate the meaning of the picture. The horn-blowing represents a rapacious crowd and signals that Christ has been captured.

It is important to note that before his first stay in Padua and his painting of the Scrovegni Chapel, whose walls, as we have seen, contain many representations of music-making, Giotto did not paint images of secular musicians or, as far as I have able to ascertain, angel musicians. For example, in his painting in the Upper Church in Assisi, which was executed in the 1290s and was his first major project, we find no representations of musical instruments. The only scene that contains an image of music-making in the cycle is the *Crib at Greccio*, in which four friars chant while Saint Francis reenacts the story of a baby's birth in a manger (Fig. 5.5).

Thomas of Celano's *First Life of Saint Francis of Assisi* reverberates with music, and we can see that this text may have been one of the inspirations of Giotto's fresco. Part 1, chapter 30, reads:

> The people all came to see and were thrilled at this new mystery as never before. The woods resounded with voices, the rocks echoed back the sounds of rejoicing. The Brothers sang, giving due praises to the Lord, and the whole night rang with sounds of jubilation. The saint stood before the crib sighing deeply, overwhelmed with love, and filled with wondrous joy. A solemn mass was celebrated over the crib and the priest enjoyed a consolation he had never known before (Celano 2000, 82-83).

Giotto chooses to place the scene in a courtyard devoid of trees, rocks, and other natural objects. The backdrop consists of marble walls and a marble floor, with an architectural canopy supported by four marble pilasters decorated with floating angels, who perhaps later might have held trumpets. While the life of Saint Francis may not be as traditional a place for musicians to appear as the *Last Judgment*, it is still significant that Giotto included so few musical elements in the cycle. Another rather oblique nod to music appears in the scene *Saint Francis Being Honored by a Simple Man* in which we see a bell hanging in the tower in the left side of the picture. The first frame of the entire cycle, the scene is set in Assisi and depicts a young Francis before he renounced his earthly belongings.[45] Two later musical additions to the Church attributed to the School of Giotto include a presentation of Miriam, sister of Moses, in the Lower Church, where Miriam

[45]For more on the origin of the scene's program, see Smart 1983, 151-152.

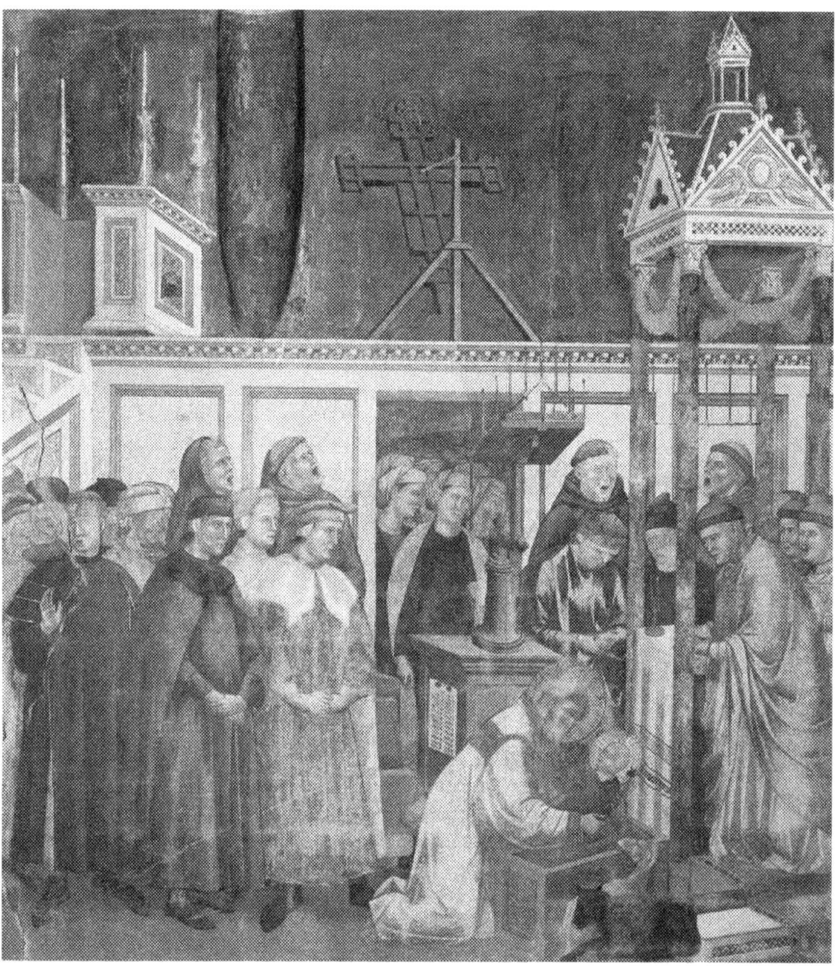

Figure 5.5: **Giotto, *Crib at Greccio.* Assisi, Saint Francis, Upper Church.**

holds a tambourine after the exodus from Egypt, and decorative medallions of the Elders of the Apocalypse, and angels, of which, according to Howard Mayer Brown (1985, 212-213), sixteen elders play cittern-like instruments, and three angels play trumpets while one sings.

On the other hand, Cimabue, Giotto's teacher, included eight angels encircling the figure of the seated Christ, seven of which blow into long-barreled trumpets, in the left transept of the Upper Basilica of Saint Francis in Assisi (Fig. 5.6).

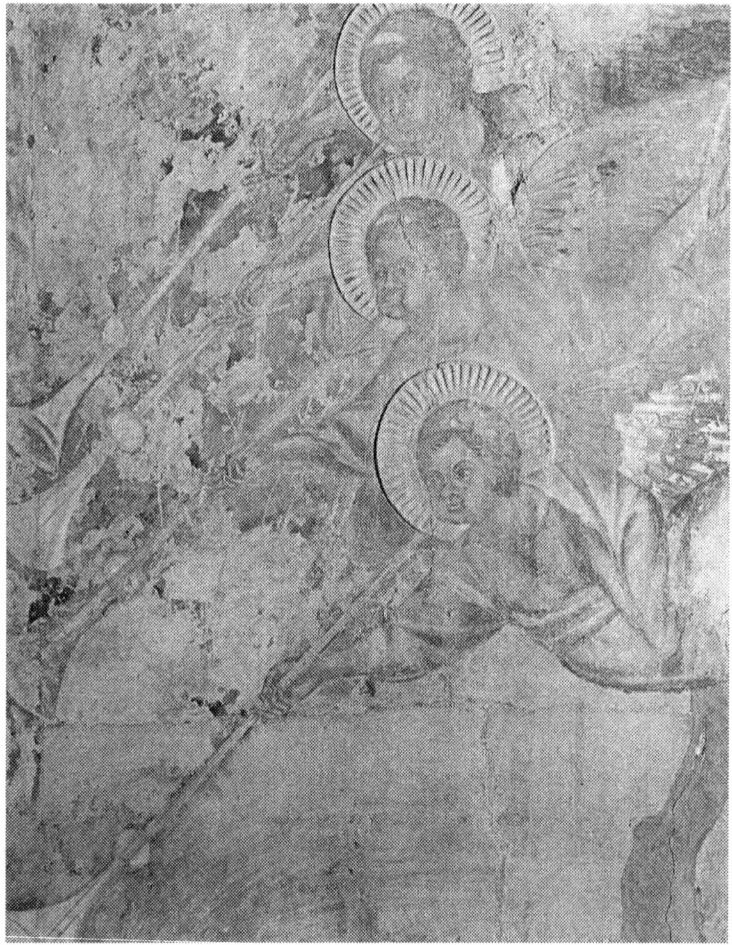

Figure 5.6: **Cimabue, Eight angels encircling the figure of the seated Christ, seven of which blow into long-barreled trumpets. Detail, three Angels. Assisi, Saint Francis, Upper Church, left transept.**

The source of this iconography is the Book of Revelation, a series of visions rather than a story cycle. The passage reads:

> And I saw the seven angels which stood before God; and to them

> were given seven trumpets. And another angel came and stood at the altar, having a golden censer; and there was given unto him much incense, that he should offer it with the prayers of all saints upon the golden altar which was before the throne. And the smoke of the incense, which came with the prayers of the saints, ascended up before God out of the angel's hand (Rev. 8:2-4).[46]

Incidentally, Simone Martini's contributions to the Assisi frescoes include a famous representation of musical bystanders, namely, the *Knighting of Saint Martin* in the Chapel of Saint Martin in the Lower Church (Fig. 5.7). In this fresco, Martini painted four men engaged in music-making: one plays two flutes, a second a small lute, and two sing behind them. Martini may have also spent time at the court of Naples between 1315 and 1319, where he painted the altar of Saint Louis of Toulouse for King Robert.[47] As previously mention and according to Scardeone, Marchetto was probably in Naples at the same time.[48]

These connections to Marchetto inspire the question, after Giotto's contact with Marchetto in Padua, did the painter begin to integrate more musical representations into his work? We have examined images of music-making found in the Scrovegni Chapel, but what of subsequent works? It is believed that after a second stay in Padua in 1309 or 1312, Giotto went first to Rome and then to Florence to work on the frescoes in the Peruzzi Chapel in Santa Croce. The Peruzzi were wealthy Florentine bankers, although no specific evidence exists regarding their commissioning the frescoes. The Peruzzi frescoes consist of episodes from the life of Saint John the Baptist and Saint John the Evangelist. These are the *Annunciation of Zacharia*, the *Birth of John the Baptist*, and *Herod's Feast*. Those of the Evangelist include *Saint John the Evangelist on Patmos*, the *Raising of Druisana*, and the *Assumption of Saint John the Evangelist*. Giotto's frescoes have suffered damage over the years, particularly at the hands of unscrupulous restorers, and because of the many floods of the Arno River over the course of the centuries.

---

[46]Bellosi 1998, 197.

[47]Martindale (1988, 216) questions whether Martini went to Naples during this period. He does not put much credence on the well-known and "ambiguous" reference to "Simone Martini miles (1317)." Martindale (1988, 178) dates the Saint Martin Chapel frescoes between 1312 and 1319.

[48]Note also that angel trumpeters grace illuminated books in the Trecento. For example, see *Apocalypse*, Royal MS 19 B. xv, ff. 13b-14, a reproduction of which is in Backhouse (1997, 109). Here we find Christ in a circular frame accompanied by seven angels blowing on long-barreled trumpets. Also see Apocalypse, Additional MS 17333, ff.10b-11 and a closely related copy in the Metropolitan Museum of Art (Backhouse 1997, 104).

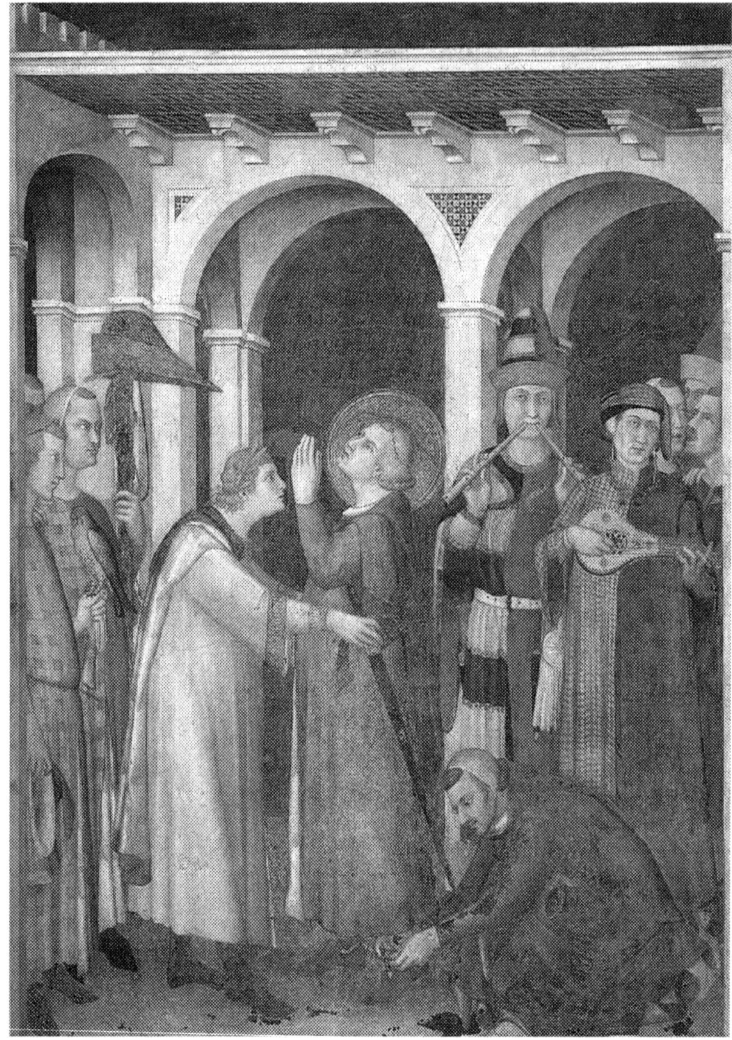

Figure 5.7: **Simone Martini, *Knighted of Saint Martin.* Assisi, Saint Francis, Lower Church, Chapel of Saint Martin.**

As he did in the Assisi frescoes, Giotto has created elaborate architectural spaces, canopies upon which he has placed standing figures. Two of the cycle's frescoes contain representations of music: the *Annunciation to*

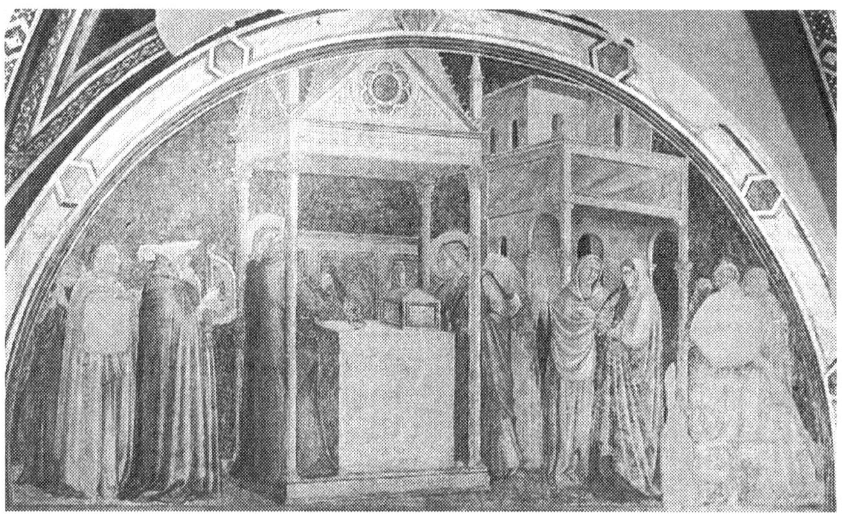

Figure 5.8: **Giotto, *Annunciation to Zachariah.* Florence, Santa Croce, Peruzzi Chapel.**

Zachariah and the *Feast of Herod.* In the *Annunciation* fresco (Fig. 5.8), Giotto introduces an elaborate ensemble consisting of three men playing a shawm and two psalteries.[49] The players occupy the left side of the picture and are balanced against two women in thick robes on the right. The musicians play "outside," in a space devoid of a canopy, while the other figures – Zachariah, the angels, and two women – are sheltered by Giotto's elegant architecture. The musicians, therefore, are separated from the others. Unlike the young musician in the *Feast of Herod,* the rightmost musician holding a psaltery is patrician and has a long gray beard. This is most likely a nod to David, who traditionally held a psaltery. The second psaltery player is young and a companion of the first, while the shawm player lurks a bit further in the background, his instrument butting up against the fresco's frame. This musical ensemble is the most complex musical group of Giotto's oeuvre to date. The presence of the musicians underscores the solemnity of the scene.

The *Feast of Herod* (Fig. 5.9) contains one of the most elegant representations of music-making in Giotto's work.[50] While Herod sits at a table, he

[49]Agnolo Gaddi includes a man playing a psaltery in the *Annunciation to Zachariah* in the Castellani Chapel in Santa Croce in Florence, painted in 1383-1385.

[50]See also Agnolo Gaddi's *Feast of Herod,* 1388, in the Louvre, Paris, in which Salome

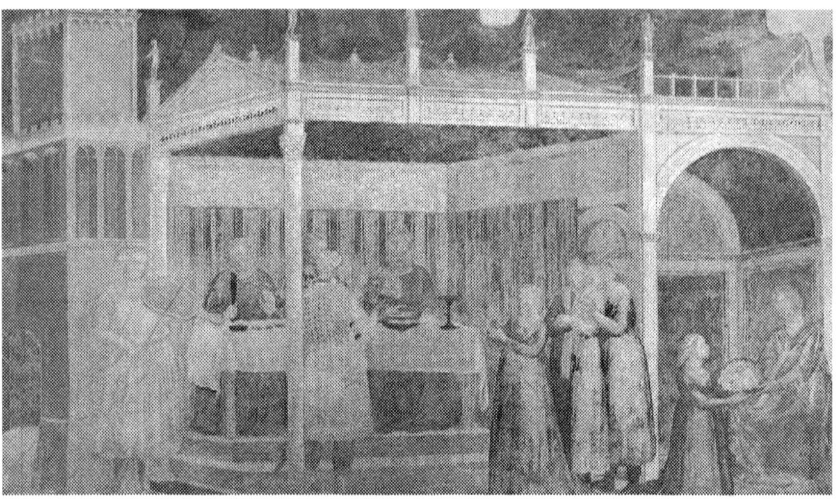

Figure 5.9: **Giotto, *Feast of Herod.* Florence, Santa Croce, Peruzzi Chapel.**

is brought the head of Saint John on a plate. A young male plays the vielle to his left, strikingly similar to the vielle played in the *Wedding Procession* in the Scrovegni Chapel. The instruments are the same approximate shape and size, and both are decorated with carvings on their sounding boards. One can discern stars of David on the case of the Scrovegni Chapel vielle player, implying, perhaps, that the instrument also communicates a spiritual message. The theme of David and music thus appears in both of Giotto's pictures. As noted, David was the most recognized musical figure in medieval iconography, appearing with a stringed instrument, in many cases a lyre. As we have seen, he is closely associated with the Psalms and music-making in the Psalm texts. Moreover, both of Giotto's vielle players stand in a similar fashion. Each steps forward onto his left leg and hunches over the instrument. The musicians wear tunics belted at the waist so that the folds are kept close to the body in order not to interfere with the playing of the instrument. Both are not situated at the center of the scene, but to the left and right, respectively, each stunningly beautiful, but at the same time not essential to the narrative. In each case, Giotto has placed the musicians in front of an unattached architectural structure – as in the

dances to the accompaniment of a musican playing a fiddle, and Pietro Lorenzetti *Herod's Feast* in Santa Maria dei Servi in Siena.

Annunciation to Zachariah scene. In the Scrovegni Chapel the musicians stand before a balcony in front of which juts a leafy branch. In the Peruzzi Chapel the vielle player appears before an arched tower, unconnected to the structure in which the dinner guests appear.

While in the Scrovegni Chapel the function of the vielle seems to heighten the sanctity of the moment, the playing of the instrument in the Herod scene heightens the evening's "festivities." A second difference is that the vielle player in the Scrovegni Chapel is a member of a trio, while in the Herod scene he plays alone, perhaps underscoring in an ironic fashion the cruelty of the scene. In the Scrovegni Chapel, although music pervades the scene, the connection between the musicians and the wedding party is not clearly made. No one seems to look directly at the musicians; rather, the solemnity of the occasion is emphasized by the procession and the music, but the party is not distracted by the music. In the Herod fresco, on the other hand, one man with knife in hand sitting at a table turns his head slightly toward the musician: he seems to be acknowledging the player, as Mozart's Don Giovanni acknowledges the musicians in Act 2 of the opera. One final point regarding the music in the *Feast of Herod*: some controversy exists regarding Salome and music in this picture. During one of the picture's many restorations in the 1400s and 1500s, a lyre was given to Salome to hold. The most recent restoration has returned to her the original jar (Baccheschi 1966, 113).

In examining Giotto's depictions of music, one can differentiate two kinds of music-making in his frescoes. First, there is implied music, the type that is perhaps a reflection of the heavens; this music does not entertain guests, or detract from the seriousness of the scene. It is the music of the spheres, as it were, or of the body, but not the use of instruments for wanton sensuality, and it is within the framework of the Boethian division of three types of music, later discussed by both Pietro and Marchetto. This is the kind of music found in the Scrovegni Chapel scenes (except for the scene under *Justice*). Second, there is actual music, as in the *Feast of Herod*, where Giotto portrays the earthly and lascivious music-making that the church fathers disapproved of, further accenting the cruelty of the scene and the disdain for human life and justice. This differentiation is important to understanding Giotto's other "musical" images, including the Scrovegni Chapel's *Annunciation*, in which scholars have argued there is musicality, and the *Last Judgment*, in which the musical angels are a reflection of the "silent" music of the heavens.

It is important to keep in mind that for the late medieval thinker, for whom the teachings of Boethius and the church fathers were transmitted through Aquinas and by extension Pietro and Marchetto, the most elevated kind of music was indeed not audible – it reverberated in the heavens.

The Stefaneschi Polyptych, a late work housed in Pinacoteca Vaticana, contains one music-making scene. Gnudi (1959, 236) remarks that it was completed during Giotto's stay in Naples in about 1333. The polyptych is painted on both sides of the wooden panel, with one side consisting of the *Crucifixion of Saint Peter*, the *Beheading of Saint Peter*, and *Christ Enthroned.* While the many angels that hover about the polyptych in the scenes bemoaning the death of Saint Peter, and those standing about Christ, do not hold instruments, in the scene of the actual beheading of Saint Peter, one soldier blows into an elaborate trumpet (Fig. 5.10).

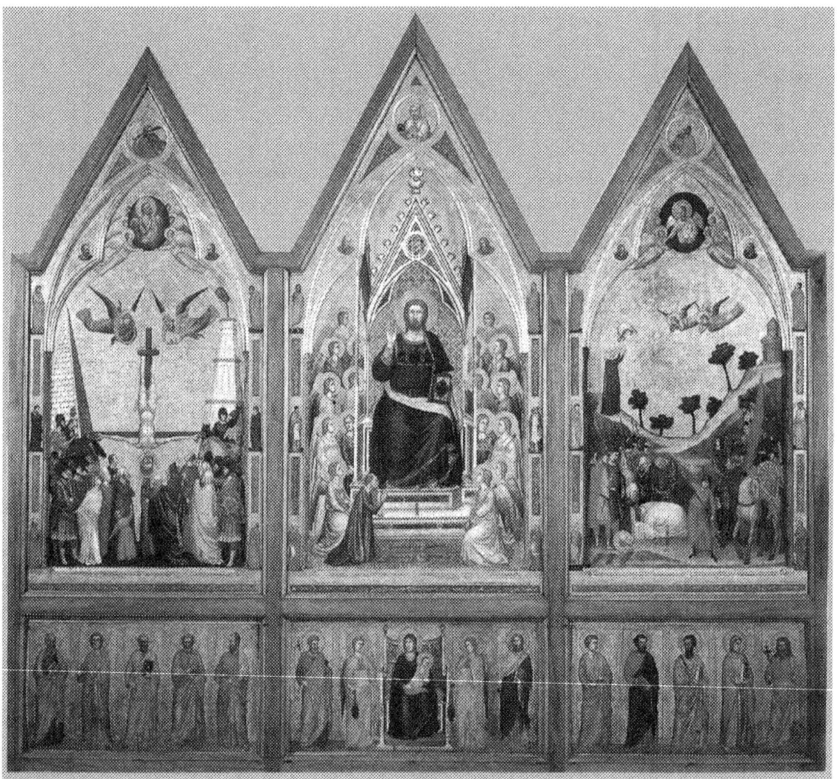

Figure 5.10: **Giotto, Stefaneschi Polyptych. Detail, beheading of Saint Peter. Rome, Pinacoteca Vaticana.**

This soldier is part of a group of men standing to the right of the fallen

Peter. A man playing a trumpet with outstretched arms is placed at the center of the scene, emphasizing his importance. A helmeted man in a red tunic has seemingly just beheaded Peter and is about to replace the sword in its holster. At the same time, three women in mourning look down upon Peter. The trumpet-playing can be interpreted in several ways. First, as was customary with Giotto, it heightens the realism of the scene. It is triumphal and meant to underscore the completion of a soldier's duty. Second, it infuses the scene with irony, as we have seen in the Peruzzi Chapel, the irony being that because of Peter's demise, the true believers will proclaim victory, a victory unmatched by the soldier's trumpeting sounds. Third, the trumpet is a visual device that unites the picture. With its black tube and red flag, it mimics the black sword that the soldier is returning to a red holster. In addition, the trumpet's outline echoes the pointed staves held by the on-looking soldiers. As in the Scrovegni *Wedding Procession*, the trumpet is aligned with a tree directly behind it, perhaps again a device used by Giotto to integrate it further into the scene. The trumpeting soldier dressed in red blows on his instrument in typical Giotto fashion. His cheeks are puffed out and he holds his instrument diagonally, with his right hand curled around its tube. Together these considerations underscore the dual conventions of musical meaning, one heavenly (unheard), and one mundane (heard), adopted by Marchetto and Pietro in Padua. Here the earthy quality of music-making accentuates the brutal deed that was just committed.

Flores d'Arcais (1995, 314) points out that "a good number of scholars do not consider the polyptych one of the master's autograph works, but the product of his workshop." She disagrees, however, and writes: "But the work's masterly conception can only have been by Giotto: at once poetry and architecture, beginning with the gorgeous grandeur of the frame, which is also a Giottesque invention of great celebrative significance for the papacy, and continuing with images from the Old Testament, the Apostles, Christ, and the Madonna."

One aspect of the trumpet player, however, does contradict Flores d'Arcais's assertion that Giotto himself completed the picture. The trumpet player holds the instrument with only one hand. In Giotto's work, we find his trumpet players holding trumpets with two hands, the right hand outstretched, holding the instrument from below, and the left hand closer to the mouth piece, positioning the instrument to the correct embrasure. This stance is most notably seen in the *Last Judgment* and in the Baroncelli Polyptych, a work that we will consider at the conclusion of this chapter. While the trumpet player conforms to the overall complex philosophical underpinnings of music described in this chapter as Giottesque, the trumpet-playing itself is not done in typical Giotto style, suggesting that it may have been undertaken by a member of his workshop. The one-handed trumpet player is found in the work of Cimabue in the Upper Basilica of Saint Francis of Assisi, where Christ is surrounded by seven angels blowing trumpets. One-handed trumpet players (and trumpets with flags attached to their barrels) are also more typical in manuscript illuminations of warring city-states in, for instance, "Faciente sembiante d'assalire i nemici" in *La cronoca figurata di Giovanni Villani.*[51]

The trumpet players found in Giotto's Scrovegni Chapel frescoes and his polyptychs reveal a palpable classical influence. The long-barreled trumpet or *tuba* was a popular motif in Roman art.[52] A well-preserved example of trumpet players is found on a relief on Trajan's Column (113 AD) in Rome. In this image, men wearing wreaths blow into trumpets, their cheeks puffed out and each holding the instrument with both hands, the left hand holding the barrel and the right near the lips of the player. Even more strikingly similar to the *Beheading of Saint Peter* is a Roman relief found on the Arch of Constantine in Rome.[53] In this scene, a soldier blows into a trumpet while a gruppetto of helmeted soldiers watch. One final Roman example that Giotto may have seen is found in the Palazzo dei Conservatori. It is of a wreathed figure holding a trumpet with two hands and blowing into an empty architectural space. As in Giotto's paintings, the trumpet players in the Roman scenes are prominent, but they are not part of the narrative, functioning instead as a device to amplify a musical atmosphere. The *tubae* are certainly triumphal and associated with military endeavors, which, once again returning to the *Wedding Procession*, does not seem particularly appropriate for that quiet scene. Curt Sachs notes that trumpets disappeared after the fall of Rome, only to reappear after the crusades. An early medieval image with long trumpets is found near Capua in an 11th-century fresco in the Church of Sant' Angelo in Formis, with angels blowing trumpets, and trumpeting angels, as we have seen, are found in medieval manuscripts.

The Baroncelli Polyptych, which is housed in the Baroncelli Chapel of Santa Croce in Florence, contains a veritable orchestra of angels. The work, signed "OPUS MAGISTRI JOCTI", is thought to have been completed around 1327, just prior to Giotto's trip to Naples (Flores d'Arcais 1995, 337). The attribution to Giotto has been debated by scholars, with some attributing the predella to Giotto's studio and to Taddeo Gaddi, who completed the frescoes in the chapel of the same name. The polyptych consists of five panels, with pointed arches at their tops. Unlike the Stefaneschi Polyptych,

[51] Rome, Biblioeca Apostolica Vaticana, *Codex Chigiano* L. VII, 296, f. 224.

[52] The *lituus*, a long trumpet with a curved bell, is also found in Roman art. For more examples, see Kinsky 1951.

[53] On musical instruments in ancient art, see Fleischhauer 1964.

which consists of three separate scenes, the Baroncelli Polyptych is uniquely conceived of as one scene, "interrupted" by the divisions of the panel frames, which gives the viewer the feeling of looking at the numerous figures through windows, their repetitive shapes like pilasters impeding the view. At the center is the *Coronation of the Virgin*, in which the Virgin sits on an elaborate throne, with four angels at her feet. The saints and angels are crowded into the panels and look toward the middle scene, almost craning their necks to get a better view. The most interesting and eye-catching gestures in the picture concern the sparkling angel musicians kneeling at the lowest level of the panel (Fig. 5.11).

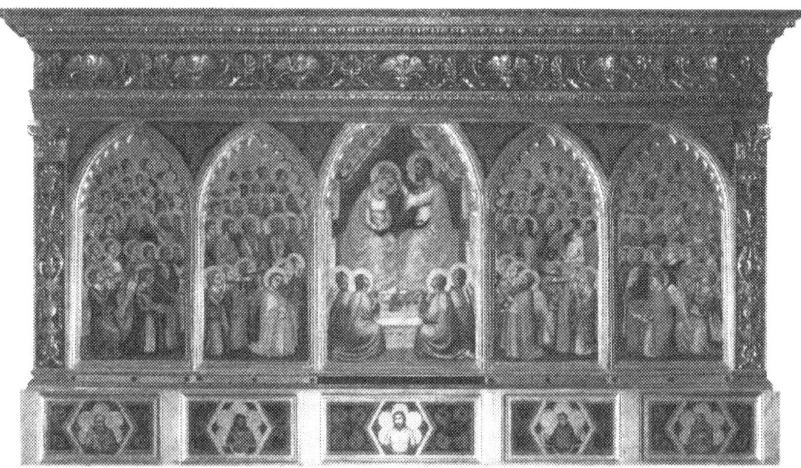

Figure 5.11: **Giotto, Baroncelli Polyptych. Florence, Santa Croce, Baroncelli Chapel.**

Of the twenty angels situated on the bottom-most row of angels, fourteen play a recognizable instrument. The twenty angels are divided into four groups by the frame of the picture. These four groups are arranged (reading from left to right) as 4 + 6 + 6 + 4 angels. The angels that do not carry instruments have their mouths open, as if singing.

In addition, angels in rows about them also appear to be singing, while their unmoving gaze is set on the *Coronation* scene. The two outermost musical angels prop themselves up on one knee, with their other legs outstretched behind their bodies. Four angels who are not engaged in music-making are seated in front of the Virgin and on the same plane as the musical angels. They are gazing up at the seated Mary and Christ instead.

The arrangement of musical angels is carefully studied, with musicians positioned with the precision of a modern-day orchestra. Giotto places the noisiest instruments in the panels farthest from the center. Moving from the left panel to the right, we find two angels blowing into long-barreled trumpets and one playing the portative organ. The next panel contains two angels blowing into reed instruments, one angel playing a psaltery, one a vielle, and one a bagpipe, perhaps, though all that is shown to the viewer is a wooden pipe and what may be the outlines of a bag.[54]

On the right inner panel, we find a woman playing a vielle, an angel playing what looks like a psaltery, shown from the back, and two reed players. The right outer panel depicts an angel playing the portative organ and two angels playing trumpets. These figures are clearly mirror images of each other: the players on the left side of the panel wear the same colored clothing as their corresponding figures on the right side. But even more fascinating is the representation of both sides of the same musical instrument within the polyptych. For example, in the left-hand panel the angel holds a portative organ with her left hand and plays the keys with her right hand. On the right side of the picture the angel is shown with the back side of the instrument facing the viewer. In this case we see the organ's bellows pumped by the angel's left hand and the organ's pipes viewed in reversed order (in terms of length of pipes). This reversal of instruments is true for all except the bagpipes. Note that the trumpet players reverse their hands on the instrument, and, in typical Giotto fashion, hold the instrument with two hands. The reed players also switch hands on their instruments. On the left side of the picture, they place their right hand closer to the mouthpiece, while on the right side, their left hand is closer to the mouthpiece. The painter has elected not to switch the hands of the vielle player (this would not represent authentic playing). Instead, like the organ, one sees two views of the instrument: on the left side the top of the instrument, on the right the underside in shortened perspective.

While Giotto's angel orchestra in the Baroncelli Polyptych is clearly much more expansive than that found in the Scrovegni Chapel's *Last Judgment* and *Annunciation*, which features reeds, trumpets, and voice, some parallel representations of musicians suggest that Giotto was the designer, if not the actual painter, of the angel musicians. In the top tier of the *Annunciation*, we find a variety of instruments, including the psaltery, lute, cymbals, and tambourine. Giotto favored mirror imaging around the seated

[54]Scholars do not agree that Giotto painted the bagpipe player. For a synthesis of scholarly opinion on this subject, see Baccheschi 1966, 115. Giotto painted a bagpipe player in the *Adoration of the Magi*, c.1320-1325, now housed in the Metropolitan Museum in New York.

Christ in the *Last Judgment.* The trumpet-playing angels at the feet of Christ and above his head are mirror images. On the left, the player holds his left hand closest to his mouth, on the right, his right hand. The same is true of the angels above his head.

Returning to Marchetto's *Lucidarium*, which contains a compendium of musical types divided into three species, we note that Giotto has included all three types in this picture: harmonic, organic, and rhythmic. The first is vocal music; the second is produced by the breath or air, like trumpet, reeds, and organ; and the third does not require air, such as the vielle. Recall also, from an earlier chapter, Machetto's description of the angel choir in the *Lucidarium*, quoting Remigius: "The vastness of music encompasses all that lives and all that does not live; this the choir of all the angels, archangels, and saints sings without end, chanting 'Sanctus, Sanctus' before the eyes of God" Herlinger (1985, 77). Giotto's and Marchetto's representations of music show marked similarities. Each, in a sense, decorated the Scrovegni Chapel: Giotto with his frescoes and Marchetto with the performance of his motet *Ave regina celorum.* Giotto's philosophy of music, as outlined in this chapter, that is, the understanding of music as something that is both heard and represented in nature and "heard" in the heavens, reflects Marchetto's prevailing philosophy of music as expressed in his *Lucidarium.*

The Scrovegni frescoes mark Giotto's new commitment to include more representations of music-making in his work, and we see for the first time in the history of premodern art the appearance of a prominent professional laic player in the scene of the *Wedding Procession.* After his time in Padua, we see Giotto including more music in his frescoes, in, for example, the Bardi Chapel and in the polyptychs mentioned earlier. However, he will never repeat in later work the pervasiveness or richness of the musical representations found in the Scrovegni Chapel, in the scenes of the *Annunciation, Last Judgment, Justice* (and by implication *Injustice*), and the *Wedding Procession.* The following chapter will explore representations of music in subsequent major art works, from the astrological walls of the Salone della Ragione to the crowning musical masterpiece, Donatello's Altar of Saint Anthony of Padua. In the process of examining these works, it will be demonstrated that the musical philosophy of Pietro and Marchetto connects these works and establishes Padua as an important source of music theory as the medieval period draws to a close and the Renaissance dawns.

Chapter 6

Representations of Music-Making from Giotto to Donatello: Transition to Renaissance Padua

After Giotto painted the monumental Scrovegni Chapel frescoes, musical figures appeared with frequency throughout the art of Trecento and Quattrocento Padua. Followers of Giotto in Padua, such as Giusto de' Menabuoi and Guariento, painted elaborate music-makers, culminating in the musical angels in Donatello's altar in the Church of the Santo in Padua. This chapter will explore the meaning of music in the Paduan artwork succeeding Giotto and its connection to early Trecento musical philosophy. The works will be seen as emerging from the tapestry of influences established in previous chapters – the Roman tradition, the philosophy of Pietro's and Marchetto's, Giotto's frescoes – and the chapter will serve as a roadmap to Padua's transition to the Renaissance in music and in art. Each example explores the representation of musical instruments and the implied sounds that they produce in the tradition of Giotto, as if captured in nature. Three primary pictorial masterpieces will be examined: the astrological frescoes in the Salone della Ragione, Giusto de' Menabuoi's frescoes in the Baptistery, and Donatello's bronze altar in the Church of Saint Anthony of Padua, also known as the Church of the Santo.

Although scholars have scrutinized the organization and significance of the Salone della Ragione frescoes as a whole, little has been written about the ten individual representations of music.[1] As was mentioned in chapter 4, Giotto was the first artist to cover the walls with twelve astrological frescoes, and the program of these frescoes was provided by Pietro. The Salone della Ragione frescoes depict the influence of the heavenly bodies on the habits, natures, and actions of all creatures. There are three primary modes of celestial action: (1) motion (*motus*), (2) light (*lumen*), and (3) influence (*influentia*).[2] Motion concerns the elliptical and circular movements of the bodies in space; a well-known effect of lunar motion is the rising and waning of the tides on earth. Light relates to the amount of hotness and coldness given off by a particular celestial body, and an obvious example of light's influence is that plants grow as a result of sunlight. *Influentia* may be defined as the terrestrial effects that are not explained by either motion or light. In contrast to the first two, these influences are invisible in nature. One famous medieval example of *influentia* is the production of metals in the heart of the earth, which is unreachable by light.

The Salone frescoes are arranged in a kind of tabular form, as a series of images of "planet's children," a sequence that finds its origin in Islamic manuscripts such as the Bodleian Oriental Manuscript 133 (Klibansky, Panofsky, and Saxl 1964, 204-205). The images are further grouped into twelve parts, reflecting the number of months in a year. Each section consists of roughly thirty images arranged in three rows of ten images each, analogous to the three decades that constitute a calendar month. They are laid out on the four walls as follows: the south wall contains the months March through July; the west wall, July and August; the north wall, September through January; and the east wall, January and February.

Each section contains a sacred element that balances the secular bent of the frescoes. Twelve apostles appear in larger spaces and dominate the other, smaller images. In the month of March, for example, we find the figure of Saint Andrew. Under the figure of March, we find a scene of Saints Francis and Dominic; under April, the same painter created an image of Saint Anthony, the patron saint of Padua. In addition to the religious figures, many frescoes display symbols relating to the virtues of justice and harmony. These more pagan elements speak to the function of the palazzo as a meeting space for governmental and other civic agencies and to the secular nature of justice.

The planets were thought to be the most influential spheres in the heavenly arena, dominating all other forces.[3] For instance, coldness is at-

[1] See Vescovini 1987 and Barzon 1924.

[2] Grant 1994, 586.

[3] The following overview of astrology is from Barzon 1924, 17-26. For more on astrological practice, see Nesle 1985.

tributed to Saturn, hotness to the sun, wetness to the moon, and dryness to Mars. Moreover, each planet also exudes a specific influence when united with the sign of the Zodiac. The planet is united with the sign when it is most luminous, or at closest distance to the earth. For instance, Venus is most resplendent in May when Taurus dominates. Therefore, Venus has its house in Taurus, Mars in Aries, and so on.

The following is a description of the images found representing the month of March, the first month of the year according to the old Roman calendar (Fig. 6.1).[4]

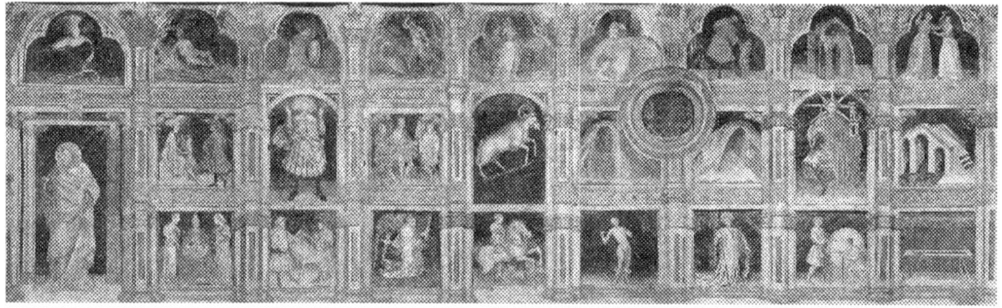

Figure 6.1: **Month of March. Padua, Salone della Ragione.**

This month will serve as a template for understanding the organization of images in each subsequent month. Reading from left to right and from top to bottom, we see a great white heron (a figure yet to be interpreted by either Barzon or Vescovini), Saint Andrew, a woman of loose ways, a hunter with a falcon, a Benediction, a warrior, a figure representing the month of March, a seller of fish, Hercules, warriors, an angel, incautious love, Aries, violence, a house, a grotto, suicide, infanticide, another grotto, the warlike character of the planet, natural inclination, Mars, knife-sharpeners, battling women, rushing waters, and textile manufacturing.

These twenty-six images capture the constellations, planetary influences, and attributes that characterize the month of March. The constellation Hercules appears brightly in the March sky; Aries and Mars dominate in March; the warrior, incautious love, natural inclination, and rushing waters refer to the influence of the sign of the Zodiac; the warriors, angel, house, grottos, warlike character of the planet, knife-sharpeners, and battling women reflect the influence of the planet, as do male violence, suicide, and infanticide; the hunt, Benediction, and selling of fish constitute the occupation of the men born under this sign; several figures are indecipherable.

[4]The following interpretations of images are taken from Barzon 1924, Vescovini 1990, Pellegrini 1990, and foldout diagrams in Fantelli and Pellegrini 1990.

Taken as a whole, this set of pictures represents the ferocity of March as a metaphor for the last blast of winter and the early turbulent, rainy weeks of spring. Furthermore, the planet Mars symbolizes a propensity for violence (as seen in the many allusions to armed conflict). Mars is represented as a seated warrior, his head within a circle of rays; he holds a tower in his left hand and a sword in his right. Of the twelve figures depicting the months, March is the only one with a musical attribute: he is represented as a hunter blowing into two horns (Fig. 6.2).

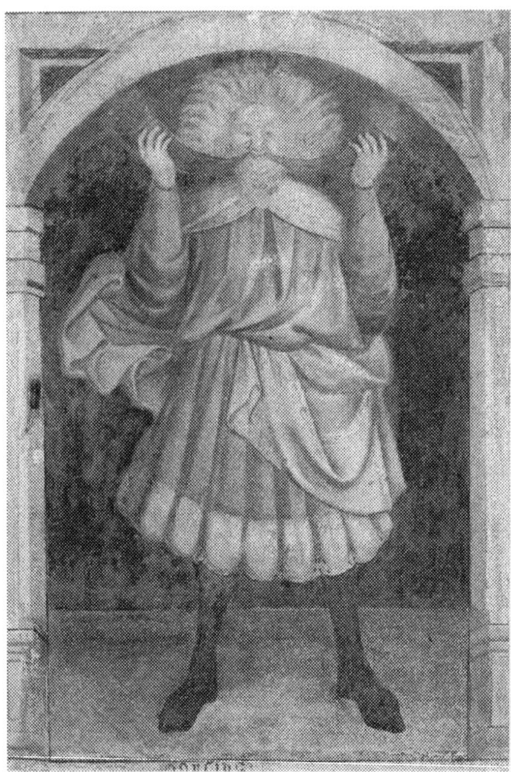

Figure 6.2: **March. Padua, Salone della Ragione.**

March's hair is in flames, and fire leaps out of the ends of the horns. Under the figure we find the word *Marcius*, which recalls the similar depiction of the "Marcius Cornator" in the small Chapel of Months in the Palazzo Ducale in Venice. The image of March blowing horns is particularly Italian and is found in Cremona, Biblioteca capitolare, "Martyrology of Adone";

Verona, San Zeno, Reliefs on porch; Pavia, San Michele, Mosaic pavement; and Ferrara, Museo del duomo, Sculptural slabs from the façade (Porta dei Mesi).[5]

Scholars interpreting this image have suggested that the blowing of horns represents the fierce winds howling in that month (Barzon 1924, 26). While this is certainly a viable reading, it does not account for the flames that surround the figure's head. I propose a new reading based on Cecco d'Ascoli's astrological poem, *L'Acerba*, an excellent source for the meaning of early Trecento astrological symbols. A prominent astrologer in Bologna, Cecco was a member of the faculty of medicine at the University of Bologna during the years 1324-1326. After several years of imprisonment, Cecco, like d'Abano before him (with whose beliefs he was surely familiar), was put to death for his heretical astrological views.

When describing "lightning, thunderbolts, flashes, and earthquakes," Cecco (1.8., lines 541-546) notes their association to the tempestuousness of the planet Mars (whose house is in March and October):

The first star [moon] with the irreverent Mars moves in stormy and thunderous time until one is against the other; then fire departs from cruel Mars, toward the cold clouds, from which the sounds exult with the inflamed veils.	La prima stella con l'empïo Marte Muove per tempo tempestati e tuoni Sin che l'una contrarii l'altro, parte Lo fuoco mosso di Marte crudele Verso le fredde nubi, onde i suoni Exultano con le infocate vele (D'Ascoli 1927, 159).

He continues (2.8., lines 547-552) his explanation of meteorological events:

Thunder is nothing but flame pushed into the bodies of cold clouds; one takes on the qualities of the other. An example is in the green branches that pop when lit on fire. Now listen to other examples.	Il tuono altro non è che fiamma spinta Entro li corpi de le nubi fredde, U' l'una qualità, da l'altra è vinta. Tu ne le verdi fronde prendi esemplo Che fanno scoppi se fuoco le lede. 'Or scolta gli accidenti ch'io contemplo (D'Ascoli 1927, 159).

Cecco's description of thunder recalls Aristotle's *Meteorologica*. For Aristotle, there are two types of exhalation (book 1): "One kind is rather of the nature of vapour, the other of the nature of a windy exhalation. That

[5]Photographs, descriptions, and histories of these images of March are found in Webster 1938. The image of March blowing a horn without burning hair is found in Roma, Vatican Library, MS Reg. lat. 1263; Calendar of Saint Mesmin; Cremona, Cathedral, Frieze on porch; Fidenza (formerly Borgo San Donnino), Relief on apse; Monreale, Cathedral, Capitals of the cloister; Parma, Baptistery, Reliefs in the triforium; and Piacenza, San Savino, Mosaic pavement in crypt. March is also traditionally depicted as pruning the vines.

which rises from the moisture contained in the earth and on its surface is vapour, while that rising from the earth itself, which is dry, is like smoke" (1931, 341b). In book 2, the Philosopher explains that thunder is caused by the collision of opposite elements: "if any of the dry exhalation is caught in the process as the air cools, it is squeezed out as the clouds contract, and collides in its rapid course with the neighboring clouds, and the sound of this collision is what we call thunder" (1931, 369a). For the Philosopher, lightning is an eruption of fire. "It usually happens that the exhalation that is ejected is inflamed and burns with a thin and faint fire: this is what we call lightning, where we see as it were the exhalation colored in the act of its ejection" (1931, 369b).

The depiction of March in the Salone represents the two Aristotelian sources of thunder and lightning: the "squeezing" through of exhalations and the collision with the clouds is captured by the blowing of two horns; the inflamed bolts of lightning caused by the dry exhalation is depicted in the fire that shoots out of the horns and the hair of March.

The next musical image in the Salone cycle appears in the month of May. This fresco consists of a winged angel blowing on a trumpet (Fig. 6.3).

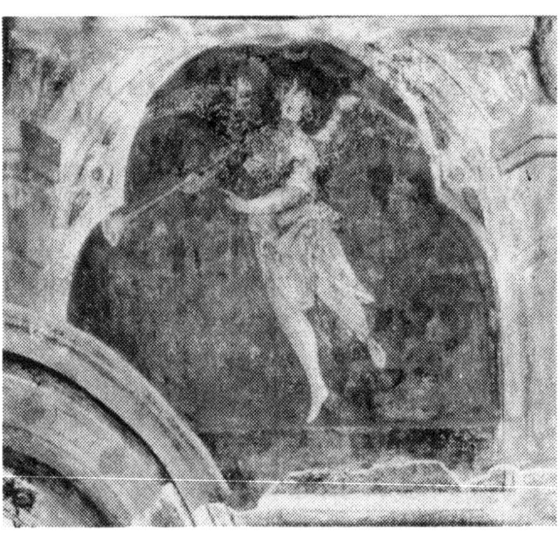

Figure 6.3: **Winged Angel Blowing on a Trumpet in May. Padua, Salone della Ragione.**

The meaning of the fresco has not yet been identified in the literature. Certainly the trumpeting angel is common in the Trecento, as seen in the trumpet-playing angels in both the *Annunciation* and *Last Judgment* in

Giotto's Scrovegni Chapel.[6] Trumpets traditionally accompany processions and celebrations in art, functioning to announce the arrival of a particular figure, such as Mary, Jesus, or the Holy Father. They also represent heavenly music and escort choruses of angels. The angel in the Salone della Ragione frescoes probably represents an announcement of forthcoming nuptials since May is traditionally the month of weddings.

A reading of *L'Acerba* provides a new interpretation of the enigmatic angel trumpeter. In 4.5., lines 3867-3872, entitled the "Problems of Physics and Meteorology," Cecco explains the reason for sounding church bells during violent storms:

'Why do people sound bells during summer storms?' Because the sound breaks the air and gets rid of pestilence. I also tell you that maligned angels envious of humans create storms because they are angry.	'Perchè d'estate, nelle gran tempeste la gente suona a stormo le campane?' Chè il suono rompe l'aria e toglie peste. Anche ti dico: gli angeli maligni, Invid'iosi delle genti umane, Fanno tempeste per certi disdigni (D'Ascoli 1927, 353-354).

Cecco (book 4.5., lines 3873-3878) then explains that playing "le divine tube" also helps to dissipate the clouds:

So that in playing the divine trumpets, they flee like broken people. Dante did not know this secret. So that in vain, I say, one should not sound each bell in anger, according to my reasonable saying.	Sì che, sonando le divine tube, Fugge lor setta come gente rotta. Questo segreto Dante non conube. Sicchè invano, dico, non si suona Ogni campana tempestando allotta, Secondo che il mio detto ti ragiona (D'Ascoli 1927, 354).

Interestingly, Cecco boasts that Dante did not know this fact when he wrote about clouds in the sonnet "Io sono stato con Amore insieme" and in the "Purgatory" of the *Divine Comedy.* Cecco's metaphor relating the weather to music is the first I have come across in the literature, and enriches the meaning of musical representations in the medieval period. Returning to the Salone della Ragione images, then, the angel trumpeter represents the dissipation of early summer storms.

Starting at the other end of the south wall and continuing on the west wall, July is the next month in the calendar to contain an image of music-making (Fig. 6.4).

Leo dominates this month, as depicted by the lion and the sun, seen resplendent on a carriage. Those born in July exhibit characteristics of

[6] For more on the iconography of trumpet-playing angels, see Hammerstein 1962, 205-217.

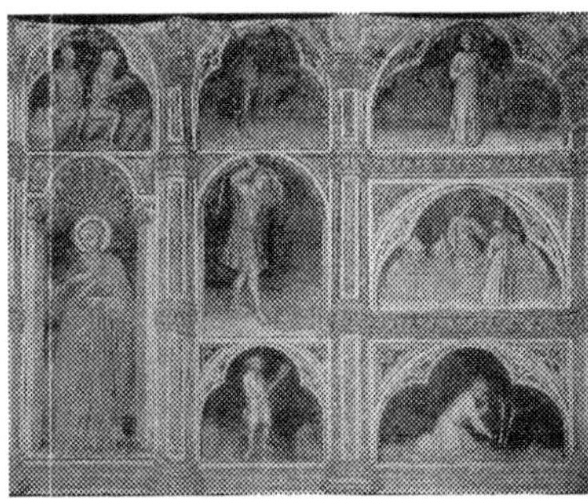
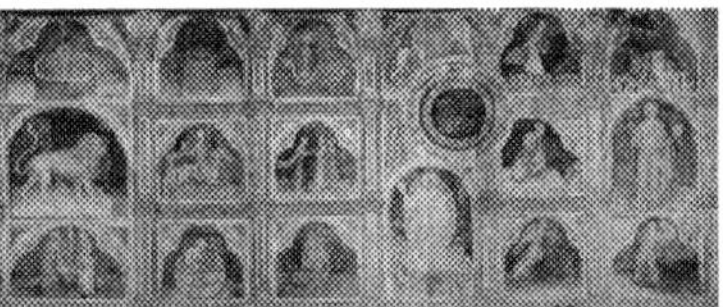

Figure 6.4: **Month of July, Padua, Salone della Ragione.**

spirituality and power. Saint Matthew begins the month. Just above the figure of July, who appears as a young, barefoot man beating the grain on the ground, is an image of a beastlike figure blowing into a horn. This fresco signifies ire and bad deeds.[7]

A second image of music appears at the beginning of the west wall in the top row of figures to the right of the sun. A man wearing a flowing red cape blows into bagpipes (Fig. 6.5).

In the Trecento, bagpipes traditionally represented the servant class. One of the most famous examples appears in Boccaccio's *Decameron*, when the servant Tindaro entertains the aristocrats on his pipes. The servant-bagpipes player is also depicted in Andrea di Bonaiuto's *Allegory of the Dominican Order* in the Spanish Chapel of Santa Maria Novella in Florence.[8] In this same tradition, the bagpipe figure in the Salone della Ragione frescoes indicates summertime entertainment provided by a member of the lower classes for the benefit of those in power. This interpretation is consistent with the notion that the Sun symbolized authority. The Sun is pictured as a seated figure on a throne with wheels (a reference to the Carrara family) and by a standing figure holding a ball in its left hand, identified as "Principe-potere."[9] July's nature is gentler than March's, as depicted by the more restrained portrayal of music. The appearance of musical figures in the month of July may be explained by the presence of the sun.[10]

The Sun has long been the symbol of Apollo, one of the most prominent

[7]Fantelli and Pellegrini 1990: first insert that appears between 32 and 33.

[8]On the meaning of music in this fresco, see Beck 1992-1995.

[9]Fantelli and Pellegrini 1990: first insert that appears between 32 and 33.

[10]Barzon (1924, 85) suggests, rather half-heartedly, that the bagpipe is "perhaps a reminder of the Sun, Apollo, who was the inventor of instruments of shepherds."

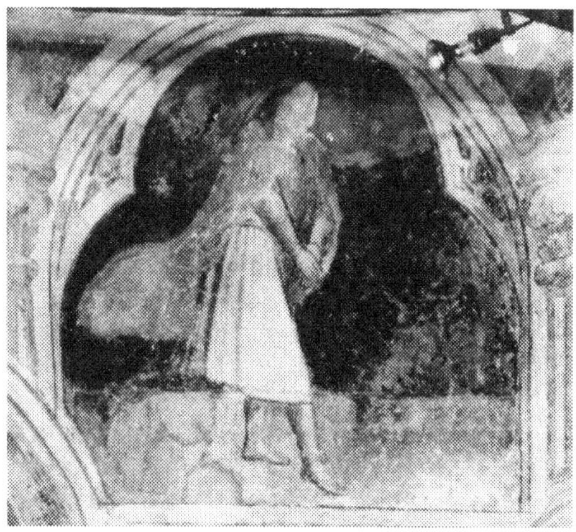

Figure 6.5: **Man Blowing into Bagpipes in July, Padua, Salone della Ragione.**

players of music in classical literature. Apollo is frequently portrayed with the lyre, as in Raphael's *Parnassus.* A fifteenth-century treatise entitled the *Kalendar and Compost of Shepherds* contains many spirited passages concerning the influence of the Sun on musical practice. For example, the author of the *Kalendar* recounts:

> And if they be never poor, yet shall love hawking and hunting with hounds and hawks and rejoice to see it. The children that are born under the Sun shall desire honor and science and shall sing very pleasantly (1930, 145).

More representations of music appear during August and September than in the other months. August, which starts at the end of the west wall and continues on the north wall, is characterized by representations of the liberal arts and the mercantile industries (Fig. 6.6).

The image of Saint Thomas marks the beginning of the scenes pertaining to August. For some as yet unexplained reason (thought to be an irreparable mistake by the artist), the personification of August has been inverted with that of September.[11]

[11]The figure of August found in the September grouping is depicted as harvesting grapes. The month of August is traditionally associated with the fruit-harvesting season.

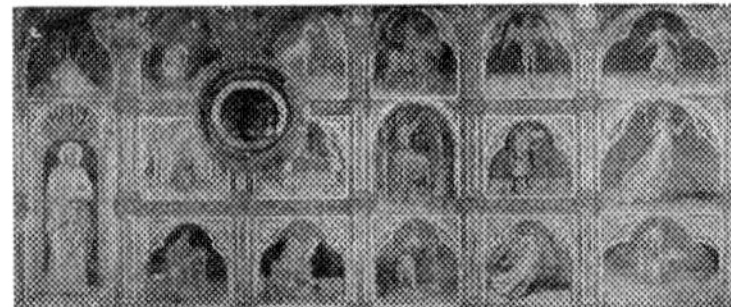

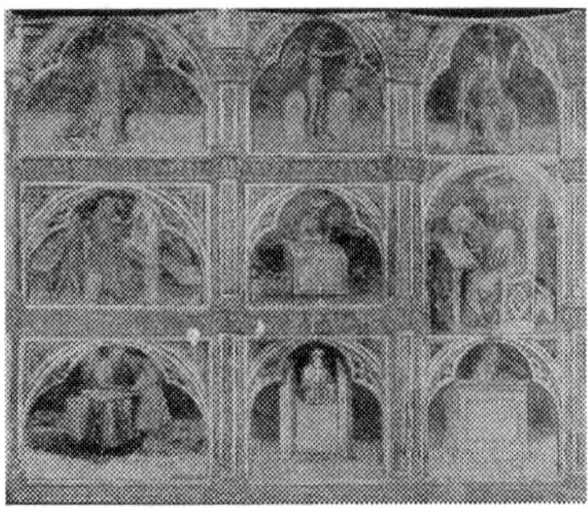

Figure 6.6: **Month of August. Padua, Salone della Ragione.**

The figure of August is followed by images of literature, writing, mathematics, geometry, music, painting, grammar, dialectic, and philosophy. Mercury has its house in the sign of the Virgin, who is dressed in a long, flowing tunic, holding flowers in her hands.

In the month of August, we find a standing musical figure grasping a tambourine in her left hand, about to strike it with her right, and singing. This is a common Trecento image: Giotto painted Miriam singing and holding a tambourine in the Upper Church of Saint Francis of Assisi. The singer-tambourine player is also prominent in Ambrogio Lorenzetti's *Effects of Good Government in the City* in the Palazzo Pubblico in Siena and Andrea di Bonaiuto's *Allegory of the Dominican Order* in Florence. Like the images in these paintings, the depiction of music in the Salone della Ragione fresco exhibits a calm, tranquil demeanor, one that personifies music as part of a well-rounded education.

Music's prominence in the month of August may be explained by the influence of Mercury. Mercury signifies reason and is viewed as the protector of the liberal arts in the tradition of the trivium and the quadrivium.[12]

At the same time, Mercury displays an affinity for poetry and music-making. D'Abano explains Mercury's dual nature in his *Geomantia*, a treatise translated into the vernacular in the sixteenth century. He writes in part 1, book 1:

> Mercury is the planet that incorporates in itself the four elements, that is, earth, water, fire, and air; [the person born under Mercury] is sociable because [Mercury] in the company of good people he is good and with bad he is bad. It denotes servants, messengers, literature, ambassadorial brigades, learning, capable people, excellent

[12]See Barzon 1924, 70, and Panofsky 1960, 199-200.

> men in manual labor, orations, games, pleasantries, pastimes, writing, scholars, particular science, and universally, painters and composers [theorists].[13]

As champion of art and poetry, Mercury is often found carrying two attributes, the flute and the lyre; he is said to have invented the latter (Mirimonde 1977, 25). *The Kalendar and Compost of Shepherds* provides a rich musical description of those born under the influence of Mercury:

> He shall love well to preach and to speak fair rhetoric language, and to talk of philosophy and geometry. He shall love well writing and to read ever in strange books, and to cast accounts of great numbers. And he shall be a gay maker of ballads, songs, meters and rhymes. He shall be perfect in the art of music and love it. He shall love measuring and meting, and shall be some great cloth maker (*The Kalendar* 1930, 147).

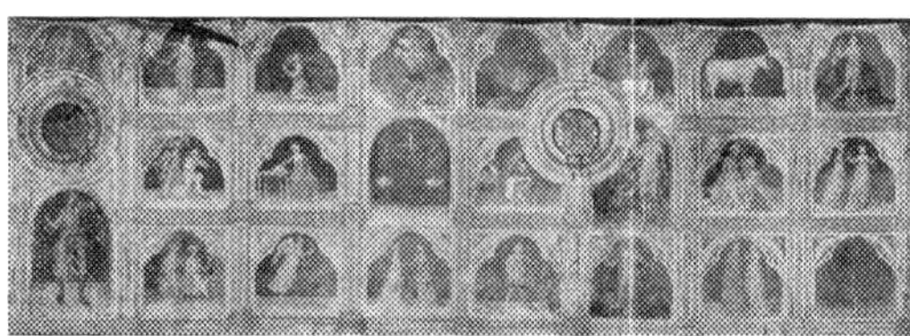

Figure 6.7: **Month of September. Padua, Salone della Ragione.**

The month of September falls under the influence of Venus and the sign of Libra. In the Salone cycle, September begins on the north wall (Fig. 6.7), announced by Saint James, who is followed by many images alluding to love: in the top row, a woman scorns her lover, and in another image the artist has portrayed the fires of love. Women dominate this month – several are shown doing housework and in prayer.

Two musical scenes decorate the month of September. Beneath the woman who declines her lover's advances, one sees the image of two men seated back-to-back playing a harp and fiddle, respectively (Fig. 6.8).

They represent instrumental music. Their hats and casual attire suggest that they are members of the lower classes, perhaps even minstrels. At the

[13]"Mercurio è Pianeta il quale ha in se li quattro elementi, cioè terra, acqua, fuoco, et aria et è comune, perché congiunto con buoni è buono, et con cattivi è cattivo ancor lui. Dinota servitori, noncij, lettere, ambasciate, dottrina, persone dotte, huomeni eccellenti in eserciti manuali, parlamenti, giuochi, piaceri, solazzi, scritture, scholari, scienza particolare, et universale pittori et musici" (D'Abano 1556, 13).

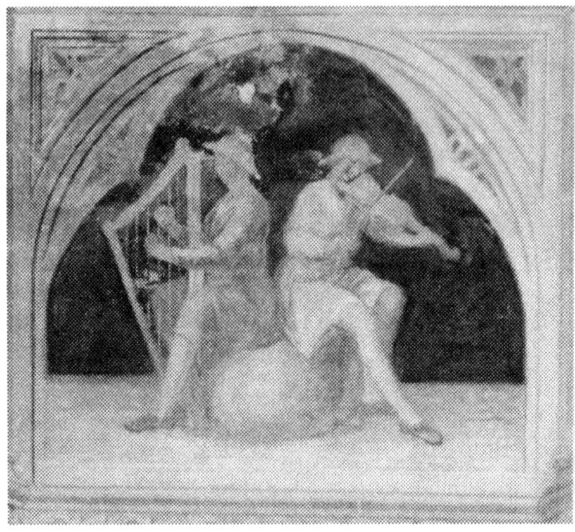

Figure 6.8: **Men Playing a Harp and a Fiddle in September. Padua, Salone della Ragione.**

other end of this row, two women dance together, holding each other's hand and moving in careful, moderate steps. As was customary during the period, their own singing accompanies their movements. In contrast to the men, these women represent the upper classes, as revealed by their flowing gowns and perfectly coiffed hair. Indeed, in their graceful movements, the dancers recall those in Lorenzetti's *Effects of Good Government in the City* in Siena. One woman is depicted in silhouette, the other has her back to the viewer. Both musical scenes reflect the sign of Libra, represented as scales in their duality, and many of the other images of the month depict two figures as well.

Libra is ruled by the planet Venus, who enjoys a rich and well-known association with music as the planet of love and sensuality. The *De Sphaera* of Firmico, another early Trecento astrologer, captures her allure:

With her ardor the gracious Venus	La graziosa Venere del suo ardore
lights up genteel hearts, whence in singing	Accende i cuor gentili, onde in cantare
and dancing and delightful feasts for love	Et danze, et vaghe feste per amore
she indicates with beautiful gazing.[14]	L'indice col soave vagheggiare

Pietro also notes Venus's connection to music in his *Geomantia*:

[14]This poem is quoted by Barzon 1924, 64.

> The planet Venus is warm, humid, and benign but of little bounty and virtue, so that it is neither good nor bad; according to the investigation, it denotes amicable people, lively young people with few worries, beautiful men and women, dances, playing, songs, revelers, falling in love, love affairs, prostitutes, sumptuous men, pomp, and fashion.[15]

Venus makes many appearances in Trecento musical texts. As the brightest star in the heavens, she is mentioned in several of the madrigals that appear in the Rossi Codex, believed to have originated in the Veneto region in the early Trecento. We read about her, for example, in the anonymous madrigals "When the dusk begins and the star in the shape of a woman appears" ("Quando l'aire comenza a farsi bruno/ et a parer la stella aparveme una donna molto bella") and "The beautiful star, whose flame is always alit in my mind" ("La bella stella, che sua fiama tene acesa sempre ne la mente mia."). Her presence at the beginning of these madrigals sets the tone for the narrator's expressions of passionate, though generally unrequited, love.

The presence of music during the rule of Libra in the Salone frescoes – and its perplexing scarcity during the sign of Taurus – is of particular interest in understanding the meaning of these musical images. Ristoro d'Arezzo's influential astrological treatise, *Della composizione del mondo*, written at the end of the Duecento, provides insight into this matter.[16]

After explaining Venus's traditional association with pleasantries (with "men of the court, and with singers of love, and instrumentalists of love and instrumentalists [in general] and with all games and pleasantries, and with all diversions, and with all the generations of instruments that provide pleasure"),[17] Ristoro notes that there is a significant difference between the influence of Venus in Libra and that in Taurus:

> And it also came with the sign of Taurus; it seems that it was useful in the world, and it also appeared that Venus dominated animals, because of lust. And let us see which of these signs is more noble, and which sign is masculine and which is feminine... (3.5).[18]

---

[15]"Venere è Pianeta caldo et humido benigno ma di poca bontà et vertù così nel bene, come nel male, secondo il quesito dinota persone amicabili, giovani allegri di pochi fastidi, belli huomeni, e belle donne; balli, suoni, canti, bagordi, inamoramenti, colloqui amorosi, meretrice, huomini lussuriosi, pompe e foggie" (D'Abano 1556, 13).

[16]On Ristoro, see Austin 1913.

[17]"...uomini di corte, e con cantatori d'amore e suonatori d'amore e suonatori e con tutt'i gli giuochi e sollazzi, e con tutte l'allegrezze, e con tutte le generazion di quelli stormenti che dilettano" (D'Arezzo 1864, 111).

[18]"Ed anche venne col segno del tauro, a parere ch'ella fusse utile nel mondo, e anche a parere che Venere avesse dominio negli animali, per cagione della lussuria. E veggiamo qual di questi segni sia più nobile, e quale segno sia mascolino e qual femminino..." (D'Arezzo 1864, 111).

Indeed, Venus in Libra is influenced by the scales of justice. For Ristoro, Libra represents justice and Taurus represents pleasantries.[19] He writes, "It seems that Venus was justice and loved justice, and this sign is called Libra" (3.5). Therefore, Libra is nobler than Taurus and "by reason we may say that Libra is masculine and Taurus is feminine."[20]

The painter of the Salone della Ragione frescoes has embraced this duality of Venus by depicting just moderation in the men playing instruments and women dancing gently to their strains in Libra and by emphasizing the amorous practices of women in Taurus.[21] Several fifteenth-century astrological treatises contain images of music during the reign of Libra and not during that of Taurus, including Biblioteca Riccardiana, 3011, f. 13v, "a male musician sitting on a horse," and Biblioteca Estense, Lat. 697, f. 6r, "a young man with lyre."[22] Conversely, the famous fifteenth-century astrological walls of the Palazzo Schifanoia in Ferrara portray Venus in the month of April accompanied by two lute players, a woman holding two recorders, dancers, and lovers.[23] As we have seen in chapter 4, Venus's association with justice also influences the reading of Giotto's seated *Justice* in the Scrovegni Chapel, and here we return to Ristoro d'Arezzo's astrological treatise, *Della composizione del mondo*, to shed further light on the Salone frescos.

The calm of September is disrupted in October by bellicose Mars and the return of warring and violent tendencies. Saint Simon introduces the month and is followed by images of arms, fighting, duels, a warrior, soldiers, and Mars astride his horse. Scorpio exerts its influence in this sign, and its huge claws are clearly discernible by the viewer from below. The woman who sits strumming a guitar (Fig. 6.9) has been described as a "woman of pleasures"[24]; under the influence of Mars, she represents seduction and power.

Dante's *Convivio* provides a provocative description of the relationship between music and Mars.[25] Written between 1304 and 1308, around the

---

[19]"...pare che Venus fosse giustizia ed amasse giustizia, e questo segno è chiamato libra." (D'Arezzo 1864, 111). The duality of Venus was commonly discussed in the medieval period. John Scotus wrote, "There are two Venuses, one the goddess of pleasure, i.e., a lustful one, whose son is Hermaphroditus, and another one who was Vulcan's wife. Thus there is a love that is chaste and one that is shameful." Quoted in Ferrante. Economou and Goldin 1975, 21.

[20]"...adunque potemo dire per ragione che libra sia mascolino e tauro femminino" (D'Arezzo 1864, 112).

[21] *The Kalendar* (1930, 146) includes this description of the relationship between instrumental music and Venus: "They shall love the voice of trumpets, clarions and other minstrelsy, and they shall be pleasant singers with sweet voice."

[22]These manuscripts are described in McGurk 1966, 37 and 49.

[23]For a reproduction of *April*, see Paolo d'Ancona 1954, plate 15.

[24]Fantelli and Pellegrini 1990: first insert between 32 and 33.

[25]The astrological portions of Dante's *Convivio* were greatly influenced by the work of

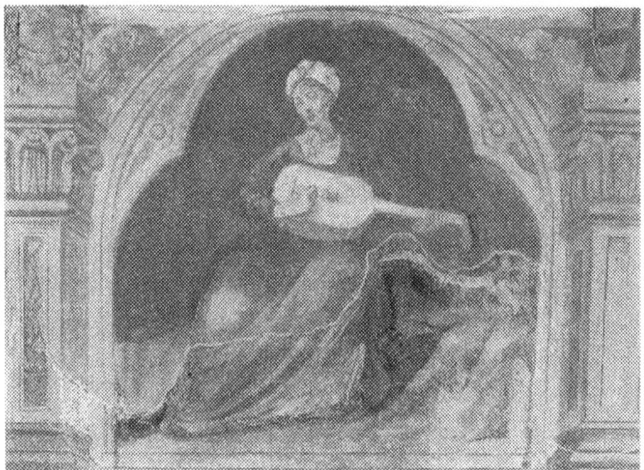

Figure 6.9: **Woman Playing a Guitar in October. Padua, Salone della Ragione.**

time of his sojourn in Padua (March-September 1306), the *Convivio* alternates between love poems and prose explanations.[26] Like Latini's *Tresor* before it, Dante's *Convivio* consists of a compilation of secular knowledge and divine wisdom. Dante fashions his narrative through the allegory of Lady Philosophy, whom he praises as an object of his devotion. Waxing Platonic, Dante notes that each individual is most familiar with the things in life that best suit him. Therefore in book 1, chapter 12, we read: "of all men a son is closest to his father; of all the professional skills medicine is closest to the doctor and music to the musician, since these are the most fully united to them."[27] In similar fashion, Dante writes about music to illuminate a point concerning the character of a philosopher:

> No one is to be called a philosopher, then, who for the sake of some pleasure is a friend of one aspect or another of wisdom, as are many who take pleasure in listening to canzoni in being students of them, or who take pleasure in being students of Rhetoric or Music, while

Arab astronomer Alfraganus. Many Arab treatises on music were translated into Latin during the thirteenth century. Of interest is Bar Hebraeus 1899. On astrology and Dante, see Zancanella 1935.

[26] Dante intended the *Convivio* to consist originally of fifteen books, of which only four were completed.

[27] Dante, *The Banquet*, translated by Ryan 1989. "... onde di tutti li uomini lo figlio è più prossimo al padre; di tutte l'arti la medicina è la più prossima al medico, e la musica al musico, però che a loro sono più unite che l'altre" (Dante 1968, 41).

> shunning and neglecting the other sciences, which all form part of wisdom (3.11.9).[28]

In book 2, chapter 13, of the *Convivio*, Dante focuses his attention on the significance of *cielo* (heaven). Dante makes clear that he will speak of the *scienza* of the heavens rather than the irrational thoughts sometimes associated with the movements of the stars. He asserts that the heavens share three principal similarities with the sciences (2.13.3-4): (1) Both concern revolutions of one body around an immobile object. Each moving body revolves only around its own center, and except for its own motion, does not move. So, like the heavens, science revolves around an immovable subject. (2) Both illuminate each other. Each sphere sheds light on objects as knowledge does. (3) Both bring about perfection to those disposed toward its attainment.

To further substantiate the scientific nature of the study of celestial bodies, Dante explains the correspondence between the order of the heavens and the sciences in the *Convivio* (2.13.8): "To the first seven heavens correspond the seven sciences making up the trivium and quadrivium: Grammar [Moon], Dialectic [Mercury], Rhetoric [Venus], Arithmetic [Sun], Music [Mars], Geometry [Jupiter], and Astronomy [Saturn]."[29]

Dante adds three more spheres to make ten. "To the eighth sphere (the sphere of the Stars) corresponds natural science, called Physics, and the foremost science, called Metaphysics; to the ninth sphere corresponds moral science; and to the heaven at rest corresponds the divine science, called Theology."[30]

Dante then explores the grounds for these assertions. In so doing, he provides the following elaborate description of Mars and music. He begins with a discussion of two primary characteristics of Mars, which concern

[28]"Onde non si dee dicere vero filosofo alcuno che, per alcuno diletto, con la sapienza in alcuna sua parte sia amico; sì come sono molti che si dilettano in intendere canzoni ed istudiare in quelle, e che si dilettano studiare in Rettorica o in Musica, e l'altre scienze fuggono e abbandonano, che sono tutte membra di sapienza" (Dante 1968, 139-140).

[29]"A li sette primi rispondono le sette scienze del Trivio e del Quadrivio, cioè Grammatica, Dialettica, Rettorica, Arismetrica, Musica, Geometria e Astrologia" (Dante 1968, 86). Ristoro d'Arezzo conceives a different partnering of planets and the liberal arts. He writes in book 8, chapter 6 of the *Della composizione del mondo*, "And there are seven liberal arts, no more, so that each planet has its own; the most vile, like grammar, will be by reason of the most vile planet, the moon; dialectic is of Mercury; and Venus will have music, and so each planet its own." ("E anche saranno sette arti liberali e non più, sì che ciascheduno pianeto avrà la sua; la più vile, come la grammatica, sarà per ragione del più vile pianeto come la luna, de la dialettica sarà di Mercurio, e Venere avrà le musica e così ciascheduno avrà la sua").

[30]"A l'ottava spera, cioè a la stellata, risponde la scienza naturale, che Fisica si chiama, e la prima scienza, che si chiama Metafisica; a la nona spera risponde la scienza morale; ed al cielo quieto risponde la scienza divina, che è Teologica appellate" (Dante 1968, 86).

the relative position of Mars in the universe and its physical nature. With regard to its position, Dante notes that Mars enjoys the *più bella relazione* ("the most beautiful relation") because it stands at the center between the Sun and the tenth sphere. Counting from the outermost to the innermost orb, Mars is always fifth (2.13.20-21) "...and so midway between all the others, that is midway between the first two, the second two, the third two, and the fourth two."[31]

With regard to its physical nature, Dante sets forth Mars's many associations with fire. Citing Ptolemy's *Quadripartite*, he notes that Mars desiccates objects and for this reason appears red in color (2.13.21). Dante then alludes to Albumasar, an Arab astrologer who stated that the burning vapors surrounding Mars signify the death of kings and the changing of the guard. Furthermore, Dante writes that Seneca witnessed a ball of flames in the heavens at the time of Augustus's death. Florence also experienced the vision of flames in the sky (2.13.22): "...in the beginning of her destruction, a figure of a cross was seen in the sky, created by a great quantity of vapors that follow the star of Mars."[32]

Dante compares Mars's two primary qualities to musical properties (2.13. 23-24). Like Mars, music exemplifies unique relationships, enjoying, for example, the *più bella relazione* with words. To Dante, "Music is entirely a matter of relationships, as is evident in the *parole armonizzate*."[33] With the term *parole armonizzate* Dante probably is referring to words that are specifically written with music in mind.[34]

[31]"...da qualunque si conmincia o da l'infimo o dal sommo, esso cielo di Marte è lo quinto, esso è lo mezzo di tutti, cioè de li primi, de li secondi, de li terzi e de li quarti" (Dante 1968, 88).

[32]"...nel principio de la sua destruzione, veduta fu ne l'aere, in figura d'una croce, grande quantità di questi vapori seguaci de la stella di Marte" (Dante 1968, 89). The reference to Florence's destruction has been much debated (Dante 1968, 89). Perhaps Dante means to portray the destruction of Florence by Totila. Dino Compagni speaks of a vermillion cross seen in the sky above the Palazzo dei Priori a few days after the entrance of Charles of Valois to Florence. This corresponds to the first years of Dante's exile. In addition, Florence was believed to have been founded by Mars, and the Baptistery in Florence was thought, during the Renaissance, to be an ancient temple dedicated to the planet.

[33]"...la quale è tutta relativa, sì come si vede ne le parole armonizzate" (Dante, 1968, 89).

[34]In 2.9.2-3, Dante also makes clear that *canzoni* were intended to be sung: "This part will be more fully understood if I explain that in the canzone form this part is generally called the "tornata" because the poets who introduced the custom of composing it did so in order that, once the canzone itself had been sung, they might turn and address it [the canzone]". ("E acciò che questa parte più pienamente sia intesa, dico che generalmente si chiama in ciascuna canzone 'tornata,' però che li dicitori che prima usaro di farla, fenno quella perché cantata la canzone, con certa parte del canto ad essa si ritornasse" [Dante 1968, 79-80]). He strengthens the musical quality of the canzona's words later when he

He explains that one achieves harmony in song when one achieves beauty in the relationship between words and music,[35] and concludes that music is the science of relations: "for the sweetness of harmony created by any one of these works [poetry or music] is in proportion to the beauty of the relationship within it" (2.13.23).[36]

With regard to the physical nature of Mars (its dryness), Dante notes that like Mars, music affects the human spirit. He explains (2.13.24), "Music draws to itself the various spirits in a person (which may be said to consist mainly of vapors of the heart) to the extent that they almost cease to carry out any of their functions."[37] He further elucidates, "To such a degree does the soul form a single entity when it hears music, that the power in all the spirits rushes, as it were, to the sensitive spirit, which receives the sound."[38] For Dante, the dryness of Mars is comparable to the heat generated by the vapors of the human heart.

Dante's commentary on the properties of music is relevant to the Salone della Ragione frescoes in several ways. First, music concerns the sacred connection between objects, both between music and text and between individual pitches. Similarly, the Salone frescoes depict the relationship between the motions and properties of the heavens and terrestrial events. Second, music acts upon the intricate workings of the human body. By comparison, the Salone frescoes capture the influence of celestial movement on the actions and emotions of natural life on earth. Third, Dante's emphasis on the importance of exploring "the science of the heavens" and "the science of music" finds a similar voice in the work of Pietro, who advocated scientific investigation into the properties of music and the planets.

The months of November and December each contain but one image of music. In November, we find a splendid portrayal of a hunter accompanied by his two dogs, blowing into a horn (Fig. 6.10).

---

notes (2.11.9), "O people who cannot grasp the meaning of this canzona, do not for that reason spurn it; rather, recognize the great beauty it has: in syntax, the province of grammarians, in the structure governing its presentation, the province of rhetoricians, and in the rhythmical form of its parts, the province of musicians." ("O uomini, che vedere non potete la sentenza di questa canzone, non la rifiutate però; ma ponete mente la sua bellezza, ch'è grande sì per construzione, la quale si pertiene a li gramatici, sì per l'ordine del sermone, che si pertiene a li rettorici, sì per lo numero de le sue parti, che si pertiene a li musici" [Dante 1968, 81]).

[35] "... e ne li canti, de' quali tanto più dolce armonia resulta, quanto più la relazione è bella" (Dante 1968, 89).

[36] "... la quale in essa scienza massimamente è bella, perché massimamente in essa s'intende" (Dante 1968, 89).

[37] "Ancora, la Musica trae a sé li spiriti umani, che quasi sono principalmente vapori del cuore, sì che cessano da ogni operazione" (Dante 1968, 89).

[38] "... si è l'anima intera, quando l'ode, e la virtù di tutti quasi corre a lo spirito sensibile che riceve lo suono" (Dante1968, 89).

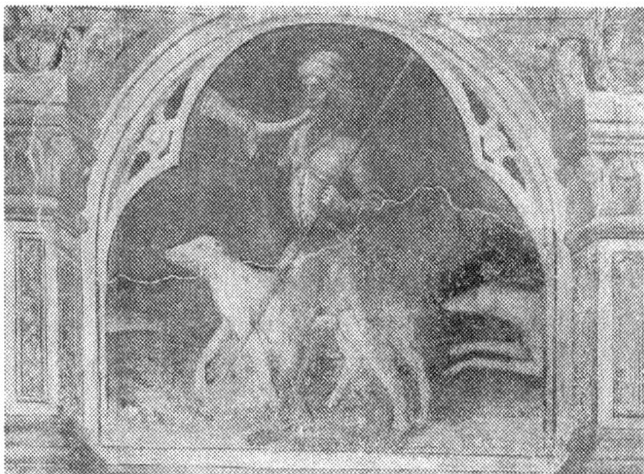

Figure 6.10: **Hunter Blowing a Horn in November. Padua, Salone della Ragione.**

He wears a hat and a red tunic and carries a sword and staff. The playing of horns is a favorite literary device in the Trecento genre of the caccia; examples include Gherardello da Cascia's caccia *Tosto che l'alba*, which describes vivid horn calls and a frenetic chase.

Cecco d'Ascoli's *L'Acerba*, book 3, chapter 15, lines 2987-2992, provides a tantalizing explanation for horn-playing during the hunt. Cecco argues that the stag delights in the hunter's music-making:

The stag finds pleasure in melody.	Il cervo in melodia si diletta,
That is why one hunter sings and plays	Sicché l'un cacciatore canta e suona
and the other pierces him with an arrow.	E l'altro mortalmente lo saetta.
And if the river or other water passes over	Se un fiume o se qualche acqua può passare,
the stag, he will regain strength; therefore,	Riprende forza, si con si ragiona
the hunters will not be able to capture him.	Che i cacciatori non lo pon pigliare.

Indeed, November, the month traditionally associated with hunting, is governed by Jupiter, another planet that exudes musical influence on earth. The *Kalendar and Compost of Shepherds* contains the following description: "He shall be happy in merchandise, and shall have plenty of gold and silver; and he shall love to sing and to be honestly merry" (*Kalendar* 1930, 143).

A harp appears at the outset of the month of December, just above the figure of Saint Matthew (Fig. 6.11).[39]

[39]The Lyra constellation is illuminated in many medieval manuscripts. See, for example, Padua, Biblioteca Antoniana 27, f. 132v., and Monza, Biblioteca capitolare F. 9/176, f. 66r. Reproductions of these images are found in McGurk 1966, plate IXa and plate XI.

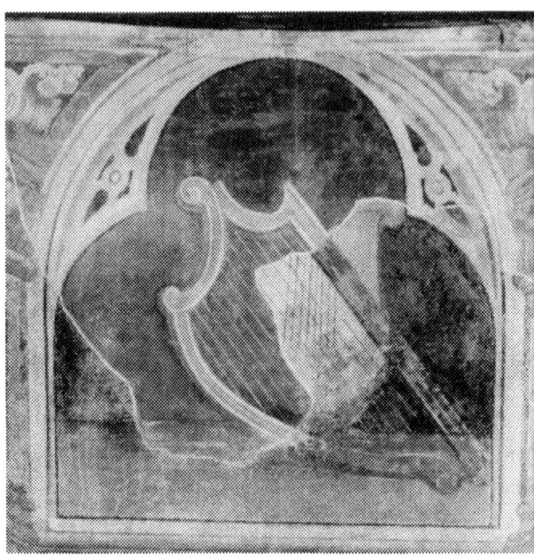

Figure 6.11: **Constellation Lyra in December. Padua, Salone della Ragione.**

It is the only image in the entire astrological ceiling to depict an instrument without its player. Vescovini suggests that the harp represents the constellation Lyra because the constellation consists of seven stars and the harp has seven strings (Vescovini 1990, 32-33). Vega, the brightest star in the constellation, emits a kind of blue luster, and was called by the ancients "Harp-Star" and "the Arc-light of the Sky." In Greek lore, the Lyra is the celestial harp invented by Hermes and given to Orpheus by Apollo (Olcott 1911, 257). Orpheus used the lyre to charm Pluto into letting his beloved Euridice out of Hell.

Though Vescovini's assertion is certainly plausible – since the top row of images in the Salone frescoes typically contain symbols relating to the constellations – the constellation Lyra is most clearly seen during the summer months, not during the month of December. I argue that the appearance of Lyra in December is a painter's error (as was the placement of the figure of September into the frescoes dedicated to the month of August, as previously mentioned). Indeed, taciturn Saturn, the planet that rules December, does not display alliances to music in late medieval sources.

Representations of music-making on the Salone della Ragione walls in Padua appear only under the influence of select planets and during select months of the year. These are the Sun (July), Mercury (May and August), Venus (September), Mars (October) and Jupiter (November). Music does not appear at all under the influence of the Moon, and its appearance in Saturn is debatable.[40]

In each instance, the artist has stressed the rational and scientific approach to music, especially in its relation to Mercury and the noble side of Venus. The musical frescoes of the Salone della Ragione capture the more tempered, moderate, and studious approach to music invoked by Pietro, Giotto, Dante, Cecco, and the Paduan school. As pictured in these frescoes, music represents education, contemplation, balance, and civic pride rather than a rambunctious renewal of the seasons like that seen in the Provençal song "Kalenda maya," for example, or even in Stravinsky's *The Rite of Spring*, a piece that thoroughly evokes the irrationality and chaos associated with the return of warmth. The Salone della Ragione frescoes stand as a unique product of pre-humanist Padua and signal the waning of the scholastic approach to the representation of the heavens and their influence. The next stage in the history of astrological ceilings will be marked by the opulence and sensuality of Renaissance themes, such as those found in the images of the Sala della Schifanoia in Ferrara.

While the Salone della Ragione frescoes weave secular and sacred iconographies together in a presentation of the days of the year, Giusto de' Menabuoi's frescoes in the Baptistery of Padua concern themselves with the Apocalypse, one of the most frighteningly vivid of sacred texts. Like medieval representations of the seasons and the planets, the Apocalypse is a familiar topic for musical embellishment. Emanuel Winternitz (1967, 29) notes that in the Middle Ages musical subjects were "limited to illustrations of the Scriptures (especially of apocalyptical themes), the Rex Psalmista, and the 150th Psalm." He outlines the subjects to include (1) the seven angels with trumpets, (2) the seven holy men playing instruments in front of the Lamb, (3) two figures flanking each of the animals with the Lamb, (4) the seven holy men, and (5) the twenty-four elders surrounding Christ in Glory. Many of these early Apocalyptic scenes are found in manuscripts, including the eleventh-century Beatus MS of Saint Sevère, Bibliothèque Nationale, Paris. Some are found in churches, such as Santiago di Compostela, Portico de la Gloria, and Chartres Cathedral, Portail Royal. Vasari notes in his *Vite* that upon being called by King Robert to Naples, Giotto painted stories from the Apocalypse in a chapel there, located in the Church of

[40]That music is allied to particular planets is substantiated by Marsilio Ficino in his *De Vita* 3.21. Ficino notes that Jupiter creates a grave constant harmony, Venus a light and lascivious one; Mercury and the Sun create moderate music. Mars, Saturn, and the Moon are assigned nonmusical voices. For more on this subject, see Tomlinson 1990.

Santa Chiara, "ordinategli (per quanto dice) da Dante," who was also in Naples at that time (Vasari 1550, 143).

Giusto de' Menabuoi's frescoes and polyptych in the Baptistery of Padua contain a fascinating array of musical representations drawn from the Book of Revelation. Together with the Scrovegni Chapel frescoes, Giusto's decorations are considered one of the greatest achievements in late medieval art. Fina Buzzaccarini, the wife of Francesco il Vecchio of Carrara, commissioned the frescoes and Giusto completed them circa 1376 to 1378.[41]

His monumental *Paradise* has been dubbed by art historian Claudio Bellinati (1994, 3) "one of the most suggestive in the world." The frescoes consist of *Paradise*; scenes from the Old Testament; images of the four evangelists; stories of Saint John the Baptist, Mary, and Christ; and the Apocalypse. Instruments and music-making are prominent in *Paradise* and the *Apocalypse* in a unique and unprecedented manner. Baroncelli's angel orchestra pales in comparison to the Mahlerian group that appears in Giusto's *Paradise* (Fig. 6.12).

To begin with, eight musical angels surround the figure of the Virgin Mary alongside her body-length gold halo (Fig. 6.13). Together with the backdrop, they provide a visual and aural border between her and the multitude of angels and important people around her. She is located before her son and functions like a musical predella, so often found in the art of this period. Thirty-eight angels (two of which are only partially seen seated behind the Virgin Mary) encircle the figure of Christ and form the third row of figures. Of these angels, thirty-one are playing discernible instruments. The remaining angels appear seated near them. The eight angels surrounding the Virgin and the thirty-two musical angels encircling Christ come together at the figure of the blue-clad Virgin, uniting the two in music. One more musician playing the psaltery appears in the crowd, and this is most likely David, who is found diagonally to the left of Christ's head.

From bottom left and moving counterclockwise, the musical angels around the Virgin play a trapezoidal psaltery, a portative organ, a fiddle, another organ, a gittern, a lute, a rebec (?), and a portative organ. Unlike Giotto's Baroncelli Polyptych, we find the instruments placed here in a more haphazard fashion. One would expect the organs, the louder or "harmonic" instruments as Marchetto would have designated them, at the bottom. But as one moves up the left side, one finds another organ tucked in below the Virgin's right hand. Also, Giusto does not imitate the subtlety of Giotto's mirror imaging, and the organs around the Virgin are played with the same hands. This is also true of the two string players above them; thus one does

[41] Giusto was a Florentine by birth and probably came to the Veneto region between 1350 and 1360. On Giusto's life, see Bettini 1960.

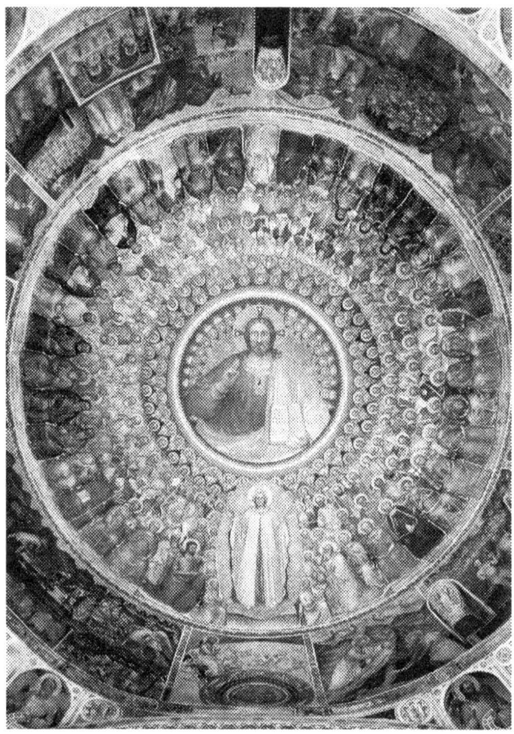

Figure 6.12: **Giusto de' Menabuoi, *Paradise*. Padua, Baptistery.**

not have the benefit of looking at the instruments from different perspectives. While the first two tiers of instruments are parallel to each other, the next two tiers are not. The instruments are gorgeous representations of originals, and we note the precise representations of the bellows and the keys of the organ, as well as the beautiful depiction of the delicate filigrees of the psaltery and the fiddles' sounding boards. The angels are dressed in white with a triangular crown, or tiara, atop their heads. A tiara, in fact, appears on the head of each musical angel in *Paradise*. The Virgin, with her uplifted arms, appears to be receiving the heavenly music that surrounds her, signifying her place in Paradise.

Moving counterclockwise from the standing Virgin Mary in the second circle around God, we find the thirty-eight angels holding the following items: (1) psaltery, (2) psaltery, (3) mirror with the reflection of the Sun in it, (4) two recorders, (5) bagpipe, (6), harp, (7) vielle, (8) a staff, (9)

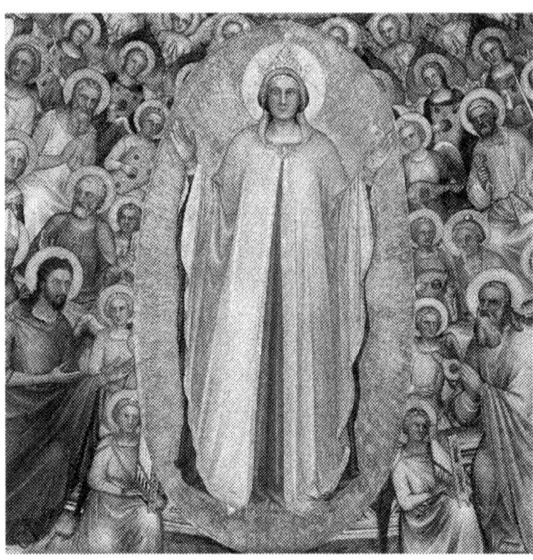

Figure 6.13: **Giusto de' Menabuoi, *Paradise*. Detail, Virgin Mary. Padua, Baptistery.**

vielle, (10) lute, (11) lute, (12) a thicker wooden staff in the angel's right hand and a shorter staff, perhaps a scroll, in the left hand, (13) a staff in the right hand and a shield with a red cross in the left, (14) organ, (15) tabor, (16) vielle, (17) drum, (18) a green branch, (19) scales in the left hand, a staff in the right, (20) psaltery, (21) psaltery, (22) psaltery, (23) dulcimer, (24) cymbals(?), (25) harp, (26) vielle, (27) lute, (28) vielle, (29) cymbal, (30) cimella, (31) bagpipe, (32) book or hurdy-gurdy, (33) drum, (34) mirror with the reflection of the Sun in it, (35) drum, and (36) psaltery. The thirty-seventh and thirty-eighth angels stand behind the Virgin.

Applying Pietro's and Marchetto's divisions of music, we find that the majority of the instruments are rhythmic, that is, they do not involve the breath: these are the psalteries, harps, vielles, lutes, organ, drums, and cymbals. There are a few wind instruments, including recorders and a cimella; and no organic music: none of the angels are singing. Of the rhythmic instruments, the psalteries are most numerous (six), followed by the vielle (five), and the lute (three).

Music abounds in the Baptistery's apse, which houses scenes from the Apocalypse. Taken from the Book of Revelation, the Apocalypse conveys the prophetic mysteries that Jesus conveyed to Saint John. Giusto's mu-

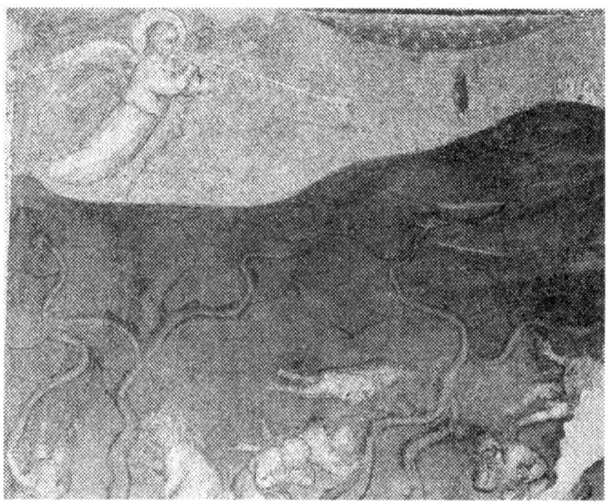

Figure 6.14: **Giusto de' Menabuoi, *Apocalypse*. Detail, first angel with trumpet. Padua, Baptistery.**

sical representations are far more elaborate and prevalent than Cimabue's musical angels in the Church of Saint Francis of Assisi. Giusto, for example, allots much more space to the trumpeting angels than did Cimabue. We recall that seven angels encircle Christ in the Cimabue picture. Giusto, instead, paints five separate scenes depicting a trumpeting angel in the context of the story in Revelation. The first angel holds the long trumpet in his left hand as he hovers above the ground (Fig. 6.14). The story recounts that after the Lamb opened the seventh seal, trumpets were given to seven angels standing before God. Revelation reads, "The first angel blew his trumpet, and there followed hail and fire, mixed with blood, which fell on the earth; and a third of the earth was burnt up, and a third of the trees were burnt up, and all green grass was burnt up" (Rev. 8:7). Giusto's second angel plays his instrument with puffed cheeks, supporting it with his left hand while his right hand holds it to his mouth in a Giottesque fashion (Fig. 6.15). Below, boats sink into a swirling blue sea, and in the background can be seen a red column of fire. ("The second angel blew his trumpet, and something like a great mountain, burning with fire, was thrown into the sea, and a third of the sea became blood, a third of the living creatures in the sea died, and a third of the ships were destroyed" Rev. 8:8).

Giusto's third trumpeting angel, who also holds the instrument in his left hand, points it towards a hilltop city, while men and women and their oxen walk below (Fig. 6.16). The top part of the painting is damaged. ("The third angel blew his trumpet, and a great star fell from heaven, blazing like

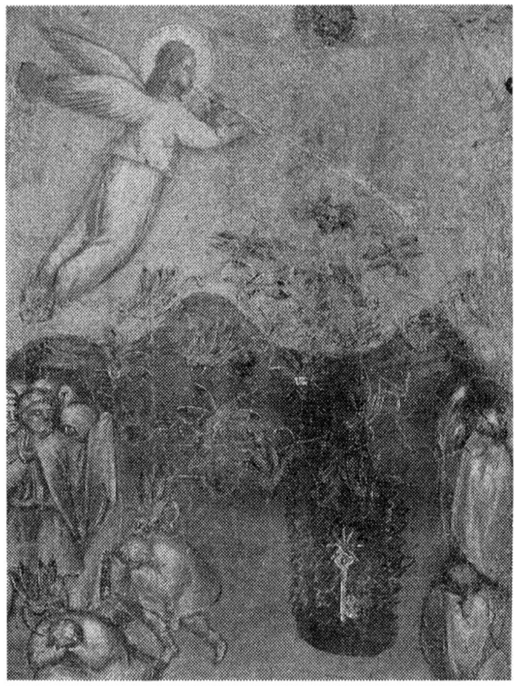

Figure 6.15: **Giusto de' Menabuoi, *Apocalypse*. Detail, second angel with trumpet. Padua, Baptistery.**

a torch, and it fell on a third of the rivers and on the fountains of water. The name of the star is Wormwood. A third of the waters became wormwood, and many men died of the water, because it was made bitter" Rev. 8:10). Floating above a devastated greenish earth, with people suffering below and in the background a burning star, is the fourth angel. ("The fourth angel blew his trumpet, and a third of the Sun was struck, and a third of the moon, and a third of the stars, so that a third of their light was darkened; a third of the day was kept from shining, and likewise a third of the night" Rev. 8:12).

A fifth trumpeting angel floats above a gold key while men cower below, and black smoke billows around the key (Fig. 6.17). ("And a fifth angel blew his trumpet, and I saw a star fallen from heaven to earth, and he was given the key of the shaft of the bottomless pit; he opened the shaft of the bottomless pit, and from the shaft rose smoke like the smoke of a great

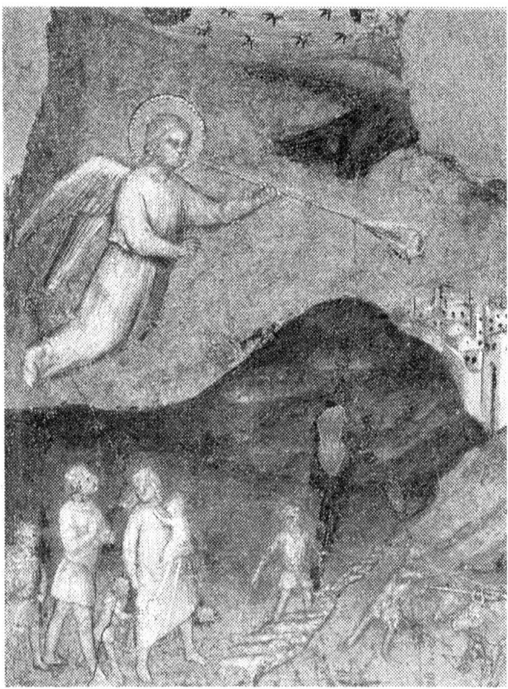

Figure 6.16: **Giusto de' Menabuoi, *Apocalypse*. Detail, third angel with trumpet. Padua, Baptistery.**

furnace, and the Sun and the air were darkened with smoke from the shaft" Rev. 9:1). A sixth angel represents the following: "Then the sixth angel blew his trumpet, and I heard a voice from the four horns of the golden altar before God, saying to the sixth angel who had the trumpet, 'Release the four angels who are bound at the great river Euphrates' " (Rev 9:13). And the seventh angel evokes these words: "Then the seventh angel blew his trumpet, and there was a loud voice in the heaven saying, 'The kingdom of the world has become the kingdom of our Lord and of his Christ, and he shall reign for ever and ever' " (Rev. 11:15).

Lastly, an orchestra of twenty-four men surrounds a seated figure of God (Fig. 6.18). Each man holds a stringed instrument in his right hand and a crown in his left. This is a remarkable pictorial aspect of the fresco for several reasons: the instrument players are not young angels but older men; the men all play the same instrument, a lute of some kind; and the men are

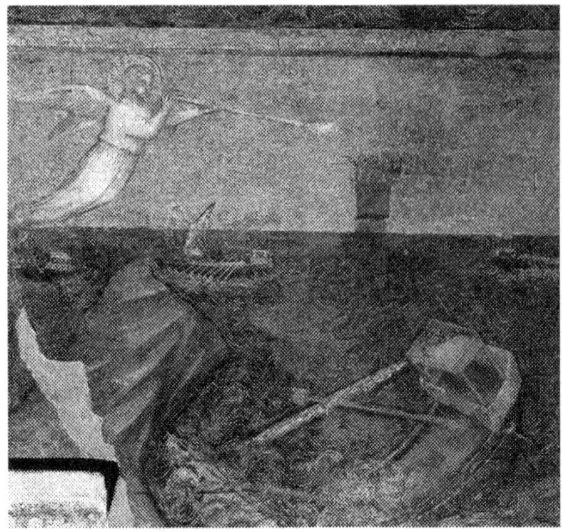

Figure 6.17: **Giusto de' Menabuoi, *Apocalypse*. Detail, fifth angel with trumpet. Padua, Baptistery.**

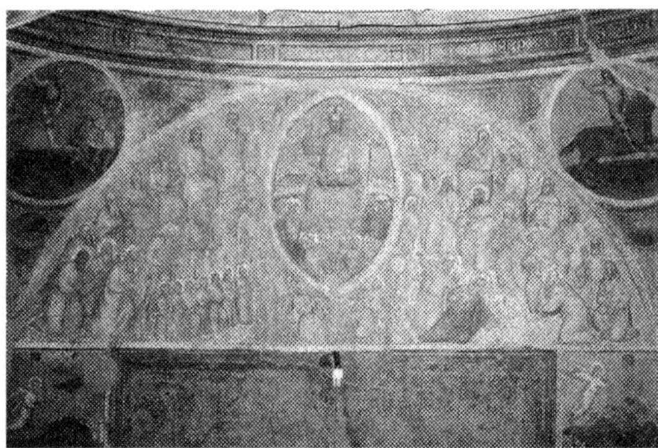

Figure 6.18: **Giusto de' Menabuoi, *Apocalypse*. Detail, God's angel and twenty-four venerable old men. Padua, Baptistery.**

not actually making music with these instruments because they are using only one hand to play. Indeed, some hold the instrument upside down by its neck. Revelation makes no mention of string players in the passage relating to Giusto's scene. Rather, the reference is to vocal music: "And the four living creatures, each of them with six wings, are full of eyes all round and within, and day and night they never cease to sing, 'Holy, holy, holy is the Lord God Almighty, who was and is and is to come.' " The twenty-four also sing: "And whenever the living creatures give glory and honor and thanks to him who is seated on the throne, who lives for ever and ever, the twenty-four elders fall down before him who is seated on the throne and worship him who lives for ever and ever; they cast their crowns before the throne, singing, 'Worthy art thou, our Lord and God, to receive glory and honor and power, for thou didst create all things, and by thy will they existed and were created.' " Giusto painted two versions of *Herod's Feast* in the Paduan Baptistery, each with musicians present. The first appears in his polyptych that was situated above the altar and was presumably painted at the same time as the frescoes. It contains a total of fifty-one scenes, one of which includes music, the *Feast of Herod* (Fig. 6.19).

This scene is found to the bottom right of the central image of the Madonna and Child. Giusto pictures a servant bringing the head of John the Baptist to a banquet table while a woman is dancing in the foreground, accompanied by a man playing a harp. Four men seated at a long table watch the grisly scene and listen to the music while eating and drinking wine. Giusto's Herod narrative is reminiscent of Giotto's in the Church of Saint Francis of Assisi. In both pictures we find a musician prominently displayed, whose strains accentuate the brutal sensuality of the action. Both artists selected "organic" (string) players for their pictures, that is, according to Trecento categorizations of music, players not required to use the voice or the breath. Giotto's *Herod's Feast*, which is quite damaged, is part of the fresco cycle devoted to the lives of Christ and Saint John the Baptist. In this version, Salome dances while two men perform on the organ and the lute and a third plays an unidentifiable instrument or sings. The musicians are placed at the foot of the banquet table to the right of the scene, on the same plane as the dancing Salome and the man holding the head of John the Baptist. The men seated at the table engage with the musicians and Salome, and appear to be clapping their hands and looking directly at the performers. This version of *Herod's Feast* is much more ornately musical, surpassing Giotto's previous rendition of the scene or that of Giusto discussed above.

Giusto's paintings, like those of Altichiero – another painter active in Padua in the last decades of the fourteenth century – seem to rely on Giotto's advances in realism and on an infusion of spiritual Gothicism, still breathing at the end of the Trecento. Sergio Bettini (1960, 12) argues that Giusto's contributions may be seen as "a musical melding of intellect and sensibility." While he chooses to paint the instruments in a realistic manner, their arrangement within the scenes is highly stylized and imaginative. The music in *Herod's Feast* in the polyptych appears to flood the scene, without the

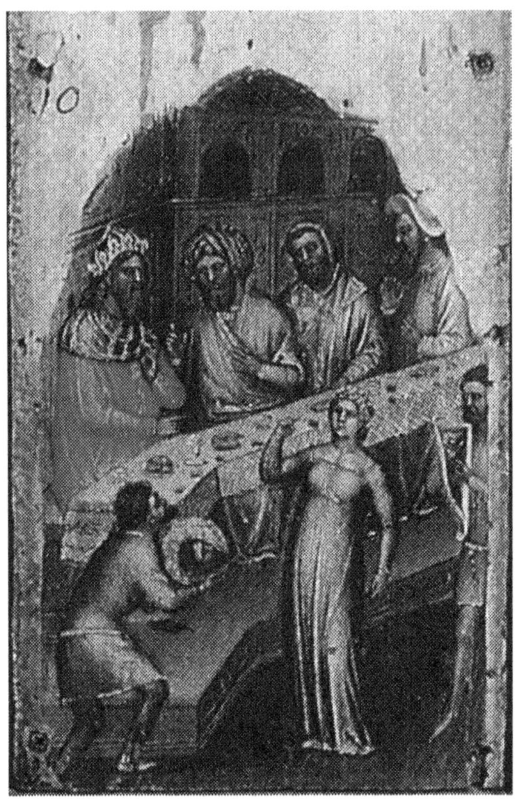

Figure 6.19: **Giusto de' Menabuoi, *Feast of Herod.* Padua, Baptistery, High Altar.**

subtlety of Giotto's more tempered approach. The irony of the presence of music – that music is both a reflection of the divine and a consort of temptation – seems to be missing in Giusto's image. Here in its debauched context, with all looking on in glee and listening to loud instruments, the music accentuates lasciviousness rather than introspection. Howard Mayer Brown (1985), in his "Ambivalent Trecento Attitudes Toward Music: An Iconographical View," argues that this ambivalence is a critical part of the iconography of Trecento music. Millard Meiss (1951, 27-44) has argued persuasively in his *Painting in Florence and Siena after the Black Death* that art became more introspective after the midcentury, an idea substantiated in Giusto's renditions of music. The musical players perform on realistic instruments, although their contributions to the scenes are primarily decorative. I view Giusto's representations of music as paradigmatic of the transitional period to the Renaissance, a time when musical figures become even further stylized and sensualized. In the Renaissance, figures making music reflect the aspect of Venus, capturing her sensual, rather than her reasonable, nature so that even within a sacred context, the musicians are ebullient, playful, and rounded, performing on realistic instruments and assuming more sensual demeanors. This trend can be best seen in our final example, the musical angels in Donatello's sculpture in the Church of the Santo in Padua, also known as the Church of Saint Anthony of Padua.

According to entries from Arca del Santo account books, Donatello completed the altar between the years 1446 and 1450. [42] The Florentine sculptor began crafting the Santo's altar after creating its bronze crucifix and while working on an equestrian monument, the Gattamelata, which stands in the Piazza del Santo. Art historians have debated the extent of Donatello's contributions to the Santo, with some suggesting that he was called to Padua to redesign the presbytery and choir. In his *Urbano da Cortona*, Paul Schubring (1903, 9-10) maintains that Donatello was summoned to Padua to "construct the tribunal of the Church of the Santo."[43] Indeed, documents published by Andrea Gloria (1895, xxi) indicate that he received payment in 1449 for "God the father and the façade of the choir and to have made the façade of the choir in marble" ("per lo dio pare e le fazè del curo e in fare fare quelo antipeto del curo de marmoro"). The façade of the choir was traditionally decorated with marble or bronze reliefs, as can be seen in a comparable choir in the Church of Santa Maria Gloriosa dei Frari in Venice (1468), executed by Marco Cozzi, a follower of the Canozi brothers. The Santo's choir, on which the Canozi worked in the year 1462 and following, burned down in 1749.

The present altar, reconstructed in 1895 by Camillo Boito, features seven bronze statues (Fig. 6.20). From left to right, we see Saint Justina, Saint Francis, Saint Anthony, Madonna and Child, Saint Daniel, Saint Louis, and Saint Prosdocimus; bronze reliefs of angels; four symbols of the evangelists; four miracles performed by Saint Anthony; the Dead Christ with two angels; and a limestone relief of the Entombment of Christ. A bronze crucifix can also be seen on the altar, although it originally belonged atop the entrance of the choir stalls. Boito based his reconstruction on the earliest known description of the altar by Marcantonio Michiel, c.1520, who noted the following:

[42]Selected entries have been transcribed by Janson 1963, 162-167; Gloria, 1895, 3-16; and Gonzati 1852-1853, lxxxv-lxxxiv.

[43]Von Bode (1902, 17) also argues that Donatello worked on the choir.

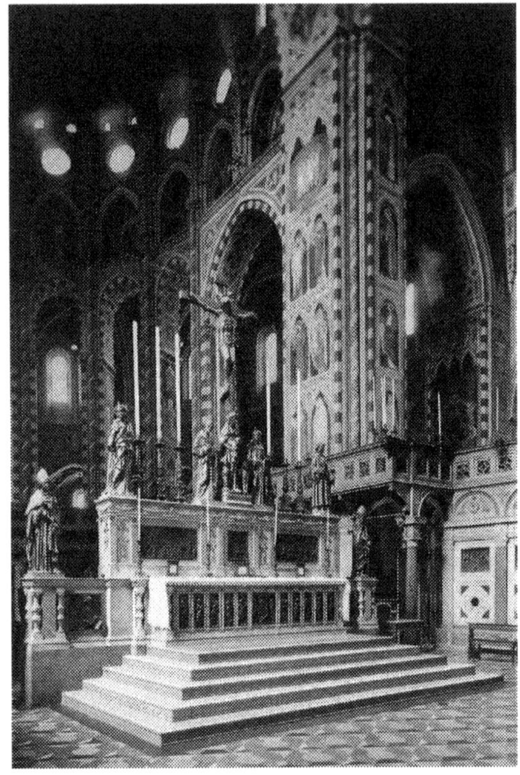

Figure 6.20: **Donatello, High Altar. Padua, Church of Saint Anthony.**

> In the church of the Santo above the high altar, the four bronze figures in the round grouped around the Madonna, and the Madonna; and below these figures on the retable, the two storiated bronze bas-reliefs in front and the two in back in bronze bas-relief, but half-length figures; and behind the altar, beneath the retable, the Dead Christ with the other figures around him, together with the two figures on the right and the two on the left, also in bas-relief but of marble (lost); [all these] were made by Donatello (Michiel 1903, 3).[44]

[44]"Nella chiesa del Santo sopra l'altar maggiore le quattro figure de bronzo tutte tonde attorno la nostra Donna, e la nostra Donna, e sotto le dette figure nel scabello le due istoriette davanti e le due da dietro pur de bronzo de basso rilevo, e li quattro Evangelisti nelli contorni, dui davanti e le due da driedo pur de bronzo e de basso rilevo, ma mezze figure, e da driedo l'altar sotto il scabello il Cristo morto con le altre figure a circo, e

Between 1579 and 1582 a new and larger altar was built under the direction of sculptors Girolamo Campagna and Cesare Franco, using the Donatello bronzes. Two subsequent modifications occurred in 1591 and 1651, and in later years parts of the altar were dispersed to other locations in the church.[45]

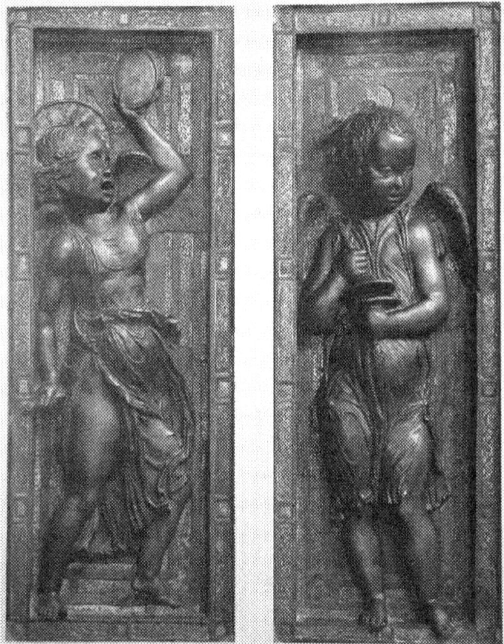

Figure 6.21: **Donatello, High Altar. Detail, panels with angel playing a tambourine. Padua, Church of Saint Anthony.**

In the present-day reconstruction, twelve musical-angel panels are beneath the altar, like a predella. While there are twelve panels, two of them contain two angels each, bringing the total number of angels to fourteen. They appear on Boito's reconstituted altar as follows, from left to right: angel playing a tambourine above its head (Fig. 6.21); angel playing two flutes; angel playing a harp; angel playing a chalumeau; angel playing a lute (Fig. 6.22); two angels singing from a score (Fig. 6.23); angel playing a

le due figure da man destra con le altre due da man sinistra pur de basso rilevo, ma de marmo, furono de mano de Donatello."

[45] Janson 1963, 171.

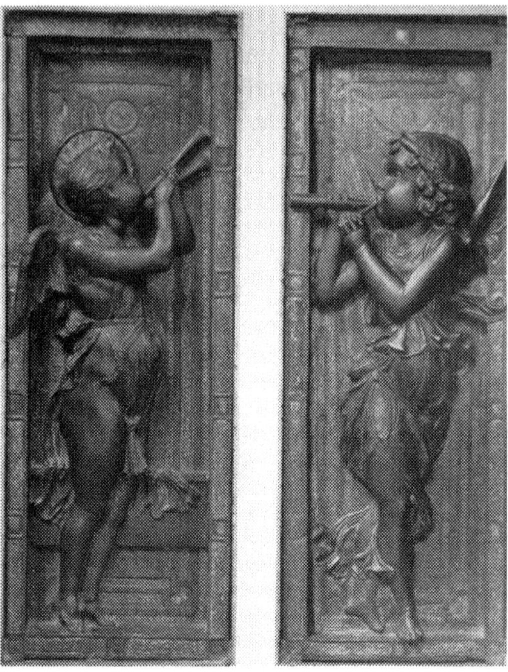

Figure 6.22: **Donatello, High Altar. Detail, angel playing a lute. Padua, Church of Saint Anthony.**

rebec; angel playing a chalumeau; angel playing cymbals; angel playing two flutes; angel putto playing a tambourine. Each relief is fifty-eight cm. high and twenty-one cm. wide. The angels were in part entrusted to Donatello's assistants to complete. Schubring (1903) assigns only two angel panels to Donatello: those of the pairs of singers. He attributes the flute players to Antonio Chellino; the harp and lute players to Urbano da Cortona; the first tambourine, cymbal, and rebec players to Giovanni da Pisa; and the second tambourine player to Francesco Valente. He makes no attribution for the remaining flute players.

Scholars have suggested several interpretations for the musical angels. Schubring (1903) believes that the artists used Psalm 150 as the source for the instruments:

> Praise him with sound of trumpet; praise him with psaltery and harp.
> Praise him with timbrel and choir; praise him with strings and organs.

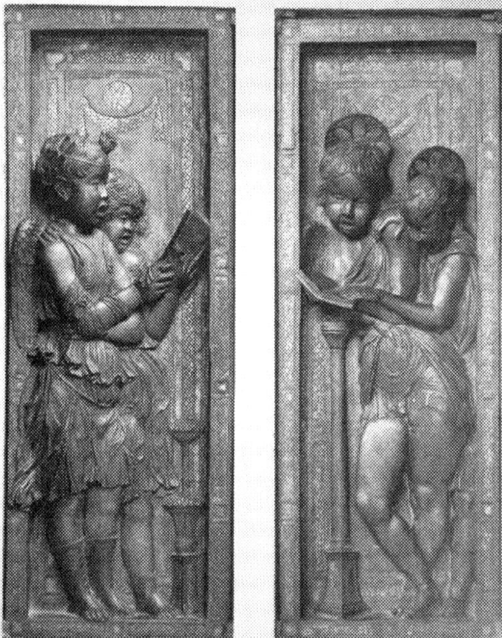

Figure 6.23: **Donatello, High Altar. Detail, angels singing. Padua, Church of Saint Anthony.**

Praise him on high sounding cymbals; praise him on cymbals of joy.[46]

Janson (1963, 179) refutes this notion, saying that not only are several instruments from Psalm 150 missing from Donatello's angels, but one cannot equate *tubae* with trumpets, as Schubring has proposed. Janson argues that the panels fall into two distinct categories: "half of them – the lute, the rebec, and the two flutes – are 'modern' and 'consonant,' i.e., they are instruments of medieval origin designed for the playing of tunes and harmonies. The rest – cymbals, tambourine, and diaulos – are 'ancient' and 'dissonant.' Their purpose was to accompany the dance."

A thirteenth-century musical office by Giuliano da Spira (1985, 213-215), yet to be considered in the art history literature, provides a link between

[46]The Latin Vulgate reads:
Laudate eum in sono tubae laudate eum in psalterio et cithara
Laudate eum in tympano et choro laudate eum in cordis et organo
Laudate eum in cymbalis bene sonantibus laudate eum in cymbalis iubilationis

Saint Anthony and Psalm 150. Spira's antiphon sung at Vespers reads, "At the sound of the trumpet, timpani, cithara, psaltery, cymbals, song, with stringed instruments and the organ, praise my heart God in mystical union with Anthony."[47] ("Sono tube, tympano, Cythara, Psalterio, Cymbalisque Deum, Choro, cordis organo, Laudet in Antonio Mystice cor meum.") In Spira's office, this antiphon introduces the singing of Psalm 150.[48] The tune accompanying the words contains anomalous wide leaps, imitating the instruments' ease in changing registers. Spira's office was familiar in the fourteenth and fifteenth centuries, as parts of it resurfaced in the music of this period. Johannes Ciconia, the *cantor* and *custos* of the Cathedral of Padua in 1403 and known for his motets praising Venice and Padua, composed a work called *O proles Hispanie* based on Spira's antiphon melody of the Magnificat for first Vespers (Durante and Petrobelli 1990, 23-24).[49] Johannes de Lymburgia, who was employed in the Veneto region around 1430, used Spira's antiphon of the Benedictus for his three-voiced motet *Gaude felix Padua.*[50] Guillaume Dufay, to whom we will return later, composed pieces based on Spira's office, employing the text of *O proles Hispanie-O sidus Hispanie* for his four-voiced motet. He also borrowed Spira's texts and music for his antiphons *Sapiente filio* and *Si queris miracula.*

Monks traditionally sang psalms before the Santo altar, as attested to by Vincenzo Rota in his poem *L'incendio del tempio di S. Antonio di Padova* (1749).[51]

Rota's many allusions to musical practice, in particular his familiarity with the violinist and theorist Giuseppe Tartini and the Grande Orchestra del Tempio di S. Antonio, shows that he was knowledgeable about music. In canto 2, verse 22, Rota (1749, 61) writes:

---

[47]"Al suono della tromba, del timpano, della cetra, del salterio e dei cembali, in coro, con strumenti a corda, con l'organo, lodi il mio cuore Dio in mistica unione con Antonio."

[48]A fifteenth-century vernacular version of the *Liber miraculorum* published by Guidaldi (1936, 24-25) contains another story connecting Saint Anthony and the psalms. A novice at Montpellier stole a richly annotated psaltery with which Saint Anthony was teaching. God admonished the boy as he was crossing a bridge, and the boy returned the psalter to Saint Anthony.

[49]Margaret Bent and Anne Hallmark (1985, 110-111) place this motet in the category of opus dubium. Ciconia also composed a motet entitled *O Padua, sidus preclarum* in praise of Saint Anthony.

[50]On this piece of music and the cult of Saint Anthony of Padua, see Lovato 1997.

[51]I have consulted two editions of this poem. They differ substantially with regard to number of stanzas and word selection. The second edition is Rome, 1753. I cite both here and will differentiate the two by date in the citations.

The choir, I say, the isolated semicircular section in front of the Cross, which includes the side where the friars sing psalms with high voices, together with the other side, where the altar is placed, on which the horrible death of the son of the divine Father is offered by the devout Clergy, called Presbytery.	Coro dico io la semicircolare pianta isolata in fronte della Croce che la parte comprende i salmeggiare fogliono i Frati con sonora voce; e l'altra insieme, ov è posto l'altare; sui cui o'offre al divin Padre l'atroce morte del figlio dal divoto Clero, chiamata volgarmente Presbitero.

While Spira's antiphon to Psalm 150 may provide a basis for the program of Donatello's musical angels, one instrument is conspicuously missing from Donatello's inventory of instruments: the organ. The player of the portative organ was a popular figure in the Renaissance, and we see this instrument prominently displayed on Luca della Robbia's *Cantoria*, which includes the text of Psalm 150 on its borders. Several new organs were installed in the area above the Santo's choir in the early 1440s. Giovanni da Vienna, a German master organ builder, was entrusted to assemble the Santo's great organ in 1443, a year before Donatello started work on the bronze crucifix (Rigoni 1936). Giovanni also constructed a smaller organ for the church in 1441. That the installations of the organs were significant to the overall refurbishing of the Santo is attested to by the fact that Francesco Squarcione, who was born in Padova in 1394 and worked in the Santo between 1441 and 1449, was commissioned to paint the wooden doors of the great organ (Gonzati 1852-1853, 54-55). He was also asked to paint the pavement near Donatello's altar, and Gonzati (1852-1853, 55) suggests that he completed a tempera picture for the antique choir. It might have been redundant for Donatello to include angels playing organs, given the recent construction of organs in the Santo.

Rota's *Incendio* (1749, 61) describes the sumptuous sounds that emitted from the Santo's organs in canto 2, verse 23:

The other side has two pilasters per band on which four instruments lean, made of thousands of pipes and sounds, decorated with gold, and shining with gentle arabesques and beautiful festoons; works of excellent deceased masters, and you hear, at the opening of the registers, trumpets, bagpipes, timpani, and tambourines.	Ha questa due per banda pilastroni, a cui quattro s'appoggiano strumenti di mille canne pregni, e mille suoni, d'oro tutti vestiti e risplendenti, con gentili rabeschi, e bei festoni; opere illustri di maestri i più eccellenti; e s'odono all'aprirsi dei registri, trombe, lire, buffon, timpani, e sistri.

Musical angels appear in only one of Donatello's miracle reliefs, the *Ass of Rimini.* Three putti play tambourines above the arches of the church, and four winged figures blow into elongated trumpets alongside the center and right-side arches (Fig. 6.24).

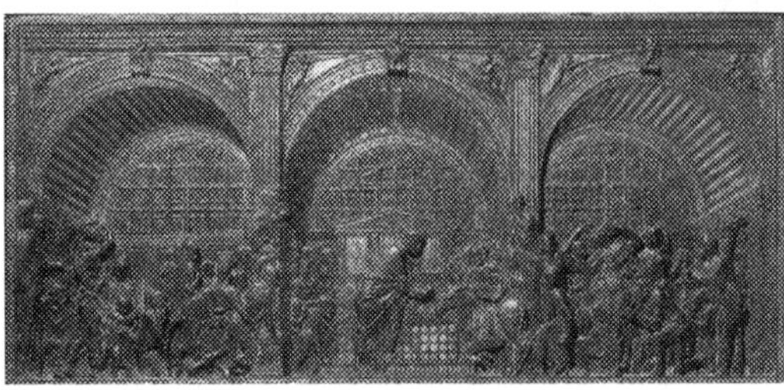

Figure 6.24: **Donatello. *The Ass of Rimini.* High Altar. Padua, Church of Saint Anthony.**

Their presence within this scene suggests that the miracle took place after Saint Anthony had presided over Mass, where music was presumably heard. A fifteenth-century version (Guidaldi 1936, 7-8) of the story reads,

> Whereas the man of God, having celebrated Mass in a chapel situated nearby, after Mass brought forth before the sight of the people the most Holy Body of Christ. And commanding silence, he said to the mule: "I bid thee, animal, and enjoin by the power in the name of thy Creator, whom, though all unworthy, I verily hold in my hands, that straightaway thou come and humbly do Him reverence, so that heretical wickedness may learn thereby how every creature is subject to the Creator, who giveth all priestly dignity upon the altar.

Cesira Gasparotto (1968, 82) describes the musical angels as announcing the triumph of Christ and writes of the scene, "The two protagonists stand isolated at the back of a large eucharistic altar, at the center of a majestic classical building: more similar to a triumphal monument than a church. Indeed, in the entrances of the three arches, the angels in flight blow into long trumpets announcing the universal triumph of Christ-Eucharist."

While the allusion to Psalm 150 is certainly relevant in considering Donatello's angels, I propose another source for the arrangement of their instruments: the *Lucidarium* of Marchetto. The *Lucidarium*, as mentioned in chapter 3, is an influential music treatise written in the second decade of the Trecento, which transmits and elaborates on Augustine's and Isidore of Seville's theories regarding the species of music. In book 1, chapter 7, called "On the Division of Music," Marchetto (Herlinger 1985, 89) describes three species of music, "harmonic, organic, and rhythmic." The first, "harmonic music," is produced "with sound that is the voice of a human being or an animal." By "sound that is voice" he means "sound of air set in vibration by the breath, perceptible to the ear, and formed exclusively by the natural instruments of a living being." In book 1, chapter 12, Marchetto discusses "organic music," which he says is "formed without natural instruments, with the breath or the impulse of air set in vibration alone, as is manifest in all artificial instruments" as in "trumpets, chalumeaus, pipes, organs, and the like" ("tubis, cimellis, fistulis, organis, et hiis similibus"). The third category is "rhythmic music," which Marchetto contends consists of all sound that is not voice, as in the "monochord, psaltery, the bell, and similar instruments" ("ut in monacordo, psalterio, tintinnabulo, et hiis similibus"). The "pulsing of strings, bells, the clattering of footsteps, and the like" ("ut pulsus cordarum, tintinnabuli, strepitus pedum, et hiis similia") belong to this group.

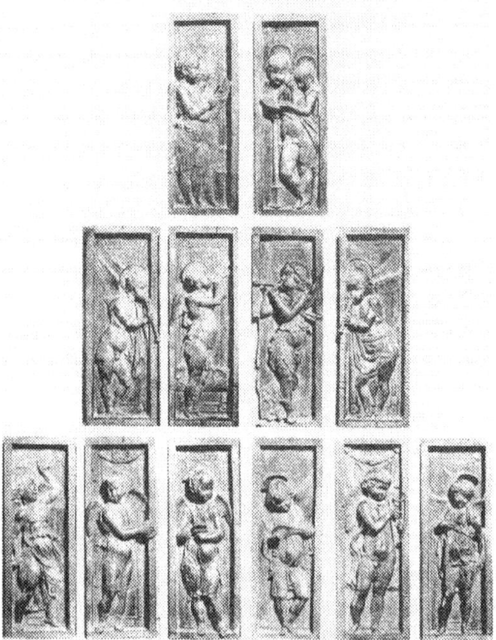

Figure 6.25: **Donatello's angel musicians arranged according to Marchetto da Padova's *Lucidarium*: harmonic, organic and rhythmic.**

If one organizes Donatello's angels according to Marchetto's hierarchy, we find that the two panels of angel singers (Fig. 6.25) represent harmonic music, the four wind players represent organic music and the six string and percussion players represent rhythmic music. Furthermore, the angels may be grouped in twos and threes in this system. The singers clearly belong together. The paired flute and chalumeau players belong in the second grouping. In the third grouping, we find two sets of three instruments: two tambourines and cymbals; and the lute, rebec, and harp.

This new grouping helps to resolve the stumbling block that is found in Boito's and Janson's reconstructions. Both proceed on the assumption that the angel panels should be considered as pairs – two flutes, two singers, and two tambourines. They run into trouble, however, when trying to arrange the three string players (rebec, harp, and lute) and the three percussion players (two tambourines and cymbals). Here the pairings break down, and we find harp and cymbals paired in Boito, and generally odd pairings of instruments in Janson, such as flutes and tambourine, and harp and tambourine.

Marchetto's species of music makes it possible to view the instruments in a more hierarchical and less linear fashion, grouped together in twos and threes. The flexibility of grouping instruments in this way mirrors the rhythmic practices of medieval and Renaissance music, in which music fluidly moved between the two meters. Janson comments on the unique versatility of the panels, arguing that perhaps "Donatello in the beginning was not yet entirely sure of their ultimate destination, in which case a uniform series of narrow panels would have had the advantage of great flexibility." The numbers of instruments also correspond to the other sculptures that form part of the altar. The four wind players in Marchetto's category of organic music correspond to the four reliefs based on the miracles of the life of Saint Anthony and the four evangelists. The six saints correspond to the six players of rhythmic music. The pairing of the Virgin and Child is mirrored in the pairing of instruments.

In addition shedding light on the arrangement of the musical angels, a close examination of the documents shows that Donatello and company may have completed more than twelve angel panels and that they were not originally all intended for the altar. Janson (1963, 177) has described the crafting of the musical angels as occurring in two phases. A document dated April 29, 1447, from the Archivio del Santo contracts Donatello and assistants for ten bronze angels at a cost of twelve ducats each. The artists also agreed to make a groove or molding around the frame of the angel panels if the officials should request it. The second phase concerns the addition of two angels, and Janson cites a June 23, 1449, entry that Donatello received payment for two additional angel panels and Dead Christ. A new consideration of this entry, however, reveals that these angels were not destined for the altar. The June 26, 1449, entry reads, "Of the said [Donatello] for God the Father and the facades of the choir CCLXXXV lira for his invoice for two angels and to cast them CXXXVI lira, XVI soldi".[52] Not only does the payment confirm the addition of two angels, it records that Donatello intended them and God the Father to belong on the choir screen and not the altar. Indeed, it is important to note that Michel mentions all the most important sculptures in the Donatello altar, but does not specifically mention the musical angels. Did they not appear on the original altar? If not, where could they have been located?

In his *Delle religiose memorie* of 1590, Valerio Polidoro describes the angels from Donatello's altar in the new structure by Campagna and Franco: "It [the new altar] also displays certain other images, of the same metal and craftsmanship, which form a few angels that graciously sing and play lauds to God."[53] It is noteworthy that Polidoro specifically describes a few angels singing and playing lauds. The fact that they were playing lauds precludes the inclusion of the percussive instruments (tambourines and cymbals), favoring those that are melodic in nature, such as flutes. The singing of psalms by the monks before the altar (as Rota's poem indicates) also suggests that the singing angels and those playing harmonic music would be more appropriate for the altar than the angels performing rhythmic music. The remaining angels may have thus been integrated together either into the choir screen or as part of the now-destroyed architectural framework that surrounded the altar. In either case, I do not believe that the angels appeared all together on the predella.

Janson (1963, 177) proposes that some of Donatello's other statues were integrated into the screen. He observes:

> If we consider the similar Quattrocento screen in S. Maria dei Frari, Venice, with its rich complement of statues, it seems reasonable to assume that the Paduan authorities, too, aspired to a monumental sculptural program for their choir screen. Perhaps they originally expected Donatello, who had participated in the work on the new choir, to carry out such a scheme, but this hope never materialized, since the master did not even live up to all of his contractual obligations with respect to the statues of the high altar.

[52] "per lo dicto (Donatello) per lo dio pare (Dio Padre) e le fazè (facciate) del coro lire CCLXXXV per sua fatura al dicto de 2 agnoleti a butarli lire CXXXVI soldi XVI" (Gloria 1895, 13).

[53] "Tengono anco certi altri quadri, che del medesimo metallo e lavoro, formano alcuni Angeli; i quali gratiosamente cantino, e suonino lodi al Signore" (Polidoro 1590, 8).

Further evidence gathered by Adolfo Venturi (1907) indicates that Donatello also sculpted bronze angel heads and angel reliefs on pilasters found in the sidewalls of the choir. He notes that Donatello worked on them as early as 1444 and that the musical and dancing angels recall the figures on the urn of Lucius Lucilius Felix of the Campidoglio in Rome, the Prato pulpit, and the Florence cantoria.

The placement of the musical angels both within the scheme of the altar and on the choir integrates the architectural space with the singers. Together the presbytery and choir form a circle within which Donatello's altar is situated. The circle and its relation to music have ancient sources including Plato's *Republic* (1941, 10.617b7): "these eight spheres sing out a single scale." In the *Paradiso*, Dante's angels encircle the world in a veil of song. Canto 27, lines 70-73, refer to the angelic Intelligences that govern the Crystalline Sphere, which is the outermost sphere, the one that while furthest from God is actually most in tune with God. Rota confirms this vision of the angelic choir in canto 2 of *L'incendio*:

Turn your gaze and your thoughts to the august and sumptuous choir, on which one may see gathered materials of great prestige of work. Here in his throne you can distinguish the majesty, the glory, the decoration, and the splendor, and the harmony, I advise you, as if you have seen Paradise descended.	Dunque il guardo piuttosto, ed il pensiere volgi all'augusto sontuoso Coro, entro di cui raccolto puoi vedere di materia ogni pregio, ed di lavoro. Quivi in suo trono scorgi alto sedere la maestà, la gloria, ed il decoro: e allo splendore, e all'armonia l'è avviso di mirarvi disceso il Paradiso (Rota, 1753, 48).

For Rota the music produced by singers in the choir should be harmonious with the architecture of the church itself:

And because harmonic music orchestrated for secular feasts is different from sacred melody which is destined for divine honors, so the harmonious symmetry of a building integrates itself with the wish of the landlord who made it his residence.	E siccome la musica armonia, che per profane feste è concertata, diversa è dalla sacra melodia, ch'ad onori divini e' destinata; così l'armoniosa simmetria debbe dell'edifizio esser formata in guisa, che completa a quel padrone, che per farvi soggiorno lo dispone (Rota, 1753, 40).

Indeed, the Santo's original choir, built by the Canozi in 1462, included intarsiated images of such instruments as the "cithara, lute, clarion, monochord, bagpipe, timpani, and trumpet" ("cetera, liuto, la chiarina, il monocordo, la sampogna, i timpani, la tromba").[54] Donatello already achieved

[54]Gonzati 1852-1853, 71.

the integration of music and space in the cantoria of Santa Maria del Fiore in Florence, where sculpted marble angels singing and playing connect the spiritual world to the mundane.

The number and placement of angels also comes into question in an examination of a drawing housed in the Uffizi's Gabinetto disegni e stampa that shows there were sixteen bas relief putti instead of twelve on the new altar. They were placed one on top of another in two spaces between columns that flank the altar (Niccoli 1932, 116-118).[55] It is not clear, however, whether these are the Donatello angels, or whether they are other angels that were sculpted for the new altar, as Polidoro observes later in his *Delle religiose memorie*: "Above sixteen columns there are sixteen bronze figures, representing sixteen angels which hold some symbols of Christ's passion."[56]

Furthermore, Polidoro makes a reference to angels and sibyls by Donatello that have not been discussed in the literature and no longer exist. He writes that "completing the superb structure, one finds two marble sibyls stretched over the frontispiece, and two angels, also in marble, which hold several symbols of Christ's passion."[57] After completing his inventory of items, Polidoro asserts, "I conclude that the construction of this so noble an altar by making it known that all the statues, the bronze pictures, which we have made note of this far, were on the old altar that was taken apart in making this one; and were all created by the brilliance and the art of the said Donatello in the year 1468."[58] Although scholars have called this date erroneous, it does correspond to the date when the Santo's choir was probably completed. Could the sibyls be the marble items that Michiel (1903) notes are now presumably lost? Perhaps only several angels were intended for the altar, as in the case of two angel lute players in Mantegna's *Saint Zeno Altarpiece* (1457-1460, Fig. 6.26) – a work often discussed in relation to Donatello's altar – or Masaccio's *Madonna and Child Enthroned*, in which two lute-playing angels also appear beneath the seated Madonna.

Series of musical angels are most notably found in Heaven and create a harmonic setting. For example, the silver altar of Saint James in the Cathedral of Pistoia displays an angel choir on either side of *Christ on the*

---

[55]Niccoli notes, however, that because of certain other inconsistencies with regard to the Donatello bronzes, these drawings may have been executed from memory.

[56]"...e sopra questi [sedici colonne] stanno sedici figure di bronzo, che rapresentano sedici Angeli, i quali portano alcuni misteri della passione di Christo" (Polidoro 1590, 9).

[57]"...dan compimento alla superba altezza due Sibille figurate in marmo, che si stendono sopra il Frontespicio, e due Angeli, pure di marmo, che portano alcuni misteri della passion di Christo" (Polidoro 1590, 8).

[58]"Emmi paruto di conchiudere la fabrica di si nobile Altare, col far sapere che tutte le Statue, e quadri di bronzo, de' quali sin'hora habbiamo fatto memoria, fossero nell'Altar vecchio, che fu disfatto nel farsi di questo; e forono formati dall'ingegno, & arte del detto Donatello, nell'anno 1468" (Polidoro 1590, 8).

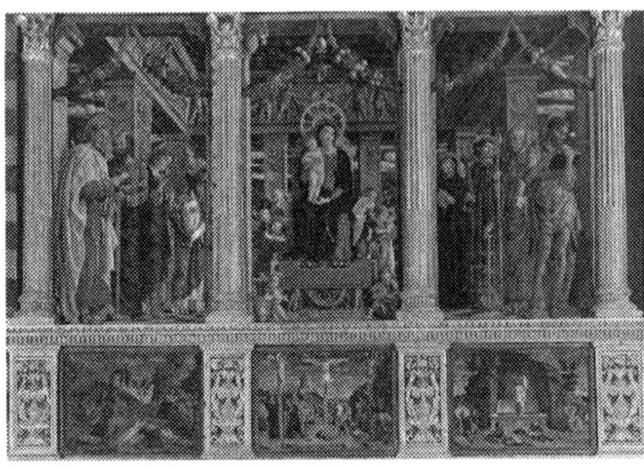

Figure 6.26: **Andrea Mantegna, *Saint Zeno Altarpiece.* Verona, Church of Saint Zeno.**

Throne. Giotto's Scrovegni Chapel frescoes depict angels in a coronation scene in Heaven. Musical angels also surround Christ in Giotto's Stefaneschi Polyptych on the high altar of the Basilica of Saint Peter. When found in a predella-like space, musical figures often comment on the scene just above them, as in Giotto's *Justice* and *Injustice* in the Scrovegni Chapel.

The number and arrangement of Donatello's angels cast doubt on David Fallows's hypothesis (1986-1987, 11) that "the work [Dufay's Mass] was composed for the consecration of Donatello's altar" ("l'opera [Dufay's Mass] sia stata composta per la consacrazione dell'altare di Donatello"). Fallows bases this assumption on his argument that Dufay composed a plenary mass in honor of Saint Anthony and that the twelve movements of the mass correspond to Donatello's twelve musical angels. In addition, he says that Dufay's Mass may be seen as consisting of two types of stylistic material which "correspond to the visible difference between standing statues and relief."[59] There are, however, at least three types of sculpture on Donatello's altar: standing statues and high and low bas relief. The connection to Donatello weakens still more when one considers that his assistants completed a majority of the work on the angels. Furthermore, no documentation appears to exist to support Fallows's notion that Donatello and Dufay might have met through Brunelleschi around the occasion of the consecration of the dome of the Santa Maria del Fiore, since Dufay composed the motet *Nuper rosarum flores* for the consecration of the altar.

While there is no evidence in Donatello's altar or the Dufay Mass that

[59]Fallows 1986-1987, 16.

a connection between the two works exists, it still remains an intriguing possibility that Dufay attended the consecration of the altar. As Fallows notes, Dufay was in Turin in June of 1450 with "novem relogiosum," who could have performed the Mass. In addition, Dufay held a personal veneration for Saint Anthony of Padua. His will dated July 8, 1474, reads: "I establish the celebration of a solemn mass of the saint by the same major vicars [as that for Easter], or a priest, a deacon, and sub deacon, in the feast of Saint Anthony of Padua in the same chapel [Saint Stephen], in perpetuity; and in this must participate the choir master of the boys and all the most eminent choristers, under the direction of the already-mentioned vicars; whoever sings the mass I have composed I assign 30 soldi, to all the others another 3 soldi and 4 denari."[60] The will also stipulates that six boys sing his motet *O proles Hispanie* lauding Saint Anthony. Dufay also composed several antiphons for the office of Saint Anthony, as earlier noted. Yet even Fallows (1986-1987, 10) admits that "the composition of a cycle for the Proper of Saint Anthony does not call for particular contact with Padua, nor even with Donatello." He continues, "We know that there was a large portrait of Saint Anthony of Padua in Cambrai, as there were in many other cathedrals in the Christian world."

Rather than the imitation of a musical genre, such as the mass, the model for Donatello's altar and angels may have been the very public veneration of Saint Anthony in fifteenth-century Padua. The Confraternity of Saint Anthony of Padua organized magnificent processionals replete with music, singing, and groups of children dressed as angels to commemorate the death of the patron saint (Gasparini 1997, 269-273). An illuminated codex of statutes compiled in 1433 describes the "confraternali con il loro corredo di angioletti." Chapter 26, entitled "The orders of the mode and formation of the procession of the glorious Saint Anthony, our protector, at the time of his feast, which will proceed with the officials and our brothers," describes the participants in the procession.[61]

It reads like a description of Donatello's altar. On the platform are found

> the said four patrons, that is, the priest who will represent Pros-

[60]Mila 1997, 359. The original appears in Houdoy 1972, 412. "Item statuo in die sancti Anthonii de Padua in predicta capella perpetuo missam de eodem sancto per tres ex ipsis magnis vicariis presbiterum scilicet dyaconum et subdyaconum solemniter celebrandam, in qua assint magister puerorum et alii quicumque sufficientiores de choro, sive sint magni vicarii sive parvi, vel capellani, ad provisionem tamen dictorum magnorum vicariorum, qui missam per me compositam decantent, quibus assigno XXX solidos, inde quilibet III solidos IIII denarios."

[61]The statutes are found in the Biblioteca Civica in Padua, manuscript B.P. 573, transcribed by Gasparini 1974, 131. "Ordene del muodo e forma della processione del gloriosissimo sancto Antonio protectore nostro al tempo della so festa, hi quali se die' proseguire per li officiali e fradelli nostri della fraia in quanto aspecta ala predicta fraia."

> docimus dressed in the most proper ornate bishop's attire one can have, the one who will represent Saint Daniel in deacon's attire, the one who will represent Saint Anthony in the hood of the minor brothers, and the one who will represent Justina with clothing of white or purple damask with a palm in hand and with a knife; all four will wear a diadem just like the saints.[62]

They are to be accompanied by angels

> dressed in long blouses, stoles, wings, and diadems, of which one plays the portative organ on the said platform and the other mans the bellows of the said organs. And all these are to be carried on the said platform by those of the said order. And if they are shown adorned in the best possible manner, they will appear better to the officials, in blouses, diadems, wings in the shape of angels, or in any other kind of way, which is the best way that they can do.[63]

The statutes specify that this group should be followed by the sacred head of Saint Anthony and his tongue.

Another description of music appears in chapter 27: "Orders of the manner in which one moves the great light, and when, and of the procession that will take place the first Sunday after the Feast of Saint Anthony the confessor, and of the offering given to the tomb." Additionally, "Before all of this there should be pipers and before the reliquary there should be trumpet players to honor the procession."[64] The solemnity of the occasion was further ensured by a law already in place in 1257 that prohibited the playing of games and dancing in the Piazza del Santo during this sacred time of the year. Girolamo Ferrari, in his unpublished *Storia di Padova* (1734) writes, "It was the case during these solemn festivities, or on other solemn occasions, that players of dice, prostitutes, ruffians and other sort of bad

[62]"...hi dicti quatro patroni, çoè quello sacerdote rapresentarà sancto Prosdocimo cum debiti e più ornadi fornimenti da vescovo se porà havere, quello rapresenterà sancto Daniele cum fornimenti da dyacono, quello representarà sancto Antonio cum la cappa da fra' menori, e quelo rapresentarà sancta Iustina cum vesta da dalmaschin biancho over de porpora e cum la palma in mane e cum el cortello, e tuti quatro cum diademe in forma de sancti" (Gasparini 1974, 131).

[63]"...ancora de do angeli fornidi cum camisi, stole, alle e diademe, delli quali l'uno sone l'organeto suso la dicta sbara e l'altro mene hi manteselli delli dicti organi; e tuti questi tali seano portadi sulla dicta sbara in li luogi dove meio parerà a quelli della dicta fraia. Ancora sea trovadi e ornadi plusor, putti serà possibele per el meior modo apparerà a quelli dela fraia over so officiali cum camisi, diademe, alle in forma de angeli e per ogni altra via al meio se porà" (Gasparini 1974, 131).

[64]"Ordine del modo se die' scuodere la luminaria granda e quando, e della processione se farà prima domenega da po' la festa de sancto Antonio confessore e della offerta se die' fare a l'archa" and (p. 133) "E che davanti tuti vada pifferi e davanti la prefata reliquia hi trombetti per honorare la prefata processione" (Gasparini 1974, 132).

people were prohibited from public dancing parties."[65] This last reference to dancing suggests that Donatello's angels are not associated with dance as part of the devotion to Saint Anthony, as Janson's rubric of instruments intimates.

Could Donatello be imitating this procession? Scholars have argued that Giotto mirrored the famous Paduan theatrical procession representing the Annunciation in his Scrovegni Chapel frescoes (Brunelli 1925). Donatello's teacher Brunelleschi was quite involved with the theater, and it is possible that Donatello gained experience with theatrical props through him. Cyrilla Barr examines a description of musical angels during the performance of an Ascension play presented at the Church of Santa Maria del Carmine in Florence. Abraham of Souzdal, a Russian bishop who attended the Ecumenical Council held in Florence in 1439, chronicled that three sacred representations with "life-sized painted angels, which were set in motion by gears and thus 'appeared to be alive,"' were placed at the highest elevation, near the roof, perhaps because it was less cumbersome than raising human beings to that height (Barr 1990, 385).[66] Music also plays an important part in Abraham's account of the play, and he mentions angels arranged around the throne of the Father holding bells, lyres, and flutes. Abraham remarks, "The children who represent the angels move around him [God the Father], while harmonious music and sweet song resound from afar." Vasari credits Brunelleschi with being the first known designer of the stage machinery used to raise and lower clouds (Barr 1990, 381).

Donatello's altar in the Santo of Padua is a work of staggering beauty and complexity. While the altar is of solid bronze, it remains flexible in its most basic sense: over the centuries its pieces have been moved, integrated with other, newer works, and displayed in many incarnations. The angels, who seem to drop in and out of the altar's history, appear to be the most mysterious elements in this regard, at this juncture relegated to an anomalous predella beneath an imposing structure. This moveable, flexible nature of the musical angels signals the new Renaissance use of musical representations as a way to enhance the drama of a scene. We may trace the evolution of the dramatic use of music – which ultimately culminates in the greatest Renaissance musical invention, opera – to the frescoes of Giotto's Scrovegni Chapel, where the *Annunciation* fresco can be seen as a realistic

[65]"Erasi già che nella ottava della sud festività, o in altre occasioni di sua solennità non potevano fermarsi nella piazza della chiesa, or di vicino sino a Ponte Corbo giocatori di dadi, nè meretrici, nè ruffiani, nè altra sorte di malagente, e che fossero proibite le pubbliche feste di balli," (*Storia di Padova*, B. P. 607).

[66]Indeed, the sacred representations of the life of Saint Anthony came into being only in the sixteenth century, when they were first printed. For more, see Alessandro d'Ancona 1891, 1.269.

rendering, as Laura Jacobus has persuasively argued, of an actual dramatic musical event: the processional feast in Padua, with the Annunciation being acted out by Paduan citizens hoisted atop platforms. As was pointed out in this chapter, the Confraternity of Saint Anthony also enacted scenes with accompanying musicians.

In Trecento Padua, then, we have seen the study of music championed as a science and the interaction of that city's celebrities Pietro, Marchetto, and Antonio da Tempo. Their formulation of the Ars Nova aesthetic, with advances in notation and the rebirth of classical musical philosophy, placed Padua at the forefront of the Italian musical map. Giotto's painting contributed to the richness of the tradition, mirroring the advances in realistic notation in his realistic rendering of musical scenes. In so doing, Giotto contributed not only to the refinement of reproducing musical ideas in a visual idiom, but also to dramatic representation, by using music to enhance the emotional impact of narrative scenes, such as those in the *Wedding Procession* and *Annunciation.* As was shown, the new advances in drama also coincided with the works of Albertino Mussato and the use of the Scrovegni Chapel as a center for the production of theatrical and musical works in the Trecento. The use of music as a dramatic tool can be traced through the work of Giusto ultimately to Donatello, whose angel musicians are in a sense movable in the context of the Santo's bronze altar. This flexibility infuses his work with new dramatic potential.

The unification of music and spectacle – inspired by classical tradition and ultimately rejuvenated in Trecento Padua – may be understood as the seed for the emergence of the genre of opera during the last breaths of the Florentine Renaissance, when a group of literate men came together to improve the quality of music. The Florentine Camerata, as these men were known, included none other than Vincenzo Galilei, whose son Galileo taught at the university in Padua. Trecento Padua, then, may be viewed as the crossroads at which musical intellectualism met dramatic emotion, as embodied in Pietro d'Abano's theories, Ristoro d'Arezzo's two-dimensional Venus, and Giotto's enigmatic *Justice.*

List of Plates

Bibliography

Alighieri, Jacopo

1895 *Il dottrinale di Jacopo Alighieri.* Ed. Giovanni Crocioni. Città di Castello: S. Lapi.

Alvarez, Giulio Bresciani

1990 "Il Palazzo della Ragione: La storia di una fabbrica civile." *Il Palazzo della Ragione in Padova.* Padova: Editoriale programma. 4-17.

Aquinas, Thomas

1948 *Summa theologica: Complete Edition in Five Volumes.* Trans. Fathers of the English Dominican Province. Vol. 3. Westminister: Christian Classics.

1975 "Justice." *Summa theologica.* Trans. Thomas Gilby. Vol. 37. London: Eyre & Spottiswoode.

Aristotle

1927 *Problemata: The Works of Aristotle.* Trans. W. D. Ross. Vol. 7. Oxford: Clarendon Press.

1928 *Metaphysica: The Works of Aristotle.* Trans. W. D. Ross. 2nd ed. Vol. 8. Oxford: Clarendon Press.

1930 *Physica.* Trans. R. P. Hardie and R. K. Gaye. Vol. 2. Oxford: Clarendon Press.

1931 *De Mundo: The Works of Aristotle.* Trans. E. S. Forster. Vol. 3. Oxford: Clarendon Press.

1930 *Meteorologica: The Works of Aristotle.* Trans. E. W. Webster. Vol. 3. Oxford: Clarendon Press.

1962 *The Politics.* Trans. T. A. Sinclair. Harmondsworth: Penguin.

1970 *Aristotle's Physics: Books I and II.* Trans. William Charlton. Oxford: Clarendon Press.

1991 *Problèmes.* Ed. and trans. Pierre Louis. 3 vols. Paris: Les belles lettres.

Atlas, Allan W.
1985 *Music at the Aragonese Court of Naples.* Cambridge: Cambridge University Press.

Augustine
1947 *De Musica.* Trans. Robert Taliaferro. Washington: Catholic University of America Press.
1957 *The City of God Against the Pagans.* Trans. George McCracken. Loeb Classical Library. Vol. 1. Cambridge: Harvard University Press.

Austin, Herbert
1913 *Accredited Citations in Ristoro d'Arezzo's "Della composizione del mondo".* Torino: G. Momo.

Baccheschi, Edi
1966 *The Complete Paintings of Giotto.* New York: Abrams.

Backhouse, Janet
1997 *The Illuminated Page: Ten Centuries of Manuscript Painting in the British Library.* Toronto: University of Toronto Press.

Bailey, L. H.
1929 *The Standard Cyclopedia of Horticulture.* New York: Macmillan.

Barberino, Francesco da
1912 *Documenti d'amore di Franscesco da Barberino.* Ed. F. Egidi. Vol 2. Roma: Presso la società.

Bar Hebraeus
1899 *Le livre de l'ascension de l'esprit... 1279.* Paris: Bouillon.

Barr, Cyrilla
1990 "Music and Spectacle in Confraternity Drama of Fifteenth-Century Florence: The Reconstruction of a Theatrical Event." *Christianity and the Renaissance: Image and Religious Imagination in the Quattrocento.* Syracuse, NY: Syracuse University Press. 376-404.

Barzon, Antonio
1924 *I cieli e la loro influenza negli affreschi del Salone di Padova.* Padova: Tip. Seminario.

Basile, Giuseppe
1993 *The Scrovegni Chapel Frescoes.* London: Thames and Hudson.
2002 "Giotto's Pictorial Cycle." *Giotto: The Frescoes of the Scrovegni Chapel in Padua.* Milano: Skira. 21-40.

Battaglia, Salvatore
1986 *Grande dizionario della lingua Italiana.* Vol. 12. Torino: Unione tipografico-editrice Torinese.

Beck, Eleonora M.
1992-95 "A Musical Interpretation of Andrea di Bonaiuto's *Allegory of the Dominican Order.*" *Imago musicae* 9-12:123-138.
1997 "Music in the Cornice of Boccaccio's *Decameron.*" *Medievalia et humanistica* 24:33-49.
1998 *Singing in the Garden: Music and Culture in the Tuscan Trecento.* Lucca: LIM.
1999 "Marchetto da Padova and Giotto's Scrovegni Chapel Frescoes." *Early Music* 27.1 (February):4-24.
1999 "Representations of Music in the Astrological Cycle of the Salone della Regione in Padua." *Music in Art: International Journal for Music Iconography* 24, 1-2 (Spring-Fall):69-84.
2001 "Revisiting Dufay's Saint Anthony Mass and Its Connection to Donatello's Altar of Saint Anthony of Padua." *Music in Art: International Journal for Music Iconography* 26, 102 (Spring-Fall):5-19.

Bellinati, Claudio
1974 "La cappella di Giotto agli Scrovegni e le miniature dell'antifonario 'Giottesco' della Cattedrale, 1306." *Da Giotto al Mantegna.* Milano: Electa editrice. 23-30.
1994 *Padua: Baptistery of the Cathedral.* Padova: G. Deganello.
1997 *Giotto: Padua felix; Atlante iconografico della cappella di Giotto, 1300-1305.* Ponzano: Vianello.

Bellosi, Luciano
1998 *Cimabue.* Trans. Alexandra Bonfante-Warren, Frank Dabell, and Jay Hyams. New York: Abbeville Publishing Group.

Benedettucci, Fabio, ed.
1991 *Il libro di Antonio Billi.* Roma: De Rubeis Editore.

Bent, Margaret, and Anne Hallmark, eds.
1985 *The Works of Johannes Ciconia.* Monaco: l'Oiseau Lyre.

Bettini, Sergio
1960 *Le pitture di Giusto de' Menabuoi nel Battistero del Duomo di Padova.* Venezia: N. Pozza Editore.

Billanovich, Giuseppe
1942-55 "Per l'edizione del 'De Cite inter Natura.' " *Bollettino del Museo Civico di Padova.* 31-44.
1976 *Petrarca e Padova.* Padova: Editrice Antenore.

Boccaccio, Giovanni
1972 *The Decameron.* Trans. G. H. McWilliam. Harmondsworth: Penguin.

Bode, Wilhelm von
1902 *Florentiner Bildhauer der Renaissance.* Berlin: B. Cassirer.

Bonardi, Antonio, ed.
1899 *Liber regiminum Padua.* Venezia: A spese della società.

Bosio, Luciano
1986 "L'eta preromana e romana." *Prato della Valle: Due millenni di storia di un'avventura urbana.* Padova: Signum. 37-50.

Brown, Howard Mayer
1984 "Saint Augustine, Lady Music, and the Gittern in Fourteenth-Century Italy." *Musica disciplina* 38:25-65.
1985 "Ambilent Attitudes Toward Music: An Iconographical View." *Music and Context: Essays for John M. Ward.* Ed. Anne Dhu Shapiro. Cambridge: Harvard University Press. 79-106.
1985 "A Corpus of Trecento Pictures with Musical Subject Matter, Part I, Installment 2." *Imago musicae* 2:179-281.

Brunelli, Bruno
1925 "La festa dell'Annunciazione all'Scrovegni e un affresco di Giotto." *Bollettino del Museo Civico di Padova* 18:100-109.

Burnett, Charles
1993 "European Knowledge of Arabic Texts Referring to Music: Some New Material." *Early Music History* 12:1-17.

Cadden, Joan
2001 "'Nothing Natural is Shameful': Vestiges of a Debate about Sex and Science in a Group of Late-Medieval Manuscripts." *Speculum* 76:66-89.

Carducci, Giosuè
1973 *Musica e poesia nel mondo elegante Italiano del secolo XIV.* Bologna: Antiquae Musicae Italicae Studiosi.

Carpenter, Nan
1972 *Music in the Medieval and Renaissance Universities.* New York: Da Capo Press.

Cassiodorus, Senator

1966 *An Introduction to Divine and Human Readings by Cassiodorus Senator.* Trans. Leslie Webber Jones. New York: Octagon Book.

Cattin, Giulio

1984 *Medieval Music I.* Trans. Steven Botterill. Cambridge: Cambridge University Press.

Cavacci, Giacomo

1927 *Historiarum coenobii Divae Justinae Patavinae libri sex.* Patavii: ex typographia Seminarii.

Celano, Thomas of

2000 *Thomas of Celano's First Life of St. Francis of Assisi.* Trans. Christopher Stace. London: Society for Promoting Christian Knowledge.

Cicero

1913 *De Officiis.* Trans. Walter Miller. Loeb Classical Library. Cambridge: Harvard University Press.

Colabich, Giorgio Fabbri, Alessandro Prosdocimi, and Giannantonio Saccomani

1964 *I recenti lavori di restauro alla Cappella degli Scrovegni.* Padova: Società Cooperativa Tipografica.

Cole, Bruce

1996 "Virtues and Vices in Giotto's Arena Chapel Frescoes." *Studies in the History of Italian Art, 1250-1550.* London: Pindar Press. 337-363.

Comotti, Giovanni

1965 *Music in Greek and Roman Culture.* Trans. Rosaria Munson. Baltimore: Johns Hopkins University Press.

Connolly, Thomas

1980 "The Legend of St. Cecilia II: Music and the Symbols of Virginity." *Studi musicali* 9:3-44.

1983 "The Cult and Iconography of S. Cecilia before Raphael." *Indagini per undipinto: La Santa Cecilia de Raffaello.* Bologna: Edizioni ALFA. 119-139.

Corsi, Giuseppe

1970 *Poesie musicali del Trecento.* Bologna: Commissione per i testi di lingua.

Cortusi, Guglielmo

1941 "Chronica de Novitatibus Padue et Lombardie." *Rerum italicarum scriptores.* Ed. Beniamino Pagnin. Vol. 12, pt. 5. Bologna: Nicola Zanichelli.

Coussemaker, Charles Edmond Henri de
1963 *Scriptorum de musica medii aevi.* Hildesheim: Georg Olms Verlag.

D'Abano, Pietro
1475 *Expositio problematum Aristotelis.* Mantua: Paulus de Butzbach.
1548 *Decisiones physionomiae.* Venezia: Cominum de Tridino.
1556 *Comincia la Geomantia di Pietro d'Abano: Tradotta dilattina lingua nel volgare idioma.* Venezia: Cominum Troiano de i Nauò.

Dall'Acqua, A.
1842 *Cenni storici sulle famiglie di Padova.* Padova: Coi tipi della Minerva.

D'Ancona, Alessandro
1891 *Origini del teatro italiano.* 3 Vols. Torino: Loescher.

D'Ancona, Mirella
1978 "The Rabbit Hutch and Political Allusions in the Visconti Hours." *Arte lombarda* 50:7-18.
1983 *Botticelli's Primavera.* Florence: Olschki.

D'Ancona, Paolo
1954 *The Schifanoia Months at Ferrara.* Trans. Lucia Krasnik. Milano: Edizione del Milione.

Da Nono, Giovanni
1934-39 *Visio Egidij Regis Patavie.* Ed. Giovanni Fabris. *Bollettino del Museo Civico di Padova* 10-11:1-30.

Dante
1868 *Della volgare eloquenza di Dante Alighieri.* Trans. Giangiorio Trissino. Milano: Presso G. Bernardoni tipografico editore.
1968 *Convivio.* Ed. Bruna Cordati. Torino: Loescher.
1989 *The Banquet.* Trans. Christopher Ryan. Saratoga, CA: ANMA Libri.

Da Padova, Marchetto
1961 *Marcheti de Padua, Pomerium musices.* Ed. Giuseppe Vecchi. Roma: American Institute of Musicology.

D'Arezzo, Ristoro
1864 *Della composizione del mundo.* Ed. Enrico Narducci. Milano: G. Daelli.

D'Ascoli, Cecco
1927 *L'Acerba.* Ascoli Piceno: G. Cesari.

Da Spira, Giuliano
1985 *Officio ritmico e vita seconda.* Ed. Vergilio Gamboso. Padova: Edizioni Messaggero.

Da Tempo, Antonio
1977 *Summa artis rithmici vulgaris dictaminis.* Ed. Richard Andrews. Bologna: Commissione per i testi di lingua.

Debenedetti, Santore
1906-07 "Un trattatello del secolo XIV sopra la poesia musicale." *Studi medievali* 2:59- 82.

Della Seta, Fabrizio
1976 "Scienza e filosofia nella teoria musicale dell'ars nova in Francia." *Nuova rivista musicale italiana* 10:357-383.

Dornpacher, Nicolò de Claricini
1951 *Ricerche sugli affreschi di Giotto nel capitolo del Santo.* Milano: Emilia Bestetti.

Durante, Sergio, and Pierluigi Petrobelli
1990 *Storia della musica al Santo di Padova.* Vicenza: N. Pozzi Editore.

Edwards, Mary
1988 "Apollo and Daphne in the Scrovegni Chapel." *Bollettino del Museo Civico di Padova* 77:15-35.

Fabris, Giovanni
1937 "Il presunto cronista padovano del sec. XV Guglielmo di Paolo Ongarello." *Atti e Memorie della R. Accademia di scienze, lettere ed arti in Padova* n.s. 53:167.

Fallows, David
1986-87 "Dufay, la sua messa per Sant'Antonio da Padova e Donatello." *Rassegna di musica veneta* 2-3:3-19.

Fantelli, Pier Luigi and Franca Pellegrini, eds.
1990 *Il Palazzo della Ragione in Padova.* Padova: Editoriale programma.

Ferrante, Joan, George Economou, and Frederick Goldin, eds.
1975 *In Pursuit of Perfection: Courtly Love in Medieval Literature.* Port Washington, New York: Kennikat Press.

Fleischhauer, Günther
1964 *Etrurien und Rom.* Leipzig: Deutscher Verlag für Musik.

Flores d'Arcais, Francesca
1995 *Giotto.* Trans. Raymond Rosenthal. New York: Abbeville Press Publishers.
2002 "Giotto after the Restoration." *Giotto: The Frescoes of the Scrovegni Chapel in Padua.* Ed. Giuseppe Basile. Milano: Skira. 13-20.

Gallo, F. Alberto
1966 *La teoria della notazione in Italia dalla fine del XIII all'inizio del XV secolo.* Bologna: Tamari Editori.
1974 "Marchettus de Padua und die 'franco-venetische' Musik des frühen Trecento." *Archiv für Musikwissenschaft* 31:42-56.
1985 *Music of the Middle Ages.* Trans. Karen Eales. Cambridge: Cambridge University Press.

Gasparini, Giuseppina de Sandre
1974 *Statuti di confraternite religiose di Padova nel Medio Evo.* Padova: Istituto per la storia ecclesiastica Padovana.
1997 "Proiezione civica del culto Antoniano e processioni cittadine nel Quattrocentro." *'Vite' e vita di Antonio di Padova: Atti del convegno internazionale sulla agiografia antoniana.* Padova: Centro di studi antoniani. 259-283.

Gasparotto, Cesira
1951 *Padova romana.* Roma: "L'Erma" di Bretscheider.
1966 "Il buono e il cattivo governo." *Città di Padova* 4:26-30.
1968 "Iconografia Antoniniana: I'miracoli' dell'altare di Donatello." *Il santo* 82.

Gatari, Galeazzo and Bartolomeo
1931 "Cronaca carrarese confrontata con la redazione di Andrea Gatari." Eds. Antonio Medin and Guido Tolomei. *Rerum italicarum scriptores.* Vol. 17, pt. 1. Città del Castello: S. Lapi.

Gennari, Giuseppe
1804 *Annali della città di Padova.* Vol. 3. Bassano: Tipografia Remondini.

Gloria, Andrea
1865 "Sulla dimora di Dante in Padova." *Dante e Padova: Studi storico-critici.* Padova. 1- 28.
1895 *Donatello fiorentino e le sue opere mirabili nel tempio di S. Antonio in Padova.* Padova: Tipografia e libreria Antoniana.

Gnudi, Cesare

1959 *Giotto.* Milano: Aldo Martello.

Gonzati, Bernardo

1852-53 *La Basilica di S. Antonio di Padova.* 2 Vols. Padova: Coi tipi di Antonio Bianchi.

Grant, Edward

1994 *Planets, Stars, and Orbs.* Cambridge: Cambridge University Press.

Guidaldi, Luigi

1936 *The Little Flowers of Saint Anthony of Padua.* Trans. George Smith. London: Burns, Oates, and Washbourne.

Hammerstein, Reinhold

1962 *Die Musik der Engel.* Bern and Munich: Frache Verlag.

Herlinger, Jan

1985 *The "Lucidarium" of Marchetto of Padua: A Critical Edition, Translation, and Commentary.* Chicago and London: The University of Chicago Press.

2001 "Marchetto of Padua."*New Grove Dictionary of Music and Musicians.* Vol. 15. London: Macmillan. 826-828.

Houdoy, Jules

1972 *Histoire artistique de la cathédrale di Cambrai.* Geneva: Minkoff Reprints.

Huizinga, Johan

1996 *The Autumn of the Middle Ages.* Trans. Rodney J. Payton and Ulrich Mammitzsch. Chicago: Chicago University Press.

Hyde, John Kenneth

1966 *Padua in the Age of Dante.* Manchester: Manchester Universtiy Press.

Jacobus, Laura

1999 "Giotto's Annunciation in the Scrovegni Chapel, Padua." *Art Bulletin* 81:1 (March):93-107.

Janson, W. H.

1963 *The Sculpture of Donatello.* Princeton: Princeton University Press.

The Kalendar and Compost of Shepherds from the Original Edition

1930 *Published by Guy Marchant in Paris in the Year 1493, and Translated into English c. 1518.*
Trans. Robert Copland. London: Peter Davies.

Kelly, Samantha
2003 *The New Solomon: Robert of Naples (1309-1334) and Fourteenth-Century Kingship.* Leiden: Brill.

Kinsky, Georg, ed.
1951 *A History of Music in Pictures.* New York: Dover Publications.

Klibansky, Raymond, Erwin Panofsky, and Fritz Saxl
1964 *Saturn and Melancholy: Studies in the History of the Natural Philosophy, Religion and Art.* New York: Basic Books.

Kohl, Benjamin
1998 *Padua under the Carrara, 1318-1405.* Baltimore and London: Johns Hopkins University Press.

Kristeller, Paul
1985 "Umanismo e scolastica a Padova fino al Petrarca." *Medioevo* 11:1-18.

Lang, Helen
1992 *Aristotle's Physics and Its Medieval Varieties.* New York: State University of New York Press.

Latini, Brunetto
1852 *The Book of the Treasure.* Trans. Paul Barrette and Spurgeon Baldwin. New York: Garland Publishing.

Lemay, Richard
1962 *Abu Ma'shar and Latin Aristotelianism in the Twelfth Century: The Recovery of Aristotle's Natural Philosophy through Arabic Astrology.* Beirut: The American University.

Litta, Pompeo
1819-83 *Celebri famiglie italiane.* Milano: Giusti.

Livy
1919 *Livy: In Fourteen Volumes.* Trans. Benjamin Oliver Foster. Loeb Classical Library. Vol. 1. Cambridge: Harvard University Press.
1924 *Livy: In Fourteen Volumes.* Trans. Benjamin Oliver Foster. Loeb Classical Library. Vol. 3. Cambridge: Harvard University Press.
1926 *Livy: In Fourteen Volumes.* Trans. Benjamin Oliver Foster. Loeb Classical Library. Vol. 4. Cambridge: Harvard University Press.

Lovato, Antonio

1997 "Tradizioni liturgio-musicali del culto Antoniano." *'Vite' e vita di Antonio di Padova: atti del convegno internazionale sulla agiografia antoniana.* Padova: Centro studi antoniani. 303-320.

Marchi, A. de, ed.

1842 *Cenni storici sulle famiglie di Padova.* Padova: Coi tipi della Minerva.

Martial

1920 *Epigrams.* Trans. Walter Ker. Loeb Classical Library. Vol. 2. Cambridge: Harvard University Press.

Martindale, Andrei

1988 *Simone Martini: Complete Editino.* New York: New York University Press.

McGurk, Patrick

1966 *Catalogue of Astrological and Mythological Illuminated Manuscripts of the Latin Middle Ages.* London: Warburg Institute.

McKinnon, James

1968 "Musical Instruments in Medieval Psalm Commentaries and Psalters." *Journal of the American Musicological Society* 21:3-20.

2001 "Augustine of Hippo."*New Grove Dictionary of Music and Musicians.* Vol. 2. London: Macmillan. 173-174.

Megas, Anastasius, ed.

1969 *Albertini Mussati: Argumenta tragoediarum Senecae; Commentarii in L.A. Senecae tragoedias.* Thessalonike.

Meiss, Millard

1951 *Painting in Florence and Siena after the Black Death.* Princeton: Princeton University Press.

Mellini, Gian Lorenzo

1984 "La regia del racconto di Giotto a Padova e il realismo." *Giotto e il suo tempo.* Milano: Federico Motta Editore. 72-86.

Meucci, Renato

1985 "Riflessioni di archeologia musicale: gli strumenti militari romani e il lituus." *Rivista italiana di musicologia* 19:3:383-394.

Michiel, Marcantonio
1903 *The Anonimo: Notes on Pictures and Works of Art in Italy Made by an Anonymous Writer in the Sixteenth Century.* Trans. Paolo Mussi. New York and London: Benjamin Blom.

Mila, Massimo
1997 *Guillaume Dufay.* Torino: Einaudi.

Minio-Paluello, L.
1952 "Iacobus Veneticus Grecus, Canonist and Translator of Aristotle." *Traditio* 8:265- 304.

Mirimonde, Albert P. de
1977 *Astrologie et musique.* Geneva: Editions Minkoff.

Moschetti, Andrea
1934 *La Cappella degli Scrovegni e la Chiesa degli Eremitani a Padova.* Milano: Fratelli Treves Editori.

Moyer, Ann
1992 *Musica scientia: Musical Scholarship in the Italian Renaissance* Ithaca: Cornell University Press.

Nesle, Solange de Mailly
1985 *Astrology: History, Symbols and Signs.* New York: Inner Traditions International.

Niccoli, Raffaello
1932 "Di due disegni che rigardano progetti del tardo cinquecento per un nuovo altare maggiore nella basilica del Santo a Padova." *Rivista d'arte* 14:116-118.

Oertel, Robert
1966 *Early Italian Painting to 1400.* London: Thames and Hudson.

Olcott, William
1911 *Star Lore of All Ages.* New York and London: G.P. Putnam's Sons.

Olivieri, Luigi
1988 *Pietro d'Abano e il pensiero neolatino: filosofia, scienza, e ricerca dell'Aristotele greco tra i secoli XIII e XIV.* Padua: Editrice Antenore.

Orsato, Sertorio
1652 *Monumenta Patavina.* Patavii: Apud Paulum Frambottum Bibliopolam.
1678 *Historia di Padova.* Bologna: Arnaldo Forni.

Ovid
1976 *Fasti.* Trans. George Frazer. Loeb Classical Library. Cambridge: Harvard University Press.

Page, Christopher
1990 *The Owl and the Nightingale: Musical Life and Ideas in France, 1100-1300.* Berkeley: University of California Press.
1993 *Discarding Images: Reflections on Music and Culture in Medieval France.* Oxford: Clarendon Press.

Palisca, Claude
1985 *Humanism in Italian Renaissance Thought.* New Haven: Yale University Press.

Panofsky, Erwin
1960 *Renaissance and Renascences in Western Art.* Stockholm: Almqvist and Wiksell.

Patavini, Rolandini
1905 "Rolandini Patavini cronica in factis et circa facta Marchie Trivixane." Ed. Antonio Bonardi. *Rerum italicarum scriptores.* Vol. 8, pt. 1. Città di Castello: S. Lapi.

Pellegrini, Franca
1990 "Gli affreschi astrologici." *Il palazzo della Ragione in Padova.* Padua: Editoriale programma. 35-37.

Pescerelli, Beatrice
1991 "Un omaggio musicale a Roberto d'Angiò." *Studi musicali* 20:173-179.

Pfeiffenberger, Selma
1966 The Iconography of Giotto's Virtues and Vices at Padua. PhD diss., Bryn Mahr College.

Petrobelli, Pierluigi
1977 "La musica nelle cattedrali e nelle città ed i suoi rapporti con la cultura letteraria." *Storia della cultura veneta: Il Trecento.* Vicenza: N. Pozza. 440-468.

Pignoria, Lorenzo
1625 *Le origini di Padova.* Padova: Pietro e Paolo Tozzi.

Pirrotta, Nino
1946-47 "Per l'origin e la storia della'caccia' e del 'madrigale' trecentesco." *Rivista musicale italiana* 48:305-323; 49:121-142.
1963 *Music of Fourteenth-Century Italy.* Vol. 4, pts. 1-2. Amsterdam: American Institute of Musicology.
1992 *Il codice Rossi = The Rossi Codex 215.* Lucca: Libreria Musicale Italiana.

Plato
1941 *The Republic.* Ed. Francis Cornford. Oxford: Clarendon Press.

Pleister, Wolfgang
1988 *Recht und Gerechtigkeit im Spiegel der europäischen Kunst.* Köln: Dumont.

Pliny
1938 *Natural History.* Trans. H. Rackham. Loeb Classical Library. Vol. 1. Cambridge: Harvard University Press.
1942 *Natural History.* Trans. H. Rackham. Loeb Classical Library. Vol. 2. Cambridge: Harvard University Press.

Polidoro, Valerio
1590 *Della religiose memorie.* Venezia.

Polybius
1922 *The Histories.* Trans. W. R. Paton. Loeb Classical Library. Vol. 1. Cambridge: Harvard University Press.

Portenari, Angelo
1623 *Della felicità di Padova.* Padova: Pietro Paolo Tozzi.

Puppi, Lionello, ed.
1986 *Prato della Valle: Due millenni di storia di un'avventura urbana.* Padova: Signum Editrice.

Randall, John Jr.
1961 *The School of Padua and the Emergence of Modern Science.* Padova: Editrice Antenore.

Renner, Ralph Clifford
1980 The *Pomerium* of Marchettus of Padua: A Translation and Critical Commentary. Masters thesis, Washington University.

Riess, Jonathan
1984 "Justice and Common Good in Giotto's Arena Chapel Frescoes." *Arte cristiana* 72:69-80.

Rigoni, Erice
1936 "Organari italiani e tedeschi a Padova nel Quattrocentro." *Note d'archivio per la storia musicale* 13:7:7-9.

Robertson, D.W.
1963 *A Preface to Chaucer.* Princeton: Princeton University Press.

Rota, Vincenzo

1749 *L'incendio del tempio di S. Antonio di Padova.* Roma: Con licenza di superiori Rota.

1753 *L'incendio del tempio di S. Antonio di Padova.* Padova: Per li Conzatti.

Rubenstein, Nicolai

1958 "Political Ideas in Sienese Art: The Frescoes by Ambrogio Lorenzetti and Taddeo di Bartolo in the Palazzo Pubblico." *Journal of the Warburg and Courtauld Institutes* 21:179- 207.

Salvini, Roberto

1953 *Giotto: The Scrovegni Chapel in the Arena at Padua.* Firenze: Arnaud.

Savonarola, Michele

1902 "Libellus de magnificis ornamentis regie civiatis Padue Michaelis Savonarole." Ed. Arnoldo Segarizzi. *Rerum italicarum scriptores.* Vol. 24, pt. 15. Città di Castello: S. Lapi.

Scardeone, Bernardino

1979 *Historiae de urbis Patavii.* Sala Bolognese: A. Forni.

Schubring, Paul

1903 *Urbano da Cortona: ein Beitrag zur Kenntnis der Schule Donatellos und der Sieneser Plastik im Quattrocento.* Straussberg: J.H.E. Heitz.

1913 *The Work of Donatello.* New York: Brentano.

Selvatico, Pietro

1870 "Vista di Dante a Giotto." *L'arte nella vita degli artisti.* Firenze: G. Barbera editore. 1-70.

Semenzato, Camillo, ed.

1987 *La Provincia di Padova: la natura, l'arte e la cultura di una terra antica.* Padova: Editoriale programma.

Sendrey, Alfred

1974 *Music in the Social and Religious Life of Antiquity.* Rutherford: Fairleigh Dickinson University.

Seneca

1920 *Epistles.* Trans. Richard Gummere. Loeb Classical Library. Vol. 2. Cambridge: Harvard University Press.

Shackleton, Nicholas

1980 "Chalumeau." *New Grove Dictionary of Music and Musicians.* Vol. 4. London: Macmillan. 111-112.

Simon, Robin

1995 "Giotto and After: Altars and Alterations at the Arena Chapel, Padua." *Apollo* 142 (December):24-36.

Siraisi, Nancy

1970 "The *Expositio problematum Aristotelis* of Peter of Abano." *Isis* 61:3 (Autumn):325.

1973 *Arts and Sciences at Padua: The Studium of Padua before 1350.* Toronto: Pontifical Institute of Medieval Studies.

1975 "The Music Pulse in the Writings of Italian Academic Physicians." *Speculum* 50:4:689-710.

Smart, Alistair

1983 *The Assisi Problem and the Art of Giotto: A Study of the Legend of St. Francis in the Upper Church of San Francesco, Assisi.* New York: Hacker Art Books.

Smolden, William

1965 *A History of Music.* London: Herbert Jenkins.

Sommer, Ignazio

1935 *Curiosità storiche Padovane.* Padova: Libreria A. Draghi.

Steenberghen, Fernand van

1955 *Aristotle in the West.* Louvain: Nauwelaerts.

Strabo

1923 *The Geography of Strabo.* Trans. Horace Leonard Jones. Loeb Classical Library. Vol. 2. Cambridge: Harvard University Press.

Stratico, Simone

1795 *Dell' antico teatro di Padova.* Padova: Stamperia del seminario.

Stevens, John

1986 *Words and Music.* Cambridge: Cambridge University Press.

Strohm, Reinhard

2001 *Music as Concept and Practice in the Late Middle Ages.* Oxford: Oxford University Press.

Strunk, Oliver

1950 "On the Date of Marchetto of Padua." *Rassegna musicale* 20:312-315.

1965 *Source Readings in Music History: Antiquity and the Middle Ages.* New York: W.W. Norton. 160-171.

Stubblebine, James
1969 *Giotto: The Arena Chapel Frescoes.* New York: W.W. Norton.
1985 *Assisi and the Rise of Vernacular Art.* New York: Harper and Row Publishers.

Supino, I. B.
1920 *Giotto.* Firenze: Istituto di edizione artistiche.

Swerdlow, Noel
1967 "Musica dicitur a moys, quod est aqua." *Journal of the American Musicological Association* 20:3-9.

Tacitus
1937 *The Annals.* Trans. John Jackson. Loeb Classical Library. Vol. 5. Cambridge: Harvard University Press.

Tertullian
1931 *Apology, de Spectaculis.* Trans. T. R. Glover. Loeb Classical Library. Cambridge: Harvard University Press.

Thomann, J.
1989 "Pietro d'Abano on Giotto." *Journal of the Warburg and Courtauld Institutes* 54:239-240.

Thorndike, Lynn
1923 *A History of Magic and Experimental Science.* New York: Macmillan.

Tintori, Leonetto, and Millard Meiss
1961 *The Painting of the Life of St. Francis Assisi with Notes on the Arena Chapel.* New York: New York University Press.

Tomlinson, Gary
1990 "Musical Modes and Planetary Song, 1480-1520."*Atti del XIV Congresso della Società internazionale di musicologia.* Torino: Edizioni di Torino. 183-188.

Vasari, Giorgio
1550 *Le vite de' più eccellenti pittori scultori e architettori.* Fascimile of the first edition. New York: Broude International Edition.

Vecchi, Giuseppe, ed.
1954 *Uffici drammatici padovani.* Firenze: L.S. Olschki.
1967 *Medicina e musica, voci e strumenti nel "Conciliator" (1303) di Pietro d'Abano.* Bologna: Istituto di Studi Musicali e Teatrali.

Venturi, Aldofo
1907 "Donatello a Padova." *L'arte* 10:276-285.

Vescovini, Graziella Federici

1986 "Pietro d'Abano e gli affreschi astologici del Palazzo della Ragione di Padova." *Labyrinthos* 9:50-75.

1987 " La teoria delle immagini di Pietro d'Abano e gli affreschi astrologici del Palazzo della Ragione di Padova." *Die Kunst und das Studium der Natur vom 14. zum 16. Jahrhundert*. Weinhein: VCH. 213-235.

1988 "Lucidator dubitabilium astronomiae." *Pietro d'Abano: opere scientifiche inedite.* Padova: Editoriale programma.

1990 "La decorazione pittorica." *Il Palazzo della Ragione in Padova.* Padova: Editoriale programma. 32-34.

Villani, Filippo

1997 *De origine civitatis Florentie et de eiusdem famosis civibus.* Ed. Giuliano Tanturli. Padova: Antenore.

Waite, William

1954 *The Rhythm of Twelfth-Century Polyphony: Its Theory and Practice.* New Haven: Yale University Press.

Wallace, William

1996 *The Modeling of Nature: Philosophy of Science and Philosophy of Nature in Synthesis.* Washington D. C.: Catholic University of America Press.

Webster, James Carson

1938 *The Labors of the Months in Antique and Medieval Art.* Evanston: Northwestern University Press.

Weiss, Piero, and Richard Taruskin, eds.

1984 *Music in the Western World: History in Documents.* New York: Schirmer Books.

Weiss, Robert

1947 *The Dawn of Humanism in Italy: An Inaugural Lecture.* London: H. K. Lewis and Co. Ltd.

Wieruszowski, Helene

1944 "Art and the Commune in the Time of Dante." *Speculum* 19:14-33.

Winternitz, Emanuel

1967 *Musical Instruments and Their Symbolism in Western Art.* New York: W.W. Norton.

Young, Carl

1933 *The Drama of the Medieval Church.* Vol. 2. Oxford: Clarendon Press.

Yudkin, Jeremy
1987 "The Influence of Aristotle on French University Music Texts." *Music Theory and Its Sources: Antiquity and the Middle Ages*. Notre Dame, Ind.: University of Notre Dame Press. 173-189.

Zampieri, Girolamo
1990 *Padova per Antenore*. Padova: Editoriale programma.

Zancanella, Angelo
1935 *Scienza e magia ai tempi di Ristoro d'Arezzo e di Dante*. Ferrara: Industrie grafiche.

Zannoco, Rizieri
1937 "L'Annunciazione all'Scrovegni di Padova (1305-1309)." *Rivista d'arte* 29:370-373.

Zdekauer, Ludovico
1913 "Iustitia: Imagine e idea." *Bollettino senese di storia e partia*. 20:344-425.

Manuscripts

Roma, Biblioteca Apostolica Vaticana, L. VII, 296, f. 224, *Codex Chigiano*.

Padova, Biblioteca Civica, ms. 607, Girolamo Ferrari. *Storia di Padova*.

Padova, Biblioteca Civica, ms. 260, Paolo Ongarello. *Cronoca di Guglielmo*.

Index

www.ingramcontent.com/pod-product-compliance
Lightning Source LLC
LaVergne TN
LVHW010553110826
845149LV00003B/649

* 9 7 8 8 8 8 3 9 8 0 3 0 5 *